FERTILIZERS, PILLS, AND MAGNETIC STRIPS

THE FATE OF PUBLIC EDUCATION IN AMERICA

FERTILIZERS, PILLS, AND MAGNETIC STRIPS

THE FATE OF PUBLIC EDUCATION IN AMERICA

GENE V GLASS

Information Age Publishing, Inc.
Charlotte, North Carolina • www.infoagepub.com

Library of Congress Cataloging-in-Publication Data

Glass, Gene V., 1940-
 Fertilizers, pills,and magnetic strips : the fate of public education in America /
by Gene V. Glass.
  p. cm.
 Includes bibliographical references and index.
 ISBN 978-1-59311-892-1 (pbk.) — ISBN 978-1-59311-893-8 (hardcover) 1. Public
schools—United States. 2. Education—United States. I. Title.

 LA217.2.G55 2008
 371.0100973 dc22

                                                                2008003133

 ISBN 13: 978-1-59311-892-1 (paperback)
 ISBN 13: 978-1-59311-893-8 (hardcover)

Cover image is *The City Rises* (1910) by Umberto Boccioni (1882–1916). Oil on canvas,
6 ft. 6.5 in. × 9 ft. 10.5 in. The Museum of Modern Art, New York. Boccioni was a
member of the Futurist movement in graphic arts that portrayed dynamic motion and
technology.

To Isaac, and Ellie, and the two J's

We may have made a mess of our century;
We hope you do better with yours.

ABOUT THE AUTHOR

Gene V Glass is Regents' Professor at the Arizona State University. He was awarded a PhD in educational psychology and statistics in 1965 from the University of Wisconsin. His early work in statistical methods led to the development of meta-analysis in the mid-1970s, now a widely used tool in medical and social science research. He was elected president of the American Educational Research Association in 1975, and was elected to membership in the National Academy of Education in 2000. Glass was a pioneer in the creation of open access scholarly journals in the 1990s. Among his many writings are *The Benefits of Psychotherapy* (with M. L. Smith & T. I. Miller), *Meta-Analysis of Social Research* (with B. McGaw & M. L. Smith), *School Class Size: Research & Policy*, and three recent books coedited with Charalambos Vrasidas: *Distance Education and Distributed Learning, Online Professional Development for Teachers*, and *Preparing Teachers to Teach with Technology*. Since 2000, he has served Information Age Publishing as a senior advisor to the founder and publisher.

CONTENTS

PART III.   WHAT ACCOUNTABILITY MEANS

PART IV.   LOOKING FORWARD

Preface

Why do certain topics and not others dominate the debates about education? Why do some questions get asked (Do home-schooled students learn more than traditionally schooled students?) and not others (Should public school teachers receive sabbaticals just like college professors?)? And why are the commonly asked questions never answered to the satisfaction of both sides in the debates?

I was trained as an empiricist and an analyst of statistics. Like many of my generation, I shared a galvanizing faith in the power of social science research to find the way to a better life for all. An early frustration with the inconsistencies in the results of research studies led me in 1976 to illustrate a statistical method that I dubbed "meta-analysis."[1] I truly believed, for a while, that the synthesis of dozens or even hundreds of

---

1. "Meta-analysis, *n*. Analysis of data from a number of independent studies of the same subject (published or unpublished), esp. in order to determine overall trends and significance; an instance of this. 1976 G. V. GLASS in *Educ. Res.* Nov. 3/2 My major interest currently is in what we have come to call ... the meta-analysis of research. The term is a bit grand, but it is precise and apt.... Meta-analysis refers to the analysis of analyses." *Oxford English Dictionary.* Retrieved June 19, 2006 from http://dictionary.oed.com

---

empirical studies into an aggregated, overall conclusion would command the attention and consent of all sides in a debate. One hundred studies when properly integrated show unequivocally that students in smaller classes learn more than students in larger classes. Can there be any doubt? I rather quickly learned in a decade that no mass of data regardless of its size or its consistency resolves debates about the best way to educate children.[2] Where education is concerned, the old adage holds true: Facts are negotiable; beliefs are rock solid.

Eventually, I came to believe that debates in education are not about achievement or test scores or preparing tomorrow's workforce at all. They are about gaining the political power to control money and secure special privileges. Behind the rhetoric lies material self-interest, a drive for comfort, and a need for security. These enduring motives are older than public education. They never change, just as the debates about public education seem never to change.

The title of this work bears obvious similarity to the title of Jared Diamond's masterpiece, *Guns, Germs & Steel: The Fates of Human Societies*, in which Diamond laid out an astounding explanation of the fate of societies based on environmental, geographic, and economic influences. It was Diamond's steadfast adherence to a set of causes that moved through history like Adam Smith's invisible hand that so impressed me. Unlike most sociological or social psychological explanatory systems that appeal primarily to human actions and choices that arise ex nihilo to shape modern society, Diamond strung together a chain of influences that few had seen but which immediately rang true—unless that reader encountered Diamond's argument already wielding some disciplinary axe to grind.

On a much smaller scale, I have come to see the continuous debates and attempts at reform of public education in Amer-

---

2.   Glass, Gene V. (1987). What works: Politics and research. *Educational Researcher, 16,* 5-10.

ica as linked to a set of influences largely unseen and unacknowledged, but when pointed out to any intelligent and objective observer strike a note of recognition and acceptance. My analysis is akin to that of the cultural materialists in anthropology, most notably its most influential proponent the late Marvin Harris, in that it combines elements of both Karl Marx (in the emphasis given to the forces of production in industrialized societies) and Thomas Malthus[3] (in the emphasis given to the implications of expanding human populations). These two forces have much to say about a wide range of phenomena that pass before our eyes in modern society, in particular, how public institutions like education emerge, grow, and recede.

It is a truism that nearly everything in life is political. However, unlike many scholars who examine education policy, I ignore for the most part the day-to-day, month-to-month, and year-to-year machinations of politicians. The minutia of which bill will make it out of Congress, or how to tweak the No Child Left Behind Act so as to make its effects on curriculum and teachers' morale less pernicious are matters for the newspapers and ephemeral academic magazines. To focus at this level of epiphenomena—the mere surface appearances of deeper driving forces—is to miss the larger picture that determines these daily goings-on. Policymakers will at most moments and in the end do what the people—the *demos*—tell them to do in a democratic society. Even in the United States, as much an oligopoly as it is a democracy—the self interest of the voting majority gives politicians their marching orders when it comes to matters as intimately personal as the education of children.

A few words about this work as a published book may be necessary. An argument that leans heavily on demography and economics can not help but document its points with numerous graphs and statistical tables. I hope that no more

---

3.   Thomas Robert Malthus (1766-1834), British demographer and political economist, who speculated on the interrelationships of fertility, productivity, and various social practices.

are presented than are necessary to substantiate the points being made. In any event, the statistical load is scarcely heavier than that of *USA Today* or other popular publications. To complain that numbers and graphs are involved in understanding how American education got to where it is today is a bit like complaining that poetry involves words. That is simply the way it is. Frequently, more data could be presented than have made their way into print. Consequently, a Web site has been created which contains supplementary information too voluminous for this publication. The site will serve at the same time as a venue for asking and answering questions about the thesis of the present work. The Web address is http://lounge.infoagepub.com/gglass.

The pages that follow are replete with footnotes. As an early adventurer into the world of online scholarly publication, I came to despise footnotes and their close relative, endnotes. Footnotes were an impossibility in the hypertext markup language (html) that was used to present most articles in scholarly electronic journals. The function once performed by footnotes then had to be performed by endnotes that appeared at the end of each article. The constant checking of sources that is typical of careful reading of scholarly work entailed annoying clicking from text to endnotes and back to text. It took John Willinsky's brilliant exegesis of the footnote to convince me that in fact they performed an essential function in scholarly writing and that they should be employed abundantly in serious work.[4] As a result, the present work contains a few hundred footnotes that record sources of information or quotations. The citations to literature in the footnotes are redundant with the entries in the References list at the end of the book. However, presenting both full citations in the footnotes and an alphabetized list of cited sources at the back allows the reader to check sources without interrupting the flow of reading to thumb through

---

4. Willinsky, John. (2000). *If only we knew: Increasing the public value of social science research.* New York: Routledge.

pages and then later to find citations quickly by first author's name. This useful redundancy seemed worth the extra space.

Part I.
The Drumbeat of Reform

Chapter One

The Endless Narrative of Education Reform

This book is about debates that never seem to end and why they don't. It is about people who insist that the sky is falling, when in fact things are about the way they have always been. It is about farms and fertilizers and tractors and how many people it takes to feed a nation; about why no one lives in the country any more and why people in the city don't want as many children as people used to want. It's about pills that prevent pregnancies and discoveries in medicine that mean that we can expect to live almost twice as long as our great-grandparents did. It is about robots that can build cars better than human hands can, and never ask for time off. It is about how people carry less money with them these days, and how the plastic card in their billfold or purse no longer seems like real money. It's about people spending themselves into debt and corporations that welcome them there, and about those who retire only to go back to work because they have out-lived their savings. It is about a nation growing older and poorer and caring less and less about the fate of those unlike themselves who were never invited here any way. And this book is about how all of these things are interrelated and

Fertilizers, Pills, and Magnetic Strips: The Fate of Education in America
pp. 3–18

under the control of some of the strongest human drives: for material comfort and for feelings of safety, drives that undergo transformations across a lifetime into the need to consume and the wish to segregate oneself from others who are different. And this book is about how all of this plays out in the arena of the public education system, long the pride of a young nation and now in danger of being abandoned.

The Calls for Reform

Reforming the public elementary and secondary schools of America is not a new endeavor. Those who come late to an interest in the education of children may think that serious discussion of reforming schools began with No Child Left Behind in 2001, or at least not before *A Nation at Risk* in 1983.[1] In fact, debates about reforming schools are as old as public education itself. What is new is the polarized political environment in which those debates are now taking place, the set of motives driving those debates, and the social and economic transformations of the 20th century that gave rise to those motives.

Criticism and reform of the education of young people was old when Quintilian (35-95 A.D.) was young.[2] The denigration of children, particularly adolescents, has been prominent in most nations since the Industrial Revolution. The background whine of crisis has been a feature of public life for decades in the U.S. Electronic media contribute to the ahistorical culture of modern America. The word "news" itself says that the "old" is unimportant. The *Times* is about today, and *die Zeitung* is now. The elderly have forgotten how things once were, and the young never knew. So it is easy to talk

1.   National Commission on Excellence in Education. (1983). *A nation at risk: The imperative for educational reform*. Washington, DC: U.S. Department of Education.
2.   "What is happening to our young people? They disrespect their elders, they disobey their parents. They ignore the law. They riot in the streets inflamed with wild notions. Their morals are decaying" (Plato, 427-347 B.C.E).

idly about education in America today as being inferior to what came before, or to fall for the jeremiads of politicians who declare the U.S. school system a failure that can only be saved by revolutionary reform.

Richard Rothstein, writing about the history of criticism of American education, reminds us of the decades old—indeed, centuries old—sport of bad mouthing public schools.[3]

More than 150 years ago, Horace Mann decried the incompetence of Boston's 14-year-olds, fewer than half of whom appeared to know that water expands when it freezes (or at least failed to indicate as much on one of the nation's first standardized tests).

- As the 19th century turned into the 20th, authorities of the University of California at Berkeley declared that something of the order of a third of all entering Freshmen were "not proficient" in English. Colleges have long accused K-12 schools of dumping incompetent students at their door; it has not been overlooked that the financial interests of these same colleges are served by declaring their students in dire need of even more education than one might have expected. Ellwood Cubberly, then dean of the School of Education at Stanford, wrote of an increasingly globalized economy in which our young people will compete against other nations in a battle of brains—100 years ago.
- Many believed that the Great Depression of the 1930s resulted in part from the failures of the U.S. education system.
- In 1947, Benjamin Fine, education editor of the *New York Times*, wrote that "Education faces a serious crisis.... We will suffer the consequences of our present neglect of education a generation hence."[4]

---

3. Rothstein, Richard. (1998). *The way we were? The myths and realities of America's student achievement.* Washington, DC: The Century Foundation.
4. Quoted in Rothstein, Richard. Ibid.

- Post-World-War II, baby boom, and Sputnik anxieties raised criticism of public education to a high pitch in the 1950s. A rash of books declaring America's school children incompetent flew from the printing presses.[5] Admiral Hyman Rickover wrote in his 1959 book *Education and Freedom* that, "education is the most important problem facing the United States today ... only the massive upgrading of the scholastic standards of our schools will guarantee the future prosperity and freedom of the Republic."
- Later, in 1962 Rickover published *Swiss Schools and Ours: Why Theirs are Better*. Ah, the Swiss, a model for America and our times—or at least for parts of Wisconsin. Rickover could not decide whether the schools of Switzerland or of England were the proper model for American education.
- In a conversation with Eric Sevareid in 1965, Walter Lippmann, intellectual, journalist, and opinion maker, proclaimed the nation's schools "inadequate."[6]
- In the 1960s and 1970s, the abandonment of phonics instruction in the elementary grades was blamed for a rising wave of illiteracy.
- In 1983 in *A Nation at Risk*, our very way of life was declared to be *at risk* of economic servitude due to the failure of public education. The downward spiral could only be stemmed by concentrating on instilling *content* and *character* into the minds and hearts of youth, and only *choice* could guarantee both, according to then Secretary of Education William Bennett.[7]

---

5. Arthur Bestor's *Educational wastelands: The retreat from learning in our public schools* (1953) followed quickly by his *The restoration of learning* (1955); Rudolph Flesch's *Why Johnny can't read* (1955) followed by *Teaching Johnny to read* (1956) and *Why Johnny still can't read* (1981). Hyman Rickover's *Education and freedom* (1959) followed by *American education, A national failure; The problem of our schools and what we can learn from England* (1963); apparently these critics' outrage was always too great for a single volume.

6. Lippmann, Walter. Conversation with Eric Sevareid, February 22, 1965. Quoted in *Bartlett's familiar quotations* (1982), p. 1013.

For reasons to be explored here, the cries to transform the U.S. public education system are reaching a crescendo. Education occupies a high position in every political party platform, though it is typically quickly forgotten after the ballots are counted. Never before has our way of life seemed so threatened, some claim. Our economy will surely be eclipsed—by the Japanese? No, that was last century's competitor; by the Chinese? the East Indians? Well, by someone surely—unless our schools are made better, tougher, more demanding. Standards must be raised, it is claimed. And competition among providers of training and education is the surest route to excellence.[8] Our very survival is said to hang in the balance. Today's cries of crisis and exhortations to reform are taking on a new and urgent character.

In an earlier time, reformers called for change within the existing structure of public education. What was wrong with American education could be cured by broadening the curriculum, or by adopting a more progressive philosophy, or by the return to the McGuffey reader and teaching reading by phonics. James Bryant Conant, then ex-president of Harvard University in the late 1950s, laid a good portion of the blame for the decline of America's schools at the door of colleges of education that trained the teachers. But always a proponent of a strong public education system, his proposals for reform scarcely went beyond altering the preservice training of teachers: fewer "Mickey Mouse" courses, some tough instruction in tests and measurements, and plenty of student teaching.

Today's reformers,[9] overwhelmingly representing a conservative political philosophy, call for nothing less than radi-

---

7. Glass, Gene V. (1986). "What works": Politics and research. *Educational Researcher, 16*(3), 5-10.

8. Herb Gintis, who along with Samuel Bowles provided the searching critique of American education in the 1970s under the title *Schooling in Capitalist America*, can be seen in the 1990s recommending competition in public education. (Glass, G. V., 1994, School choice: A discussion with Herbert Gintis. *Education Policy Analysis Archives, 2*(6). Retrieved January 24, 2007 from http://epaa.asu.edu/epaa/v2n6.html

cal change. Parents should be free to choose public or private schools and have their choice financed by public monies. Any adult with a bachelor's degree and a short course in teaching should be allowed to teach in the nation's schools. All schools should compete for students and those that can not compete successfully should be closed. No longer is the assumption made by would-be education reformers that our nation must have a universal system of free public education. While branding the public school system a failure, politically conservative reformers propose not to abolish it but to change its financing and its composition radically. The form they propose would better serve the interests of one special group, the majority class. These same advocates of reform have learned to cloak their proposals and legislation in the mantle of concern for the poor so as to make their efforts appear less self-interested. "Choice" is claimed to be for the benefit of the poor who must escape the failing urban schools. But for a variety of reasons, the poor can seldom take advantage of choice; the suburban middle class can.[10] Freedom and justice, liberty and equality are in constant opposition, and conservatives opt for liberty. George Will, the conservative political columnist described the tension accurately:

> Today conservatives tend to favor freedom, and consequently are inclined to be somewhat sanguine about inequalities of outcomes.

9.   When I write here of the conservative and neoconservative critics of public education, it is persons such as former Secretary of Education William J. Bennett (1985-1988), Bennett's former Assistant Secretary of Education Chester Finn, and now their many like-minded colleagues such as Caroline Hoxby, Eric Hanushek, Jeanne Allen and the like to whom I refer. They are followers of the laissez-faire economic and social philosophy of Milton Friedman, the most influential economic theorist of the last 50 years who is credited with the invention of the notion of school vouchers.

10.   Michael Apple has been one of the most eloquent voices warning how conservative education reformers are contributing to ethnicity, race, and class divisions in American education. Apple, Michael W. (1993). *Official knowledge: Democratic education in a conservative age.* New York: Routledge & Kegan Paul. Apple, Michael W. (1996). *Education and cultural politics.* New York: Teachers College Press. Apple, Michael W. (2001). *Educating the "right" way: Markets, standards, God, and inequality.* New York: Routledge/Falmer.

Liberals are more concerned with equality, understood, they insist, primarily as equality of opportunity, not of outcome.… Liberalism increasingly seeks to deliver equality in the form of equal dependence of more and more people for more and more things on government. Hence liberals' hostility to school choice programs that challenge public education's semimonopoly.[11]

The inequalities in American education mirror the inequalities in American life more generally. They are, as Jonathan Kozol described them, savage; and they appear to be getting worse.[12]

Experimental or "pilot" voucher programs are introduced as "means-tested," but proponents really want universal vouchers. And yet the American public school system goes on, a wretched monopoly of government schools some claim, sustained and protected by the power hungry collective of elementary and secondary school teachers known as the National Education Association. There are strong elements of political theater in this contest between conservatives and liberals.[13, 14]

---

11.   Will, George. (2007, May 31). The case for conservatism. *Washington Post*, p. B7.

12.   Kozol, J. (1991). *Savage inequalities: Children in America's schools*. New York: HarperCollins.

13.   Smith, Mary Lee, with Miller-Kahn, Linda; Heinecke, Walt; Jarvis, Patricia F.; & Noble, Audrey. (2003). *Political spectacle and the fate of American schools*. New York: Routledge/Falmer.

14.   The public debate over education is so shot through with "disinformation" that even dedicated observers need a program to identify the players. Conservative critics of public education generally reside in privately funded "think tanks" not associated with universities. Liberal education policy analysts generally reside in centers located in public or private universities. Policy analysts in the federal government at the official, nonpolitical level are typically liberal. This division is likely a legacy of the huge expansion of the federal civil service by Franklin D. Roosevelt after the Great Depression. Liberal education policy centers recently formed a consortium, the Education Policy Alliance, to focus their efforts: http://educationpolicyalliance.org/. The Education Policy Studies Laboratory (http://www.educationanalysis.org) and the Education and the Public Interest Center (http://education.colorado.edu/epic/) recently formed a Think Tank Review project (http://thinktankreview.org) to counter the messages emanating from conservative quarters.

Extravagant claims are made for the potential benefits of supposed inventions: charter schools, vouchers, online virtual schools, tuition tax credits, and the like. Proposals advanced by would-be reformers travel under false colors. As I shall describe, these actions stem largely from economic and material interests colored strongly by class conflict and racial suspicion and animosity. These are dangerous charges to level against any political opponent because they go directly to motives that are largely hidden from the view of social scientists and pollsters. Indeed, the claim that "classism" and racism underlie much of contemporary education reform efforts goes to motives of which the reformers themselves would be offended to be accused. And yet, in our ordinary daily lives, we see and hear the evidence again and again that one group wants nothing to do with the other: not to live by them and not to send their children to the same school.

If the basic causes of the cry to reform the public education system are hidden from view, then perhaps they can be inferred from a pattern of tell-tale evidence. For example, if reforms touted as vastly superior in the benefits they confer on students' knowledge do in fact lack any compelling evidence of their effectiveness, then the causes of why they are favored by some must be sought elsewhere. And if reforms once instituted are seen consistently to favor one class of students while leaving another in diminished circumstances, then one legitimately asks why this is allowed to continue. To take a second example, one reads repeatedly in the press about how U.S. school children score far below their counterparts in Europe or Asia. They are portrayed as lazy, dull, being taught by incompetent and unmotivated teachers. If all of this has been shown by careful research to be unfounded, one can legitimately ask why the self-flagellation continues. And if the self-criticism is consistently tied to proposals for reform that would greatly favor one group at the expense of another, one properly inquires into the motives behind the criticism.

The drumbeat of education reform is unrelenting. The message of this book is that it is not to be understood for what it purports to be. It must be listened to closely and interpreted in light of economics and politics.

Fertilizers, Pills, and Magnetic Strips: Technology Driving Culture

The invention of technologies shapes culture in ways that are often unpredictable at the birth of the invention. Television killed dance bands; the Internet is killing used book stores.

What do fertilizers, pills, and magnetic strips have to do with public education in America? Part metonyms,[15] part causes themselves, these three elements are at the core of the forces that have created American culture in the early 21st century. And any institution as pervasive as public education is certain to both reflect and be shaped by the larger culture in which it is embedded. Some will say that education itself is a major force shaping our culture, but I doubt it. Some will say that the primary function of the schools is to shape youth into the forms required to preserve the larger culture that surrounds them. I suspect they have it right.

The observations I wish to make here are that the major issues of American education policy at the beginning of the 21st century (school choice in its various forms including homeschooling, vouchers, charter schools, and open enrollment; high-stakes testing; tuition tax credits; various privatization proposals; commercial ties between public schools and numerous vendors of products to children; the commercialization of schooling itself; English language exclusivity laws) have arisen from powerful forces acting over decades.[16] The rural to urban migration, the control of conception and the

---

15. Metonymy: "a figure of speech which consists in substituting for the name of a thing the name of an attribute of it or of something closely related." *Oxford English dictionary* (1971, p. 398).

extension of life expectancy, and the spread of uncollateralized personal credit are among the most powerful forces that have shaped American life and American education in the past century. These forces are not the ideas created in the minds of educationists or philosophers or one brand of psychologist or another. Indeed, the days when a Dewey or a Freud carried great influence in the classroom are long since past. The forces of which I speak are far more fundamental to human needs and desires: the pursuit of material self-interest, monetary advantage, comfort, and security.

It is often regarded as impolite or unfair to make claims about people's motives in political debates—and of course even those who think this may find it an impossible rule to abide by in all cases. They would have us confine ourselves to the facts when arguing an issue of public policy, as though the personal interests of the protagonists were not themselves facts of sometimes overpowering importance. But people's actions are scarcely comprehensible without thinking about what drives them and what personal interest is served by their acting thus. Even less can their behavior be predicted without an understanding of what motivates them.

Cultural materialism—to oversimplify it, the theory that explains culture as deriving from the drive for dietary protein[17]—seems less relevant today than a concept that might be named a "culture of consumption"—which views the obvious details of culture as essentially the result of human's embracing technology to satisfy the drive for long life, comfort, and pleasure. So the infanticide of the ancients that

---

16.　The analysis presented in this book focuses on Kindergarten through grade 12 public education. The politics and economics of higher education (with the exception of community colleges) are so different that separate analyses are required. Indeed, public higher education—dominated as it is by large multipurpose research universities—is increasingly no longer "public" in the original sense of the word. The percentage of university budgets derived from taxes dwindles in nearly every state and falls below 10% in many states where the leading institutions even petition legislatures to be freed from all public regulation.

staved off starvation has been replaced by the anti-natalism of modern times that frees us to pursue satisfaction of the drive for larger homes, faster cars, and cruises.

Americans' drive for consumption is a powerful force shaping culture in myriad ways and determining in fundamental ways such institutions as schools. The exploitation of that drive has been conscious economic policy of the U.S. government for nearly 100 years. In 1929, shortly after assuming the office of President of the United States, Herbert Hoover spoke thus to a gathering of advertising executives: "You have transformed people into constantly moving happiness machines that have become the key to economic progress."[18] At the turn of the 21st century, the happiness machine was running full tilt. By the end of the previous century, happiness no longer included the births of several children per family. Financial and economic concerns were mentioned by three of every four women seeking an abortion in a survey of over 1,000 women in 2004.[19]

Modern education debates are shaped by powerful economic and demographic forces that have been over a century in the making. They include the rural-to-urban migration in industrialized societies, which itself was rooted in the increasing productivity of agriculture during the early 20th century,

---

17. Harris's theory holds that humans are motivated by a few basic biological and psychological drives that lead the species to produce things and reproduce themselves. These activities of production and reproduction are the root causes of the varied cultural forms that arise in human society. Among sociologists, parallel ideas go under the name of "historical materialism," in which production of material goods is seen as pivotal in shaping social institutions and norms. See Harris, Marvin. (1979). *Cultural materialism: The struggle for a science of culture.* New York: Random House.

18. Stevens, D. (2005, August 12). On every box of cake mix, evidence of Freud's theories. *New York Times.* Retrieved November 24, 2005 from http://movies2 .nytimes.com/2005/08/12/movies/12self.html?ex=1132894800&en= 50eefa3934e4d1da&ei=5070

19. Finer, Lawrence B., Frohwirth, L. F., Dauphinee, L. A., Singh, S., & Moore, A. M. (2005). Reasons U.S. women have abortions: Quantitative and qualitative perspectives. *Perspectives on sexual and reproductive health, 37*(3), 110-118.

itself being the result of the invention of artificial *fertilizers* in 1910 and the rapid expansion of farm machinery in the early decades of the century. Closely linked to the transition from a rural culture to an urban and suburban culture is the desire to limit family size. This desire was given the wherewithal to accomplish its aim by the invention of the birth control *pill* in 1953 and the legalization of abortion in 1973.

The desire to increase life expectancy—surely innate in the human species—finds the capacity to do so in the extraordinary discoveries of medical science, both through pharmaceuticals and the development of other effective means of curing disease. The remarkable advances of the past 50 years—roughly since the introduction of the Salk vaccine for poliomyelitis in the mid-1950s—will pale along side of the strides that will be made possible by the mapping of the human genome. Changing family sizes and increasing life expectancies add up to changing demographics. As has been pointed out *ad nauseam* in every discussion of the nation's future, America is growing older on average.

The efficiency due to *robotics* of the manufacturing sector relative to the service sector of the economy is putting increasing pressure on all public institutions for accountability. The bureaucratic language of accountability pervades contemporary public institutions of all types: goal setting, standards, zero-based budgeting, formative and summative evaluation. Education, nursing, police and fire protection, recreation services, mental health services, and many others are being subjected to intense scrutiny of their finances and their effectiveness because they constitute ever larger proportions of the gross domestic product.

Credit has become the blessing and the curse of modern economic life. The spending and saving habits of middle class America that result from the ready availability of unsecured personal credit are exerting enormous economic pressure on the middle class. Average credit card holder debt now exceeds $10,000. The creation of the system by which small amounts of unsecured credit could be extended to individuals depended on the invention of cheap telecommunications that starts with a *magnetic strip* on a plastic card. To the burden of self-inflicted debt must be added the strain on middle-class finances incurred by the rash of predatory and reckless subprime mortgage lending of the first decade of the 21st century that resulted in an epidemic of foreclosures and the collapse of the housing market. To be sure, borrowing on housing equity that was more speculative than real to feed an appetite for college tuition and luxuries contributed to the financial straits in which the middle class found themselves. But these consequences of a periodic housing boom only contributed marginally to the economic pressures experienced by the middle class. A hyperconsuming middle class culture producing growing debt and eradicating savings quickly loses sympathy for expensive public institutions that attempt to serve the common good. Neoliberal economic philosophy seeks to transform the common good into a commodity that can be designed, manufactured, and counted like any industrial product.

To complete the picture of America at century's turn, add immigration and a steeply rising differential birth rate as Hispanics[20] rise from being a small minority class to a major social and political influence. As poor Hispanics move closer to demographic majority status, the wealthier White majority—with fewer children than in past decades, and growing debt while facing an increasing life expectancy—finds it more

---

20.   Nomenclature for race and ethnicity in America is as complex an issue as the very concept of race itself. No one set of choices for names pleases everyone. I have, however, elected to follow the lead of the U.S. Census, who in turn have followed the Statistical Policy Directive #15 of the Office of Management and Budget in designating four racial categories (*American Indian or Alaskan Native, Asian or Pacific Islander, Black,* and *White*) and two ethnicities (*Hispanic* and *Not of Hispanic Origin*). The term *Black* will be used in particular when referring to information stemming primarily from the Census; *African American* will often be used in more general discourse. At certain points it will be important to utilize the term *Non-Hispanic White,* as it is used in the Census; otherwise, *White* will be used as a synonym. See http://www.census.gov/population/www/socdemo/race/racefactcb.htm for further information.

and more unappealing to support the institutions that are stewards of "other" people's children.

The result is that these very powerful forces are degrading public institutions in their many forms, foremost among which is the traditional public education system. It is not clear what might slow or reverse this trend. Neither new education policies themselves nor philanthropy on the part of the rapidly growing super-rich segment of society seem powerful enough to deflect these forces. Least of all will the market forces of competition among schools, supposedly leading to the invention or adoption of business models, reverse the trend toward a weakened and degraded public education system.

It is necessary for at least two reasons to point out the connections between a handful of technological advances and an institution like public education: (1) policies widely advocated in democratic institutions ranging from local school boards to the U.S. Congress have been put forward as solutions to a crisis in educational attainment that threatens national prosperity and security (indeed, national preeminence itself), when in fact these policies have likely arisen from different, less honorable motives, namely, the desire of White voters to preserve wealth, consume material goods, and provide a "quasi-private" education for their children at public expense; and (2) an aging U.S. White population is entering retirement with about $100,000 net wealth including equity in their home, with the prospect of inheriting some $50,000 on average from their own parents, a life expectancy of 30 to 40 years, and a strong wish to reduce their taxes and, hence, the costs of all public services including education. Fertilizers, pills, and magnetic strips have served as major forces shaping population, politics and policy. Will they continue to be a primary influence shaping public education in America? For the next two or three decades, I think they will. No one can claim to see much beyond that.

Any attempt to explain something as complex as the forces that are changing the nation's education system presents first what might be called the "point of entry" problem. Where in the huge flow of forces and influences over decades if not centuries does one step in and attempt to draw a coherent and credible picture of school at the beginning of the 21st century? Enter too far back in time, and risk losing one's way in the retelling of quaint stories and ephemera. Enter too near the present, and risk drowning in the enormous pool of minutiae that comprise the contemporary scene. No theory exists to guide an investigator to the most promising points of entry; they are all more or less arbitrary. Only the eventual explanations of the dynamics and effects offered can justify one choice over another. I choose to begin in the vicinity of the beginning of the previous century, at a moment when this society stepped into a torrent of technological, followed by cultural, changes that ultimately led to the education system we have today.[21]

My contention is that technology in the service of economic productivity, better health, and the drive for creature comforts has determined culture, even in such details as seemingly remote as the purposes to which schooling is put and how it is delivered. This observation is hundreds of years old, and probably older. Among other things, my argument identifies certain forces shaping education that are too often ignored, and it exposes other rationalizations for education

---

21.   It has been particularly difficult for some—in particular, my students who are steeped in the constructivist and "culture-is-all-things" philosophy of the day—to accept the importance I place on the transformative power of technological invention. But I do see these and closely related inventions as *primus inter pares* among all the forces shaping modern life. Indeed, a birth control pill would have no effect on demographics if laws or customs forbade their sale, or production, or use. But the question of the influence of the culture in which the pill functions would not even be asked were it not for the pill itself. Consequently, these classes of inventions—fertilizers, pills, magnetic strips, and robots—are the sine qua non of societal change. In much the same way will historians look back on these decades with their concern about climate change, for example, and see that exhortations to change lifestyle—drive less, turn the thermostat down (or up)—will mean little compared to technological inventions still unimagined.

reform as hypocritical or intentionally misleading, as political spectacles that hide actual intentions. Among these distractions is the claim that the U.S. education system is in crisis. As the crisis was declared, the "accountability" movement in education was taking shape. Soon, a return to "basics" with high-stakes testing and "choice" in the form of vouchers, charter schools, tuition tax credits, open enrollment, home-schooling and the like, was declared to be the salvation of American public education and of America itself. As an aside, a contention I do not wish to defend here is that this accountability movement has had a devastating effect on public education, it is destroying the richness of a curriculum that has taken decades to develop, it is obliterating the professional autonomy of teachers, and it is dimming the personal hopes and dreams of hundreds of thousands of children. I believe all of these things to be true; and not simply true but obvious to millions of parents, teachers, and students throughout the country.

As a group, educators tend to be dreamers. They dream of better days and healthier, more competent children. Under the pressure of serving dozens of children with increasingly urgent needs, teachers too often fall for the promises of experts with simple answers who paint rosy pictures of a world where all children learn, where the race and social class achievement gap disappears, where every child is a winner, and where no child is left behind. Reality may be less rosy. There may be no simple answers, nor any at all, as to how to rescue America's public schools from their fate: segregated along racial and social class lines; pressured always to do more with less; blamed repeatedly for the failures that are more rightly the fault of corporations and politicians; and treated like the whipping boy of ideologues and media pundits. How did we come to be in this mess? Will knowing its causes make any difference? What is its fate, and are there other possibilities?

Chapter Two

Transforming Education: *Ordo Ab Chao*

Americans have always looked on their public education system with a combination of hope and alarm. But not until the latter half of the 20th century were attempts to change public education introduced as solutions to a crisis. The proof of the alleged breakdown of the education system was said to be found in declining test scores and international score cards that showed U.S. students falling behind competition from around the world. Closer examinations of test score data showed that nothing approaching a crisis ever existed. Creating the impression of a failing system depended on invidious and invalid comparisons of college applicants from different decades, students taking tests under vastly different conditions, or large heterogeneous populations of students compared to small privileged groups like the high school students of Finland or Austria. In fact, U.S. students, as a whole, were doing quite well, and better than in the past that was frequently glorified. But closer examinations of test data do not lend themselves to television sound bites and newspaper headlines. And the public continues to receive the message that reform is needed to avert a crisis. What if American pub-

Fertilizers, Pills, and Magnetic Strips: The Fate of Education in America
pp. 19–55

lic education were not in crisis? What if it were in fact true that U.S. students were indeed smarter as a group than their predecessors had ever been? What if the U.S. public schools are actually the envy of most nations? Would the American public be as willing as they are to listen to would-be reformers telling them how their schools must undergo massive changes?

The Rhetoric of Crisis

The rhetoric of "crisis" is so prevalent and persistent in debates about education that the arguments as to whether the crisis is real or "manufactured"[1] for political purposes must be revisited again and again. Reformers[2] dress their proposals as solutions to the problem of a failing public education system. The putative failure is demonstrated by graphs and tables of declining achievement scores and climbing drop out rates. Staggering percentages of pupils are said to be illit-

---

1.   The notion of "crisis" has a history in political and economic theory, such as, in the writings of Antonio Gramsci, or more recently in such books as James O'Connor's *The meaning of crisis: A theoretical introduction*. But the sense in which the word is used here is non-technical, ordinary language, as it emanates from the mouths not of political theorists but of politicians. My colleague David Berliner has referred to "manufactured crises," and this is the topic here examined. Berliner, David C., & Biddle, Bruce J. (1995). *The manufactured crisis: Myths, fraud, and the attack on America's public schools*. New York: Addison-Wesley.

2.   Tamim Ansary (2007) pointed out that in common parlance as well as in the political spectacle of education debate, the verb "reform" is used as a synonym for "improve." "He is a reformed alcoholic." "She is a reformed sinner." The Reformation was undertaken to correct the evils of Medieval Catholicism, and so on. To call oneself a "reformer" is to present oneself to the public as one who is concerned, well meaning, insightful; a reformer has an answer to a problem. In a literal sense, "to reform" means simply to change the form of, for better or worse. To speak of those who wish to change public education in fundamental ways, with major implications for its cost or who shall bear its costs, as "reformers" then, is neither to prejudge that a legitimate problem exists that would be corrected by the proposed changes or that the proposals themselves have any merit. My colleagues and students objected to using the name "reformer" to refer to the conservative critics of public education, preferring usage such as "proposals to change education" or "seeking to transform schools."

erate or "illnumerate," as proven by one large-scale testing or another. College professors complain bitterly about the poor education that incoming Freshmen received in high school. High school teachers complain that middle school education is failing, and the middle schools blame elementary schools. The blame game eventually reaches parents who suddenly learn that they are responsible for the decline of the West. With such an abysmally bad supply of talent to populate America's workforce, the country will soon be eclipsed by the industrious, hard working students of ... (fill in the latest nation with a 10% growth rate for its economy). Our nation is in crisis. By the time the public has finished listening to this litany of failure, they are ready to consider virtually any plausible sounding solution: school vouchers, more private education to compete with the monopolistic public school system, charter schools freed from the stultifying bureaucracy of public education, and so on. Ironically, parents often endorse these reforms for the "nation's schools" that they believe to be failing while rejecting them for their own children's school, which they regard as adequate or better.

The old adage, "If it ain't broke, don't fix it" acquired a new corollary in the rhetoric of conservative reformers: "If you want to fix it, declare it broken." Education, welfare, and later, Social Security (FICA) have all been declared "broken" and in need of repair. Neoconservatives have been widely accused of creating chaos to justify intervention and Draconian controls, the Iraq War being only one of the most recent examples. Indeed, *Ordo ab Chao* (or "order out of chaos") has lost its teleological references and acquired Machiavellian connotations.[3]

Our Nation is at risk. Our once unchallenged preeminence in commerce, industry, science, and technological innovation is being overtaken by competitors throughout the world.... The educational foundations of our society are presently being eroded by a rising tide

---

3. "*Ordo ab Chao*" was a motto of Freemasonry in use as early as the late 14th century, where its meaning was completely different from the current meaning of using chaos in deceptive and manipulative ways in order to seize power.

of mediocrity that threatens our very future as a Nation and a people.... Others are matching and surpassing our educational attainments. (*A Nation at Risk: The Imperative for Educational Reform*, 1983)

The word "crisis" had an auspicious introduction into the language of American politics. On January 20, 1981, in his first inaugural address, President Ronald Reagan spoke of the nation's crisis: "In this present crisis, government is not the solution to our problem; government is the problem." The crisis that Reagan was referring to in his address was an economic crisis, brought on by escalating interest rates. Treasury bonds with 20-year maturity were yielding 13% interest; inflation was spiraling upward, seemingly out of control. Two weeks before Reagan's inaugural address, the prime interest rate hit an all-time high, 20.50%. He went on: "These United States are confronted with an economic affliction of great proportions. We suffer from the longest and one of the worst sustained inflations in our national history. It distorts our economic decisions, penalizes thrift, and crushes the struggling young and the fixed-income elderly alike. It threatens to shatter the lives of millions of our people."

"Crisis" was soon to become the favored metaphor for debates about education and the U.S. economy. Under the direction of Secretary of Education Terrell Bell, the publication on April 26, 1983, of *A Nation at Risk*[4] declared the U.S. public education system broken and in urgent need of repair. America's alleged preeminence in science and technology was said to have been overtaken. Neither the height from which the nation fell nor the depths to which it was alleged to have fallen were seriously questioned. "Crisis" was invoked as the reason to reform education.

---

4.   Charles Silberman published *Crisis in the Classroom* in 1970, but this much discussed book during the 1970s focused on the deadening effects of an outmoded curriculum and the inequities among races in the U.S. school system of the 1960s. Never did he suggest that the cure for America's supposed failing educational system was to privatize schooling or introduce competition into the system. Silberman's crisis was not about the economy nor did it succeed in drawing politicians into the debate about American education.

When the report was released in April 1983, it claimed that American students were plummeting academically, that schools suffered from uneven standards, and that teachers were not prepared. The report noted that our economy and national security would crumble if something weren't done. But the sobering report received immediate publicity for an almost comically accidental reason. As commission member Gerald Holton recalls, Reagan thanked the commissioners at a White House ceremony for endorsing school prayer, vouchers, and the elimination of the Department of Education. In fact, the newly printed blue-cover report never mentioned these pet passions of the president. "The one important reader of the report had apparently not read it after all," Holton said. Reagan had pulled a fast one, for political gain.

Reporters fell on the report like a pack of hungry dogs. The next day, "A Nation at Risk" made the front pages.[5]

The U.S. public education system was said to be near the bottom of the world rankings in academic achievement. Its economy was in danger of being wiped out by the Japanese economy, which, it was claimed, reached its exalted status due primarily to its superior education system. Educators rushed to Japan to discover the secret; they found kindergartens packed with 45 and 50 children and cram schools (*juku*) prepping high school students for gruesome college entrance exams. Rather than being shocked by what they saw, the visitors from the West actually entertained notions of importing such unfortunate practices. In 1985, Assistant Secretary of Education Chester Finn followed others to Japan for the purpose of learning the secrets of success of the Japanese education system: "They've demonstrated that you can have a coherent curriculum, high standards, good discipline, parental support, a professional teaching force and a well-run school. They have shown that the average student can learn a whole lot more."[6] Herbert J. Walberg, an educational researcher and member of the study team wrote that the Japanese system was the solution to the U.S.

---

5. Ansary, Tamim. (2007, March). Education at risk. *Edutopia*, 3(4), 49–53.
6. Richburg, Keith B. (1985, October 19). Japanese education: Admired but not easily imported. *Washington Post*, p. A1.

problems of poor performance: "I think it's portable. Gumption and willpower, that's the key."[7] Six years after *A Nation at Risk*, Vice-President George Herbert Walker Bush convened a national summit of education; politicians and business leaders attended; no educators were invited.[8]

Today our economy is supposedly threatened by "outsourcing" of telemarketing and engineering jobs to India, where engineers work for about $10,000 a year. American school children are told that they must compete with Chinese students if our economy, indeed our very culture, is to survive—forget that the Chinese economy flourishes primarily because of its seemingly inexhaustible supply of cheap labor and the fact that it pegs its currency to the U.S. dollar in order to maintain trade balances favorable to Chinese industry. Our school children are alleged to be dumb and getting dumber. Educators are blamed for nearly every problem with the nation's economy, but they are never praised when the U.S. jobs index rises or the gross domestic product exceeds expectations.

In times of crisis, the public may look to unlikely places for solutions. Bill Gates and his wife, on account of their

7.   Richburg, Keith B. (1985). *Op cit.*, p. A4.
8.   Nearly 20 years after the creation of "The Sandia Report" (Sandia National Laboratories. (1993). Perspectives on education in America: An annotated briefing. *Journal of Educational Research, 86*(5), 259-310) whether or not this document debunking the conservative's claims of an education crisis was suppressed by the George H. W. Bush administration is still being hotly debated. It is known for certain that Berliner and Biddle's *The manufactured crisis* (1995) was stimulated by the Sandia Report, that the authors of the report insist that they were threatened by officials in the Bush administration if they published their report, that the Bush administration officials involved continue to deny that anyone was threatened, and that the report was handled in a most unusual fashion by the U.S. Department of Education. See Bracey, Gerald. (2007, December 3). Righting wrongs. *The Huffington Post.* Retrieved December 9, 2007 from http://www.huffingtonpost.com/gerald-bracey/righting-wrongs_b_75189.html. Ravitch, Diane. (2007, December 5). Is U.S. education better than ever? *The Huffington Post.* Retrieved December 9, 2007 from http://www.huffingtonpost.com/diane-ravitch/is-us-education-better-_b_75441.html. Bracey, Gerald. (2007, December 5). Diane does Rush. *The Huffington Post.* http://www.huffingtonpost.com/gerald-bracey/diane-does-rush_b_75696.html

enormous wealth, are listened to as experts on the state of the American educational system. But their facts are often difficult to verify and their advice can be naïve. Gates, speaking with Eli Broad through the Strong American Schools project, claims that the majority of new jobs being created will require college education or advanced training.[9] The Bureau of Labor Statistics own studies indicate that by 2015 approximately 13 million new jobs will be created that do not require post-secondary education. The number of new jobs that will require at least a bachelor's degree is approximately 6 million—hardly the majority. Melinda Gates advises that all students in the U.S. should graduate from college. That the media report such utterances as news testifies to how firmly the grip of crisis has taken hold of the American psyche.

Americans' memories are short and few who quaked at the Jeremiahs shouting crisis in the early 1980s recalled the Sputnik crisis of the late 1950s. The launching of the unmanned satellite by the Russians on October 4, 1957, struck fear into the hearts of Americans who had been fed a constant diet of "Red Scare" news and entertainment since the end of WWII. Public education was said to bear much of the blame for the nation's decline in scientific and technical expertise that could allow a backward country like Russia to win the race to space. Congress responded by passing the National Defense Education Act in 1958 aimed primarily at financing the college and postgraduate training of tens of thousands of young men and women in foreign languages and scientific and technical fields. When the nation was again declared to be at risk in 1983, few were around to pronounce the earlier effort to upgrade American education a failure. Critics are few when the money is flowing in their direction.

---

9.   "In a country where two-thirds of new jobs being created require higher education or advanced training, these troubling trends make it harder for students from *all walks of life* to get a job and attain a middle class lifestyle."—Bill Gates. Retrieved November 1, 2007 from http://www.edin08.com/uploadedFiles/get-the-facts.pdf

Test Scores Are Alleged to Prove There is a Crisis

Proof that the nation was in a state of crisis was sought in the results of achievement test scores, domestic and international. Would-be reformers made much of a decline in SAT (Scholastic Aptitude Test[10]) and ACT (American College Test[11]) scores across the decade of the 1970s, immediately preceding the publication of *A Nation at Risk*. After leaving his position as Secretary of Education, William Bennett wrote that during the decades of the 1950s through the 1980s "we probably experienced the worst educational decline in our history. Between 1963 and 1980, for example, combined average Scholastic Aptitude Test (SAT) scores—scores which test students' verbal and math abilities—fell 90 points."[12] Bennett—once referred to by the *Wall Street Journal* as "Washington's most interesting public figure" even before his gambling problems became public knowledge—viewed the rising tide of mediocre education as a virtual war on our culture and our children. Only conservative proposals stood a chance of stemming the tide. *Ordo ab Chao.*

The only problem with these declarations of crisis was that there were no solid facts in the SAT scores to support the claim of the failure of the U.S. educational system. Largely ignored in the brouhaha over declining SAT scores was the fact that the test was not designed to reflect what students were learning in school; quite the opposite. The intent of its creators decades ago was to build a test that would reveal a student's aptitude

---

10.   The SAT test was known colloquially for years by the name "Scholastic Aptitude Test," but as notions of "aptitude" have fallen out of favor and more egalitarian concepts such as "skill" have been embraced, the Educational Testing Service that produces the SAT seems no longer to claim that its test measures aptitude. On the ETS Web site where 37 of its products (tests) are described, the word "aptitude" does not appear, although an SAT subtest is said to measure "reasoning."

11.   ACT, Inc., which no longer uses the American College Test appellation, fearlessly refers to its test as a measure of the "ability to complete college-level work" (http://www.act.org/aap/).

12.   Bennett, William J. (1992). *The devaluing of America: Fight for our culture and our children.* New York: Simon & Schuster. (p. 55)

for learning primarily abstract verbal and mathematical content beyond high school, and that the test would not give an advantage to students who happened to attend one type of high school rather than another. The resulting test and its successors over the decades resembled an IQ test, to put it bluntly, not a test of secondary school achievement. Typical questions drew on abstract reasoning with ordinary or common content that supposedly any 17 year-old would have encountered in life inside or outside of school. For many years—and during the period of the "Great Decline"—the Verbal portion of the SAT relied on the use of analogies to test aptitude. The words in the analogy would be relatively familiar, but the relationships among them had to be grasped through reasoning not specifically taught in school. For example, typical Verbal questions might look like thess:

1. *doctor* is to *hospital* as

    a) *petal* is to *flower*
    b) *horse* is to *farm*
    *c) *professor* is to *college*
    d) *criminal* is to *jail*
    e) *food* is to *restaurant*

2. *fawn* is to *deer* as

    a) *trumpet* is to *orchestra*
    *b) *puppy* is to *dog*
    c) *cat* is to *kitten*
    d) *eagle* is to *nest*
    e) *spoon* is to *fork*

A typical SAT Math item would resemble the following:

A rectangle has one side equal to 5 units and a different side equal to 13 units. The perimeter of the rectangle could be which of the following?

    I. 18
    II. 24
    III. 36

a) I only
b) II only
*c) III only
d) II and III only
e) I, II, and III

If one started out to write a test that would reflect the learning that had taken place in high school, questions about Steinbeck, the League of Nations, and isosceles triangles might appear. But these are precisely the kinds of question that were not being asked of SAT takers in the 1960s and 1970s as the SAT average was slipping downward.

The rising SAT and ACT scores after 1985 should no more have been taken as a positive evaluation of U.S. public education than the declining scores of the 1960s and 1970s were a negative message (see Exhibits 2.1 and 2.2). These score averages were greatly influenced by, among other things, fluctuating percentages of students in various social classes and ethnic or racial groups electing to attend college. Even before Bennett's citing the SAT decline as the bellwether of a crisis, a blue-ribbon panel had been formed in 1975 by the College Entrance Examination Board—the owner of the SAT—to research the decline. The panel was chaired by W. Willard

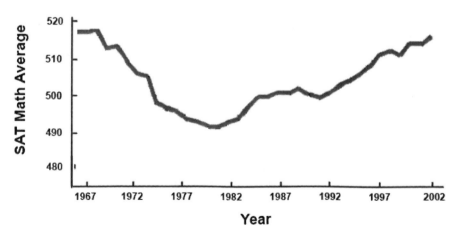

Exhibit 2.1.   SAT Mathematics score average for U.S. test takers, 1967-2002.

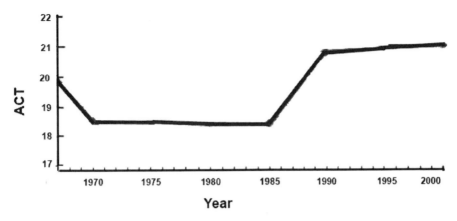

Exhibit 2.2.   ACT score average for U.S. test takers, 1967-2001.

Wirtz, who had served as Secretary of Labor from 1962 to 1969 in both the Kennedy and Lyndon Johnson Administrations. The panel attributed most of the score decline to shifts in the population of test takers: more African American students, more students from the lower ranks of high school graduating classes, and more female students. The vice-chairman of the blue-ribbon panel, former U.S. Commissioner of Education Harold Howe II, even published an article with the title "Let's Have Another SAT Decline." The opening up of postsecondary education to traditionally excluded classes of students was a good thing, he maintained. Equity and diversity were being served; more of it will be better, even if the SAT continues to drop.

It did not continue to drop, however. The SAT average leveled off at about the same time the panel was completing its work. As the nation's economy improved in the late 1980s and throughout the 1990s, more jobs were available and fewer academically marginal high school graduates chose to wait out a poor job market by spending time in college. Indeed, movements in such indicators as college admissions test scores have always told more about what types of students are choosing to apply to colleges than they reveal anything about the effectiveness or quality of our nation's elementary and secondary schools.

National Assessment of Educational Progress as an Evaluation of U.S. Schools

The National Assessment of Educational Progress (NAEP) was designed to overcome weaknesses of things like college admissions tests as measures of the school system's performance. By drawing representative samples of all students in the nation, NAEP—also known as "The Nation's Report Card"—provides the best available paper-and-pencil test evidence on the question of the accomplishments of the nation's schools, and even that evidence is not very good.

Since the late 1970s, NAEP scores have shown consistent gains with only infrequent reversals. Consider the trend in reading-scale scores from NAEP for White and Black 9-year-olds[13] from 1971 to 1999 in Exhibit 2.3. Average reading-scale

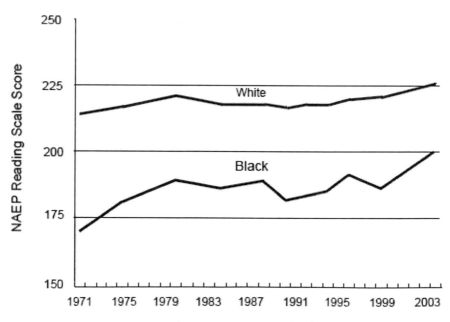

Exhibit 2.3.   NAEP scale scores for reading, 1971-2004 for White and Black pupils age 9. From U.S. Department of Education, Institute of Education Sciences, National Center for Education Statistics, National Assessment of Educational Progress (NAEP). Retrieved January 31, 2007, from http://nces.ed.gov/nationsreportcard/ltt/results2004/age_9_math_avg_score.asp

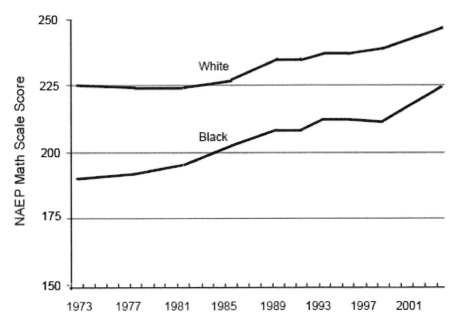

Exhibit 2.4.   NAEP scale scores for math, 1971-2004 for White and Black pupils age 9. From U.S. Department of Education, Institute of Education Sciences, National Center for Education Statistics, National Assessment of Educational Progress (NAEP). Retrieved January 31, 2007, from http://nces.ed.gov/nationsreportcard/ltt/results2004/age_9_math_avg_score.asp

scores also increased for Hispanic students from 183 in 1975 to 193 in 1999.

Exhibit 2.4 shows NAEP math scale scores for the period 1978 to 1999. These scores similarly rose consistently for both young White and Black students. Other NAEP data clearly dispelled any claims that America's school children were losing ground compared to their predecessors in reading, math, and science. A dramatic pattern of decreasing scores on "hard science" subject matter (physics and chemistry) and steeply

13.   NAEP data for 9-year-olds are presented here because they are least contaminated by problems of exclusion and demographic shifts in the school population that data for 13 and 17-year-olds suffer from. In spite of these problems, data for the older students generally show the same trends as are found in the data for 9-year-olds.

increasing scores on biological sciences subject matter gave evidence of a welcome shift in the curriculum being taught in the elementary and secondary grades rather than any worsening in the quality of instruction.

This seemingly good news from NAEP was not universally welcomed. Indeed, it tended to be ignored in the media, the very media that give front-page space to the fallacious reports of a crisis in America's schools. The refusal of NAEP scores to decline in accord with critics' wishes initiated the most embarrassing chapter in the history of this half-century-old endeavor. A National Assessment Governing Board (NAGB) was created by Congress in 1988 under the George H. W. Bush administration. Among its many duties was the task of declaring the absolute level of students' achievement inadequate, or more accurately, failing to achieve "proficiency." This was a task that the cooler heads that governed NAEP since its inception in the 1960s steadfastly refused to undertake. They knew it to be meaningless and an open door to political manipulation. And that is precisely what it became.

It hardly matters that such judgments and labeling of absolute score levels are notoriously arbitrary and political,[14] or that four different bodies (National Academy of Sciences, National Academy of Education, Government Accounting Office, and an independent panel of scholars) declared the "standard setting" by NAGB to be specious. The arbitrary labeling of NAEP levels as failing persists and has entered popular consciousness. Now one hears of NAEP primarily in connections with its labels: Basic, Proficient, Advanced. The Education Roundtable of the Indiana Legislature wrote "in Indiana, only about 30% of students achieve NAEP Proficient.

---

14.   Glass, Gene V. (1978). Standards and criteria. *Journal of Educational Measurement, 15*(4), 237-261. An updated version is available at Glass, Gene V. (2003). *Standards and criteria redux.* Retrieved June 19, 2007 from http://glass.ed.asu.edu/gene/papers/standards/

Indiana students need to be challenged."[15] When it became clear that NAEP scores were not going down, those who wished that they do so decided to declare them "not good enough," even when they rose.

From its inception until around 1980, NAEP was located at the Education Commission of the States in Denver, Colorado.[16] The project was largely influenced up until that time by its founder, Ralph W. Tyler, and a committee of statisticians and mathematicians led by John W. Tukey of Princeton University. Tukey, as chair of the very influential Analysis Advisory Committee (ANAC), guided the project in a manner largely faithful to Tyler's original conception. "Tyler's idea of critical evidence of learning was measurements of increase in knowledge and skill (performance) by the individual student. Evidence of national progress could simply be aggregates of those increases. Tyler's view of behavioral objectives and goal-based evaluation shaped NAEP theory and practice at first but political pressures later moved NAEP toward more conventional aptitude testing."[17] In the mid-1980s, with the Reagan administration firmly in control of federal education policy, a "request for proposals" was released by the U.S. Department of Education (DOE) that altered the course of NAEP considerably. Whereas state-by-state comparisons had originally been anathema to NAEP and whereas "grading" NAEP test performance had consistently been seen as not only technically impossible but

---

15. *Indiana's P-16 Plan for Improving Student Achievement.* Resolution Adopting Guidelines for Setting ISTEP+ Passing Scores. October 12, 2004

16. For an exhaustive history of NAEP, see Jones, Lyle V. & Olkin, Ingram. (Eds.) (2004). *The nation's report card: Evolution and perspectives.* Bloomington, IN: Phi Delta Kappa Educational Foundation. For a perspective on and critique of what NAEP ultimately became, see the review of Jones & Olkin (2004) by Robert E. Stake: Stake, Robert E. (2007, February 4). NAEP, report cards and education: A review essay. *Education Review, 10*(1). Retrieved February 17, 2007, from http://edrev.asu.edu/essays/v10n1index.html

17. Stake, Robert E. (2007, February 4). NAEP, report cards and education: A review essay. *Education Review, 10*(1). Retrieved February 17, 2007, from http://edrev.asu.edu/essays/v10n1index.html. (p. 2)

counterproductive by Tukey and ANAC, it was now clear that the DOE was intent on finding a contractor who would deliver both.[18] The department found a willing set of hands in the form of the Educational Testing Service (ETS).

It was clear from the moment that ETS became the new contractor for NAEP that things would change. Not only would the states be compared with each other with respect to NAEP performance—indeed, Secretary of Education Terrel Bell (1981-1985) created his famous "wall chart" that mapped states performance much like a weather map—but NAEP performance would also be graded. Percentages of correct answers would receive a grade, such as A, B, C, … F, or they would be labeled with the invented euphemisms chosen to make this whole system easier to swallow: Advanced, Proficient, and Basic.

As noted before, the central problem with this grading of NAEP performance is that it is technically impossible to do it in any objective, rational, or nonarbitrary way. John Tukey knew this well and resisted (indeed at times mocked) all attempts to turn NAEP into a "report card." I was commissioned by the Carnegie Corporation, a major source of funds for NAEP, at Tukey's urging to investigate the many proposed methods of "standard setting" for achievement tests and report to ANAC. In the published paper that resulted from that research, the conclusion was reached[19] "that the only sensible interpretations of data from assessment programs will be based solely on whether the rate of performance goes up or down. Interpretations and decisions based on absolute levels on performance on exercises will be largely meaningless, since these absolute

---

18.   The author was a member of ANAC from 1975 until 1978. If this account differs from other official accounts, it must be recognized that highly politically charged situations will be seen differently from different vantage points.

19.   Glass, Gene V. (1978). Standards and criteria. *Journal of Educational Measurement, 15,* 237-261. The entire issue of the journal was devoted to the publication of the paper and responses by a large number of researchers and scholars expressing various degrees of agreement and disagreement. An updated version of the paper is available at http://glass.ed.asu.edu/gene/papers/standards/

levels vary unaccountably with exercise content and difficulty, since judges will disagree wildly on the question of what consequences ought to ensue from the same absolute level of performance, and since there is no way to relate absolute levels of performance on exercises to success on the job, at higher levels of schooling, or in life. Setting performance standards on tests and exercises by known methods is a waste of time or worse."[20] Advice of this sort was ignored by the powers that took over NAEP and gave the contract for its implementation to ETS in the early 1980s.

One of the first major changes in NAEP was the formation in 1988 of the aforementioned National Assessment Governing Board (NAGB) under the chairmanship of Chester E. Finn Jr., the assistant secretary for research and improvement of the DOE. NAGB set to work to achieve the impossible, namely, the setting of performance standards for NAEP on a set of exercises so that performance could be labeled "passing" or "failing." America wanted to know whether its children were "passing" their tests or whether they were "failing" to learn their lessons. No matter that every teacher knows how arbitrarily drawn the line is between passing and failing, between the As, Bs, Cs, etc. Different graders give wildly different grades to the same performance. A "commendable" essay to one professor is "inadequate" to the eyes of a second professor. Everyone has a clear idea of what constitutes "passing" work, but everyone's clear idea is different from everyone else's. No matter. NAGB held the sword and NAEP would be forced into the Procrustean bed of "criterion referenced" testing whether it made sense or not. "NAGB essentially was a lay group, neither technical nor professional, quite unaware of the difficulty and danger in its new commitment to set cut-score standards of student competence, namely for *Basic, Proficient,* and *Advanced* performance. The commitment was

---

20.   Glass, Gene V. (1978). *Op cit.*, p. 259.

political, not educational."[21] NAEP's staff and subcontractors were told to determine the passing rates that correspond to Basic, Proficient, and Advanced achievement on each exercise, and that is what they did. The Nation would now have a report card.

Early grades on the Nation's Report Card were unfavorable. Large percentages of students failed to reach the Proficient level. However one may have wished to soften the blow of a Basic label, it was clearly read by the American public as "Failed." The conservative reformers had the evidence they desired: America's public schools were failing to educate their students; radical measures would be called for to transform a nation in crisis into a nation of achievers.

Not everyone accepted this conclusion. In particular, experts in educational measurements and evaluation moved to review NAGB/ETS's standard setting procedures (methods of determining what is known as the "cut-score," the demarcation between competence and incompetence). Three different efforts were undertaken to evaluate the process that led to the grading of America's school system. The National Academy of Sciences had its doubts and launched an investigation. The General Accounting Office at the direction of Congress in the early 1990s launched a similar study of the NAEP performance standards. The most technically competent and thorough investigation was a study conducted by an independent team of measurement and evaluation specialists consisting of Daniel Stufflebeam of the Evaluation Center at Western Michigan University, Richard M. Jaeger, then of the University of North Carolina at Greensboro and since deceased, and Michael Scriven, the well-known philosopher and leading evaluation methodologist. The team contracted with NAGB to conduct an evaluation of the performance standards. Stufflebeam, Jaeger, and Scriven's findings were stunning: NAGB had

---

21.   P. 7 in Stake, Robert E. (2007). NAEP, report cards and education: A review essay. *Education Review, 10*(1). Retrieved February 17, 2007, from http://edrev.asu.edu/essays/v10n1index.html

- "failed to produce dependable achievement levels for use in interpreting [math] NAEP results";
- "NAGB failed to produce evidence that the users of NAEP results can and are likely to make appropriate use of the levels in reaching valid conclusions about the meaning of NAEP results and that they find the levels meaningful and useful";
- "the technical difficulties are extremely serious and not mere academic complaints about finer points of test design and interpretation. Consequently, the resulting standards, which are due to be released in spite of the project's technical failures, must be used only with extreme caution."[22]

Both the National Academy of Sciences report and the GAO evaluation[23] of NAGB's standard setting agreed with the Stufflebeam team in substance if not in stridency. The National Academy of Sciences study found "the current process for setting NAEP achievement levels ... [is] fundamentally flawed."[24] Stufflebeam, Jaeger, and Scriven went on to question the technical competence of NAGB to oversee the cut-score setting attempt, and they went so far as to suggest to Congress that the membership of NAGB be reconstituted. NAGB's own internal technical advisory group had earlier issued a mildly critical report on the standard setting and was fired by the governing board. Stufflebeam, Jaeger, and Scriven's study overlapped this first internal study. The draft report was mildly critical. This group was also immediately

22.   Vinovskis, Maris A. (1998). *Overseeing the nation's reportcard: The creation and evolution of the National Assessment Governing Board (NAGB)*. Retrieved February 17, 2007, from http://www.nagb.org/pubs/95222.pdf
23.   General Accounting Office. (1993). *Educational achievement standards: NAGB's approach yields misleading interpretations*. The report went on to say: "GAO found that NAGB's 1990 standard-setting approach was procedurally flawed and that the interpretations that NAGB gave to the resulting NAEP scores were of doubtful validity."
24.   Nambury, S. R.; Pellegrino, James W.; Bertenthal, Meryl W.; Mitchell, Karen J.; & Jones, Lee R. (Eds.). (2000). *Grading the nation's report card: Research from the evaluation of NAEP*. Washington, DC: National Academies Press.

fired by the NAGB, presumably to prevent the report from being finalized and circulated. However, someone leaked the preliminary report to Congress and the GAO was asked to do its own evaluation. It did, and in response to an explicit question from the Congress, as to whether it agreed with the Stufflebeam team's report, it replied that it did. "Congress was not amused by NAGB firing the evaluators they had hired just because of mild criticism. We never received an apology (or the final payment on the contract)."[25]

The NAEP performance standards were set ridiculously high. Mathematics standards were the most egregiously misplaced. The majority of fourth and eighth grade students were labeled Basic or less, a clear message that teachers had failed to impart "proficiency" to their charges. In 1990, nearly 85% of fourth graders failed to reach the level of "Proficient" on the NAEP Math test. In 1996, "accommodations" were introduced for the learning disabled, limited English proficient, and other students. Proficiency rose to 21%; and by 2007, 39% scored proficient or higher. Of course, the standards themselves were being manipulated and schools were drilling students on test-like exercises. But the rise in scores was attributed to No Child Left Behind by some. Few bothered to note that when NAEP performance was equated to test performance on certain international assessments, hardly any nation broke the 50% barrier for "Proficient." Sweden, one of the highest performing nations in the world on tests of literacy, would have barely qualified a third of its students as "proficient" in reading.[26]

NAEP, an interesting and promising experiment in its inception that intended to start a national conversation about

25.   Personal communication from Michael Scriven, October 20, 1997.
26.   Rothstein, Richard; Jacobsen, Rebecca; & Widler, Tamara. (2006, November). *'Proficiency for all': An oxymoron.* Paper prepared for the Symposium, "Examining America's Commitment to Closing Achievement Gaps: NCLB and Its Alternatives," sponsored by the Campaign for Educational Equity, Teachers College, Columbia University. (p. 13)

curriculum and the goals of education, slowly turned bad. Too visible to be ignored by politicians, it gradually was turned to political purposes. The content of its exercises first became secondary then eventually was ignored altogether in favor of comparisons of the performance of racial groups and states. Promises by its creators—principally the educational psychologist and curriculum researcher Ralph W. Tyler—that NAEP would never be used to make state-to-state comparisons were broken in 1990 when control of NAEP had shifted completely from foundations to government agencies.

> So, it is my speculation that the history of NAEP would not have changed much had education and measurement professionals waged a much more vigorous fight against unvalidated interpretation. Hundreds of thousands of educators, legislators, and citizens wanted to do what they could to help education. They wanted to believe they had good indicators of educational progress. Steered away from trusting the nation's teachers, and like Terrel Bell, presuming a faulty wall chart (read "report card") better than none at all, they aligned with NAEP's view of educational progress. NAEP-makers didn't appreciate how people can fixate on a technical icon. They failed to appreciate the consequences. Of course an invention may turn grotesque.[27]

When the best available evidence, NAEP, on the progress of public education in America failed to satisfy political desires for empirical proof of the failure of the public schools, the Reagan and George H. W. Bush administrations co-opted the messenger and turned it to their purposes. America's public school system was declared a failure, and NAEP performance standards were said to provide the proof. And to this day, the unvalidated and specious performance labels remain the

---

27.   Stake, Robert E. (2007). NAEP, Report Cards and Education: A review essay. *Education Review*, 10(1). Retrieved January 31, 2007, from http://edrev.asu.edu/ essays/v10n1index.html. When Stake predicted many of these consequences nearly 40 years in advance, few listened and fewer still believed him. See Stake, Robert E. (1970). National assessment. Pp. 53-66 in Gene V. Glass, *Proceedings of the 1970 International Conference on Testing Problems*. Princeton, NJ: Educational Testing Service.

main message that the public receives about how the schools are doing.

International Assessments "Prove"
There Is an Education Crisis in the U.S.

When domestic assessments failed to provide support for the claims of a crisis, the focus became international assessments.[28] In 1967, the International Association for the Evaluation of Educational Achievement (IAEEA) published its first reports on the mathematics achievement of high school students in 12 nations. The international assessments were the brainchild of Torsten Husén, an educational psychologist and measurements expert at the University of Stockholm. Husén was the lead investigator on the IAEEA from 1962 to 1978 as it grew from a dozen to 20 countries. Seven reports were published during his tenure.

To some, statistics from these assessments of achievement during the 1970s, 1980s, and 1990s appeared to prove that the "tide of mediocrity" was rising. Economist Eric Hanushek,[29] a critic of U.S. public education, wrote that "In the international exams of math and science that have taken place since 1970, the U.S. has been at best in the middle of the pack, at worst well below average. At the same time it has become the world's economic superpower. How to reconcile these

28.   TIMSS (which now stands for Trends in Mathematics and Science Study) and PIRLS are part of the International Association for the Evaluation of Educational Achievement. PISA (Programme for International Student Assessment) is a project of the Organization for Economic Cooperation and Development.
29.   Hanushek is the Paul and Jean Hanna Senior Fellow of the Hoover Institution at Stanford University. The Hoover Institution draws its mission statement from the words of Herbert Hoover who articulated the purpose and scope of the Institution at its inception in 1959: "Both our social and economic systems are based on **private enterprise** from which springs initiative and ingenuity.... Ours is a system where the Federal Government should undertake no governmental, social or economic action, except where local government, or the people, cannot undertake it for themselves."

diverging trends? The answer is that the quality of the labor force is just one aspect of the economy that contributes to economic growth. Expanding education in a developing economy … is unlikely to foster much growth if the economy fails to simultaneously acquire the market structures and legal and governance systems that are necessary for a high-performing economy. The U.S. has an abundance of these attributes, and they appear to compensate for the shortcomings of its education system."[30]

The eminent education historian Lawrence Cremin attempted to account for the extraordinary vigor of the criticism of schools following the publication of *A Nation at Risk*: the criticisms of the 1980s "were putatively buttressed by data from cross-national studies of educational achievement."[31] A nation, if not at risk then certainly in a high state of anxiety over its economic problems in relation to emerging world markets, could easily be convinced that its trouble stemmed from an inferior education system. Few would attribute the nation's economic problems to decisions at the Federal Reserve Board, in the board rooms of the nation's mega-corporations, or, Heaven forbid, in the Congress. After all, the public schools were close at hand, familiar; and who really understood what the Federal Reserve Board does or was privy to the private goings-on in corporate board rooms? Each day children brought home to their parents evidence of the incompetence of their teachers and the children themselves. Americans were prepared in the 1980s to believe the worst about its schools, and an army of statisticians and social scientists would oblige them. When the Japanese economy sunk into recession in the 1990s and the U.S. emerged again as the dominant economy in the world, the credit was given to "market structures and legal and governance systems," not to the education system preparing the American workforce.

---

30. Hanushek, Eric A. (2002, Fall). The seeds of growth. *Education Next*, 10-17. *Education Next* is an in-house publication of the Hoover Institution.
31. Cremin, Lawrence A. (1990). *Popular education and its discontents*. New York: HarperCollins. (p. 6)

These structures and systems that Hanushek credited are the free trade measures enacted by the neoconservatives and extended by the neoliberals and that are contributing to the eradication of the middle class and to the transformation of today's public institutions for the worse.

The international comparative assessments were widely believed to demonstrate that U.S. students, often 4th, 8th, and 12th graders, were near the bottom of worldwide rankings of nations in reading, math, and science. The rankings might as well have appeared on the sports pages of the daily newspaper; the same competitive mentality was eagerly devouring the world rankings in science, math, and soccer. In Great Britain where rankings of schools on tests were routine in the press, the tallies were referred to with the same name as the weekly soccer rankings: the league tables. Extremely complex questions of test design and statistical sampling were routinely glossed over in the race to declare the U.S. a failure, and new reasons to declare a crisis were found.

> U.S. Twelfth-Graders Rank Poorly in Math and Science Study. (Ethan Bronner, *New York Times*, February 25, 1998, p. A-1)
>
> American 12th-graders scored at the very bottom of the rankings. (William Raspberry, *Washington Post*, March 12, 1998, p. A-15)
>
> Poor academic showing hurts U.S. high schoolers. (T. Henry, *USA Today*, February 25, 1998, p. 1-A)
>
> Hey! We're No. 19! (John Leo, *U.S. News & World Report*, March 9, 1998, p. 14)

Gerald Bracey has tirelessly debunked the claims emanating from the international assessments.[32] Where the comparisons were not patently invidious, they were often senseless.

---

32.   Bracey, Gerald W. (1998). *TIMSS, rhymes with "dims," as in "witted," KAPPAN.* Retrieved November 8, 2005 from http://www.pdkintl.org/kappan/kbra9805.htm. Bracey, Gerald W. (2000). The TIMSS "Final Year" study and report: A critique. *Educational Researcher, 29*(4), 4-10. Bracey, Gerald W. (2003). *On the death of childhood and the destruction of public schools: The folly of today's education policies and practices.* Portsmouth, NH: Heinemann.

Science and math assessments in TIMSS were conducted in the metric system (the U.S. being the only nation that does not teach exclusively in the metric system); in one assessment, the U.S. was one of only four nations not allowed to use calculators; and in the "12th grade assessment" of math/science literacy, American students averaged 18.1 years of age. In four of the other twenty nations, students were almost 19 years of age, in six they were over 19, and in two they were over 20, with Iceland garnering first place for the eldest cohort tested, 21.2 years, about the average age of U.S. college juniors. In the 16 nations that participated in the physics assessment, only the Russian Federation's students were quite a bit younger than American students (16.9 years versus 18.0), but Russia only tested 2% of them (compared with 14% in the U.S.). Students in Denmark, Italy, Austria, Germany, and Switzerland were all older than 19 on average and had 1 or 2 more years of schooling than U.S. high school seniors. Moreover, in the U.S. only 22% of 18-year-olds are in secondary school. For the 14 nations whose scores on TIMSS exceeded the U.S. in the test of general knowledge, the average percentage of 18-year-olds in secondary schools was 60%.

The Programme for International Student Assessment (PISA) in 2003 showed that U.S. 15 year-olds scored 18th in reading and 21st in science out of 41 nations, exceeding Denmark, Germany, Austria, Spain, Norway, and the like, where one hears less talk of education crises. Immediately one questions how validly students' reading performance could be compared across different languages? Translations might preserve meaning, or most of it. But how could they possibly be made equivalent in terms of reading difficulty or level of vocabulary? Were young German students quizzed on passages from Schiller while U.S. 15-year-olds puzzled over Shakespeare, or does one use Schlegel's translations of Shakespeare—acknowledged to be the best and different at the same time—to compare U.S. and German reading skill? And how does one make reading passages comparable in complexity between Farsi and Finnish, or between Swedish and Swahili? Such questions seem absurd on their face. When I asked to examine a few passages from the tests in English and in German (since I can read both with some facility), I was told that the questions were proprietary and could not be released to the public.[33]

The PISA test was administered again in 2006. Nearly a half million 15-year-old students in 57 countries took a 2-hour test comprising both multiple-choice and open-ended test items. Reading, mathematics, and science knowledge was tested. One of the key features of PISA 2006 was the opportunity to examine changes over 3 and 6 years in reading by comparing current scores with earlier assessments. Unfortunately for the U.S., improperly printed directions in the test booklet sent examinees to wrong pages and their results had to be thrown out. Apparently no one in the U.S. Department of Education or employed by the printing contractor proofread the test booklets. One wonders how accurate directions were in the dozens of other languages in which the test was printed.

Like all international assessments dating back to the early 1970s, PISA has its share of absurdities, inconsistencies, and misinformation. The U.S. scored above Israel and Norway in science on the 2006 PISA, but scored below Azerbaijan and Ireland in mathematics. From 2003 to 2006, Mexico gained 21 points in mathematics while France was losing 15 points; Austria went up 20 points in science while Japan declined by 17 points. What possible policy implications could such information hold? Repeatedly, when such fluctuations have been examined, the source of the inconsistencies has been found to lie in the vagaries of how the tests were administered or how samples of students were selected, non-response rates, the selection of "replacement" samples, and other details quite

---

33.   Personal communication, February 1, 2007, from Ina V. S. Mullis, TIMSS and PIRLS International Study Center codirector: "Since the majority of the 10 passages and their associated questions are secure to measure trends, and the instruments are translated by the national centers in the participating countries (more than 40 countries and more than 60 languages), these are proprietary materials for several reasons and not accessible via the web."

unrelated to the functioning of the school systems in the respective nations.[34] The Republican administration in the White House at the time of the release of NAEP scores in 2004 touted NAEP gains (Exhibits 2.3 and 2.4 above) as proof of the benefits of No Child Left Behind. But PISA scores for the U.S. in science show no gain whatsoever from 2003 to 2006: 491 in 2003 versus 489 in 2006, statistically virtually identical. (See Appendix B.)

Even when more recent assessments showed U.S. students excelling in math and science, politicians continued to issue jeremiads as though good news is no news. TIMSS results from 2003 revealed that only three places (Hong Kong, Latvia, and Lithuania) had larger gains in eighth-grade math than the U.S. and that U.S. eighth graders ranked ninth out of 44 nations in science. Nonetheless, while reporting these results, a *New York Times* editorial warned that if America "fails to take school reform seriously, American children will fall further and further behind their peers abroad."[35] As recently as late 2006, the U.S. Department of Education issued press releases decrying the latest international achievement rankings in which America's public schools failed to beat the competition. TIMSS and PISA results from 2003 showing the U.S. lagging half the nations in the worldwide assessment continued to be featured 4 years later on the U. S. Department of Education Web site as though they were fresh and urgent news.

That journalist Paul Farhi, a *Washington Post* staff writer, could devote an entire column in 2007 to the debunking of the U.S. defeat in the international assessments attests to the resiliency of the myth that American education has failed.[36]

34.   Lowell, B. Lindsay, & Salzman, Hal. (2007). *Into the eye of the storm: Assessing the evidence on science and engineering education, quality, and workforce demand.* Washington, DC: The Urban Institute.

35.   Happy talk on school reform. (2005, October 25). *New York Times.* Retrieved June 12, 2006 from http://www.nytimes.com/2005/10/22/opinion/22sat3.html?_r=1&oref=slogin

The international assessments have been a major source of support for this myth. Farhi identified and rebutted nearly a half dozen unsubstantiated charges against U.S. public education supposedly based on data like those collected in TIMSS and PIRLS:

1. "U.S. students rate poorly compared with those in the rest of the world.
2. "U.S. students are falling behind.
3. "U.S. students won't be well prepared for the modern workforce.
4. "Bad schooling has undermined America's competitiveness.
5. "How we stack up on international tests matters, if only for national pride."

Do U.S. students score poorly? Graduate School of Education, University of Pennsylvania, researchers Erling Boe and Sujie Shin, on whom Farhi relied extensively for his analysis, disagreed.[37] Erling and Shin called the pronouncements of U.S. failure in the international assessments "greatly exaggerated"[38] (see Exhibit 2.5). Boe and Shin aggregated results from several international assessments[39] conducted over the years and showed that U.S. 4th, 8th, 9th, and 10th graders performed at a level statistically equal to or above most industrialized nations. In no subject matter (math, reading, science, or civics) was a majority of nations above the U.S. in

36.   Farhi, Paul. (2007, January 21). Five myths about U.S. kids outclassed by the rest of the world. *Washington Post*, p. B2

37.   Boe, Erling E., & Shin, Sujie. (2005). Is the United States really losing the international horse race in academic achievement? *Kappan, 86*(9), 688-695.

38.   Boe, Erling E.. & Shin, Sujie. (2005). *Op cit.*, p. 688.

39.   Boe and Shin aggregated results from six international assessments: Reading Literacy Study (RLS 1991); Progress in International Reading Literacy Study (PIRLS 2001); Third International Mathematics and Science Study (TIMSS 1995); Third International Mathematics and Science Study — Repeat (TIMSS 1999); Programme for International Student Assessment (PISA 2000); and Civic Education Study (Torney-Purta, J., Lehmann, R., Oswald, H. and Schulz, W., 2001).

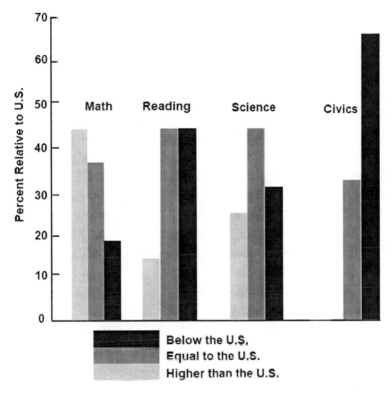

Exhibit 2.5. Aggregated achievement for U.S. 4th, 8th, 9th, and 10th graders compared to other nations. Adapted from Boe and Shin (2005); "Equal" means "not statistically significantly different."

measured achievement. Only 13% of the nations scored statistically significantly[40] higher than the U.S. in reading, 25% in science, and none in civics. The entire U.S. population of school children are performing at levels equal to those of tiny and economically privileged nations such as Canada, Scotland, Finland, Sweden, Germany, and France. Indeed, if one takes the performance of White students in the U.S. as if they constituted an economically and linguistically homogeneous nation, the White U.S. would be seen to outscore all seven G7

40. A statistically significant difference is one that exceeds a limit of uncertainty that takes the unreliability of probabilistic sampling into account. A statistically insignificant difference could disappear in subsequent sampling.

nations[41] in reading and all of the G5 nations except Japan in science and math. Entire states and regions of the U.S. with more population than many of the nations included in the international assessments can be singled out; they outscore any nation.[42] It is poverty and discrimination that threatens American education; not bureaucracy and teachers unions.

Two of the myths that Farhi identified address the question whether the schools are preparing workers for a highly technical, science-based globalized economy. Among the loudest critics of the nation's schools are those who have little experience in or grasp of what a high-tech economy involves. Politicians team with scientists, who are convinced that America is doomed if it ignores their discipline, to prescribe more mathematics, more physics, and more biology for high school students. Indeed, the loudest cries for more science seem to emanate from those, like politicians, who know next to nothing about it. And gentle demurs from scientists and engineers who report that most of the high school curriculum is irrelevant to the growth of the contemporary economy are branded as anti-intellectual or even unpatriotic by those convinced of the failure of the school system. Proposals by no less than Bill Gates to emphasize more mathematics and science in high school prompted this frank reply to postings on an internet discussion forum by a computing science professor:

> I'm Norm Matloff, a computer science professor at the University of California, Davis. I recently joined this group, but haven't had much time to read most of the posts, let alone reply. But I feel I really must reply on the issue of math.
>
> Math has been and is a big part of my life. All my degrees were in math. After my doctorate, I became a math professor, later a statistics professor, both professions that are clearly mathematical. Later still I

41.   The G7 nations are U.S., Canada, France, Germany, Italy, Japan, and the United Kingdom. The G5 were U.S., France, Germany, Japan, and the United Kingdom, superseded by G7 and G8 when Russia joined the group of leading economies.
42.   Berliner, David C. (2006). Our impoverished view of educational reform. *Teachers College Record, 108*(6), 949-995.

moved to computer science, a field which is putatively mathe-matical....

Those who say that most jobs that seem to be "mathematical" in actuality rarely use math are correct. Most engineers, for instance, never use calculus in their work--quite contrary to what most people would expect for such a basic freshman subject in engineering curricula. And I would say that fewer than 1% of computer science graduates ever do any kind of formal math in their entire careers.

This is even true in research. There are over 30 faculty in my department. At most six or seven of them use college-level math in their research; most never use it, and in fact would plead ignorance if you asked them to work a calculus problem, much less something like, say, group theory....

I do believe that standardized tests have value, but that all-too-familiar problem of "teaching to the test" is very, very real.

Let's again use calculus as our example. Most of the better students in high school nowadays do take calculus there, as an Advanced Placement (AP) course. AP is death to careful, thoughtful inquiry. There is a rush to cover the entire material by May, when the national AP exams are given, thus no time to stop and ask, "What does this really mean?" And since the AP exam is given in a multiple choice format, there are very few test problems that probe the "What does this really mean?" issues. And in turn, since these are not on the national AP exam, the teachers have no incentive to cover them, and the students have no incentive to think about them. ...

I just read today that Congress wants to spend $43 billion (yes, billion not million) in the next few years on improving math and science education at the K-12 level. I believe that money would be much better spent in numerous other areas.[43]

This professor's assessment of the needs of workers in a high-tech economy is not atypical. At present, for every one worker in "computers-physical-life sciences" in the U.S., there are more than 10 workers in "security-food service-janitorial-retail sales-trucking."[44] But candid assessments are rare in a highly charged political environment where masses fear for their children's future and worship the ineffable complexities of fields they never understood.

---

43.   Retrieved December 11, 2007 from http://groups.yahoo.com/group/eddra/.
44.   U.S. Department of Labor, Bureau of Labor Statistics. http://www.bls.gov/oes/

When *Newsweek* journalist Fareed Zakaria asked Singapore's Minister of Education Tharman Shanmugaratnam to explain why Singapore's young pupils top the world rankings in science and math but few excel in the sciences or professions or even business later in life, the minister replied:

> "[There are two] meritocracies.... Yours [U.S.] is a talent meritocracy, ours is an exam meritocracy. There are some parts of the intellect that we are not able to test well—like creativity, curiosity, a sense of adventure, ambition. Most of all, America has a culture of learning that challenges conventional wisdom, even if it means challenging authority. These are the areas where Singapore must learn from America."[45]

International assessments have contributed two things: the opportunity for chicanery by politicians, and the opportunity for employment for statisticians and psychometricians. Beyond that, they have distracted educators from real problems and real progress. Indeed it is remarkable that otherwise thoughtful observers of schooling would think that these gross comparisons of nations so utterly different in hundreds of respects could contribute to understanding how to improve America's schools. It is disheartening to those who think seriously about education in all nations that these periodic Olympics of test taking have become the focus of the public's attention to education. Ironically, Americans are slow to challenge the authority of the paper-and-pencil exams that so often constitute the sole criterion by which U.S. schools are judged. One truly wonders how all these numbers and races could benefit the effort to improve schooling and its contribution to the general welfare.

---

45.   Zakaria, Fareed. (2006, January 9). We all have a lot to learn. *Newsweek International Edition.* Retrieved February 17, 2007, from http://www.msnbc.msn.com/id/10663340/site/newsweek/

Education and the Economy

Some economists wish to attribute the threat to U.S. economic superiority and the growing income disparity within the U.S. to the effects of education in an increasingly technologically sophisticated economy. Better educated workers gain in income faster than less educated ones; more and better education for all will lift all boats, so it is thought. As an educator and one who sees almost daily the near irrelevance of most education to any form of productivity growth, I am quite skeptical of such claims. Merely demonstrating increasing earnings for those who acquire more schooling will not dispel my skepticism. Schooling has more to do with winnowing to select the *right* personalities and licensing that keeps certain labor markets from being flooded than it does have to do with imparting skills truly related to economic productivity. When employers were asked to look at the actual questions on a high stakes graduation math exam, they were nearly unanimous in their opinion that the skills tested were irrelevant to functioning in their company. In Exhibit 2.6, two of the questions posed to employers in 10 different sectors of the economy are shown along with their responses to the statement, "My employees use this type of mathematics in their daily work." As an example of how the data in Exhibit 2.6 are interpreted, consider Question 2 on graphing linear equations, the stock and trade of most elementary algebra courses. Of the 43 employers surveyed across such employment sectors as health care, law, banking, and engineering, only three employers reported that their employees used this type of mathematics in their daily work.

Many of the calls for more instruction in this subject or on that topic in the public schools emanate from special interest groups. One does not often think of groups of teachers and professors delivering opinions on the school curriculum as being special interest groups, but in fact they sometimes function as just that. When the National Commission on Mathematics and Science Teaching for the 21st Century spoke

Question 1. Of the following choices, rational numbers, integers, whole numbers, irrational numbers, which of these could not be classified as the number representing the number of people in a room?

Question 4. Which statement is true about the graphs of these equations?
$$3y = -12x + 6$$
$$-2y = 8x - 4$$
a) The lines are parallel.
b) The lines are perpendicular.
c) The lines intersect at a 45 degree angle.
d) The lines are indeterminate.

	Health Care	Law Firms	Food Indust	Whole-sale	Gov Agency	Retail Sales	Construct	Banking	Serv Indust	Engin	Totals & %
Q1	2/6*	0/3	0/3	0/3	0/6	0/4	1/3	0/4	1/7	0/4	4/43 9%
Q4	0/6	0/3	0/3	0/3	0/6	1/4	1/3	0/4	1/7	0/4	3/43 7%

Exhibit 2.6. Numbers and percentages of magagers responding affirmatively to the statement, "My employees use this type of math in their daily work. Two of 6 employers in the health care sector reported that Q1 measured a skill used by employees in their industry. Based on Glass, Gene V., & Edholm, Cheryl A. (2002). *The AIMS test and the mathematics actually used by Arizona employees.* Tempe, AZ: Education Policy Studies Laboratory, Arizona State University. Document #EPSL-0210-122-EPRU.

of the future of not just school curriculum but of the very well-being of the U.S., they saw an urgent need for more of what they had to give: "The future well-being of our nation and people depends not just on how well we educate our children generally, but on how well we educate them in mathematics and science specifically."[46] Ironically, when science and engineering graduates employed in the field are surveyed, fewer than half of them report that their preparation in their major is "closely related" to the skills required on their job.[47]

---

46. National Commission on Mathematics and Science Teaching for the 21st Century. (2000). *Before it's too late: A report to the nation from the National Commission on Mathematics and Science Teaching for the 21st Century.* Washington, DC: U.S. Department of Education. p. 5.

47. Lowell, B. Lindsay, & Salzman, Hal. (2007). *Into the eye of the storm: Assessing the evidence on science and engineering education, quality, and workforce demand.* Washington, DC: The Urban Institute.

Whaten Federal Reserve chairman Ben Bernanke sought to explain the growing income disparity in America in terms of differences in educational attainment, economist Paul Krugman labeled his reasoning "fallacious":

> the fallacy he fell into tends to dominate polite discussion about income trends, not because it's true, but because it's comforting. The notion that it's all about returns to education suggests that nobody is to blame for rising inequality, that it's just a case of supply and demand at work. And it also suggests that the way to mitigate inequality is to improve our educational system—and better education is a value to which just about every politician in America pays at least lip service.
>
> The idea that we have a rising oligarchy is much more disturbing. It suggests that the growth of inequality may have as much to do with power relations as it does with market forces. Unfortunately, that's the real story.
>
> Should we be worried about the increasingly oligarchic nature of American society? Yes, and not just because a rising economic tide has failed to lift most boats. Both history and modern experience tell us that highly unequal societies also tend to be highly corrupt....
>
> And I'm with Alan Greenspan, who—surprisingly, given his libertarian roots—has repeatedly warned that growing inequality poses a threat to "democratic society."[48]

The Crisis That Never Was

The crisis rhetoric continues to dominate debates about America's public education system. Regardless of the facts concerning test score trends, critics insist that U.S. school children are ill-prepared to compete in the high-tech economies of the future. The idea of a nation's education system in crisis had to be invented. An emergency had to be declared to legitimize radical changes that certain political interests were attempting to impose on the U.S. public schools. In actual fact, there was no crisis of the type that these political forces

---

48.   Krugman, Paul. (2006, February 27). Graduates versus oligarchs. *New York Times*, p. A20.

sought to use as their wedge to insert a conservative agenda into the education policy issues of the time. Declaring crises is now recognized as a tactic of diminishing credibility in political contests.

> We have an Administration that falsely hypes almost every issue as a crisis. They did it on Iraq, and they are doing it now on Social Security. They exploit the politics of fear and division. (*A Democratic Blueprint for America's Future*, an address by Senator Ted Kennedy at the National Press Club, January 12, 2005)

In truth, the crisis in our schools was a political invention that stemmed from motives unrelated to averting economic defeat at the hands of Japan (Germany, India, etc.). The threat of the Japanese economy has gone away, but the rhetoric of crisis in American education remains. My colleague David Berliner has argued this point successfully in his 1995 book with Bruce Biddle titled *The Manufactured Crisis: Myths, Fraud, and the Attack on America's Public Schools*. And still the beat goes on. As though the debate is fresh, authors can still reprint tables of old assessment results supposedly documenting a "social problem in need of remedy"[49] and selectively cite arguments about their interpretation in seeking to establish support for standards-based reform. As Hinchey and Cadiero-Kaplan[50] observed, "No matter how hard researchers Berliner and Biddle worked in *The Manufactured Crisis* (1995) to debunk the idea that public schools are failing wholesale, and no matter how many others have followed in their footsteps trying to make the same point, continued alarms raised by government and others have helped create a

---

49.   Kosar, Kevin. R. (2005). *Failing grades: The federal politics of education standards.* Boulder, CO: Lynne Rienner (p. 201). See the review by Camilli, Gregory. (2006). Review of Kosar, Kevin R. *Failing grades: The federal politics of education standards. Education Review.* Retrieved May 1, 2007 from http://edrev.asu.edu/reviews/rev469.htm.

50.   Hinchey, Patricia H., & Cadiero-Kaplan, Karen. The future of teacher education and teaching: Another piece of the privatization puzzle. *Journal for Critical Education Policy Studies, 3*(2). Retrieved February 4, 2007, from http://www.jceps.com/?pageID=article&articleID=48

climate in which the challenge to schools as public institutions can not only be made, but can be widely perceived as reasonable."

If one surrenders the notion of a crisis of low achievement, if U.S. schools are credited with doing a commendable job of teaching students, then where does one look to discover the forces that truly drive the movements attempting to transform public education? The search for the motivations behind the most salient school reform proposals is the subject of the next four chapters.

Part II.
Fertilizers, Pills, and
Magnetic Strips

Chapter Three

Fertilizers and Tractors: The Rural to Urban Migration

Technological invention transforms human life: the Clovis spear point (11500 B.C.E), the plow (3000 B.C.E), the horse collar (300 B.C.E), Gutenberg's printing by movable type (1450), nitroglycerine (Alfred Nobel, circa 1860), the automobile engine (Wilhelm Maybach, 1900); and at a later time, penicillin (Alexander Fleming, 1928), the birth control pill (Julian, 1940 and many others), chlorpromazine (Delay & Deniker, 1952), and lovastatin (Akira Endo, 1976). Few inventions have so impacted modern America and accelerated the pace of change as has the little known Haber process that led to the invention of artificial fertilizers. Humans change the world by invention, and the world they create changes them.

The roots of the reformers' zeal to transform modern education do not lie in the crisis politics of the 1980s, but rather they reach back more than 100 years to the agrarian society out of which America grew. My primary purpose here is not to recount the history of American education in the 20th century. That is a project pursued interminably and often redundantly

Fertilizers, Pills, and Magnetic Strips: The Fate of Education in America
pp. 59–73
Copyright © 2008 by Information Age Publishing

by others. Rather, my purpose in citing data on the revolution in food production, the growth of the comprehensive high school, and the rapidly increasing rate of high school graduation is to document the enormous changes in occupations and social life attendant to the transformation of agriculture by technological invention. This transformation was eventually to alter more than just high schools and vocations; it profoundly changed how couples felt about one of the most important decisions any family faces: whether to bear children, and how many children to bear.

It is difficult for people of nearly any age today, well more than 95% of whom live in cities or suburbs, to imagine the rural society that was America before 1900. The rural-to-urban migration actually started slowly in the 19th century during the Industrial Revolution (though in England it was nearly completed by 1900 due to the scarcity of land and the rising population). The lives of the great-grandparents and great-great-grandparents of today's Baby Boomers were mostly spent on farms, raising much of the food that they ate, often clearing land and turning the soil with the help of horses, reading what little there was to read by kerosene lamp, pumping water from wells, and communicating if at all by posted letters. "The farmers of Washington's day had no better tools than had the farmers of Julius Caesar's day; in fact, the Roman ploughs were probably superior to those in general use in America 18 centuries later."[1] The limited productivity of agriculture demanded that the vast majority of the population engage in the production of food. Farmers may have sold limited amounts of wheat and corn or an occasional pig or cow, but the vegetables they ate, the bread they baked, and the milk and butter they consumed were produced on their property by their own hands. All this would change when agriculture became more productive.

---

1.   Thompson, Holland. (1921). *The age of invention: A chronicle of mechanical conquest. Chronicles of America, Volume 37.* Retrieved February 13, 2006, from the Gutenberg Project: http://www.gutenberg.org.

Beginning in about the 1830s, limited amounts of Peruvian bat guano were first imported to Britain and the U.S. to be used as commercial fertilizers. The price was high due to the cost of transporting the fertilizer from South America. Cheap and abundant fertilizer could increase the yield of an individual farm and create excess product that could be sold on the market. So-called "natural" fertilizers would always be in limited supply, hence, their price would be great. A fertilizer concocted at reasonable cost out

Fritz Haber (1868-1934)
German Chemist

of elemental substances available everywhere would revolutionize agriculture, and much more. Food production got its big boost from the invention of the Haber process in 1908.[2] A now virtually forgotten German chemist named Fritz Haber invented a process for producing ammonia from nitrogen in the air and then transforming the ammonia into nitric acid used in the production of artificial fertilizers. The Haber process was patented in 1910 and commercial production started immediately. After the Allied blockade of Germany in WWI cut off supplies of nitrates from Chile, large scale production of ammonia by the Haber process began in earnest, primarily in the production of explosives. After the war, ammonia production was confined to more peaceful uses, primarily for fertilizers.[3] Cheap artificial fertilizer meant more fertile land. More fertile land meant fewer farmers needed to grow crops. Excess population migrated to cities. It could be argued that

2.   The late economist and philosopher Kenneth E. Boulding once referred to the invention of the Haber process as perhaps the most important event shaping the 20th century. Personal communication, 1972.

3.   Ammonia is among the most heavily produced inorganic substances. In 2000, more than 109,000,000 metric tons of ammonia were produced worldwide. More than 80% of that amount was used in the production of fertilizers.

the invention of the Haber process was the most revolutionary invention since the plow in 3000 B.C.E.[4]

U.S. Rural to Urban Migration

In 1900, America comprised 5,000 more communities than in
the year 2000. The demise of small rural America is a one of
the most transformative events of the 20th century. Scarcely
anyone is unaware that the first half of the 20th century was
characterized by the rise initially of urban centers, then of
suburban sprawl. The march of the U.S. populous from farms
to cities continues even into the 21st century. This transition
can be seen in the Department of Agriculture Census of Agriculture data on numbers of farms and ranches in Exhibits 3.1
and 3.2. The number of farms and ranches in the U.S.
declined by roughly 20% even in the last quarter of the 20th
century. This decline can be attributed in part to the rise of
corporate farming, which removes population from rural to
urban and suburban areas. In a nation of 300 million persons,
barely 2 million ranches and farms are home to a tiny proportion of the population. In 1995, only 15 of every 1,000 persons
in the U.S. resided on farms.[5]

Fewer hands were needed to tend the farms and raise the
nation's food. Fertilizers were responsible for increasing
yields of food per acre. Artificial fertilizer use was slow to be
adopted by American farmers in the 1910s and early 1920s.
Prejudices in favor of more "natural" organic fertilizers kept
usage of ammonia based fertilizers low at first. From 1910 to
1919, manufactured fertilizer sales in the U.S. amounted to a

---

4.   The plow pulled by animals made possible the production of more food by
fewer persons; the surpluses controlled by an elite group that defended its position with arms marked a milestone in the stratification of ancient societies. Prior to
the plow, everyone was a farmer and ate all that they produced.

5.   Farm residence = An occupied one-family house or mobile home is classified
as a farm residence if: (1) the housing unit is located on a property of 1 acre or
more, and (2) at least $1,000 worth of agricultural products were sold from the
property in 1989.)

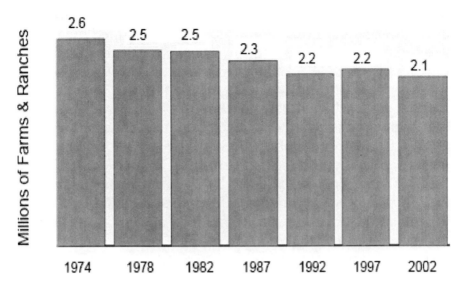

Exhibit 3.1.   Number of farms and ranches in the U.S. for selected years, 1974-2002. From U.S. Department of Agriculture, National Agricultural Statistics Service. http://www.nass.usda.gov/Census_of_Agriculture/2002/Quick_Facts/ranch.asp

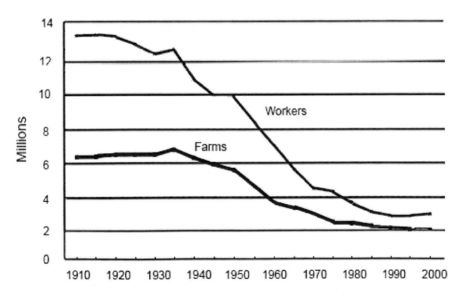

Exhibit 3.2.   Numbers of farms and farm workers for selected years, 1910-2000. From U.S. Department of Agriculture, National Agricultural Statistics Service. http://www.nass.usda.gov/Census_of_Agriculture/2002/Quick_Facts/ranch.asp

yearly average of about 6.5 tons; that figure grew slightly to 6.8 tons on average during the 1920s, but remained there during the 1930s, largely on account of the depressed economy. During the years of WWII and subsequently, ammonia-based fertilizer production and use increased rapidly. The effects of increasing productivity from the use of artificial fertilizers were most pronounced on nitrogen dependent crops such as corn, fruits, and vegetables. Wheat, the most abundant crop in the U.S. and worldwide, constituting about one fifth of the world's crops, was less affected by the use of artificial fertilizers. The wheat stalk grew too tall when stimulated by the fertilizers and the plant tended to fall over and rot in the fields.

Not all of the remarkable transformation of farm work was due to the advent of artificial fertilizers, however. Many technological advances that can be grouped under the heading "mechanization" played an important role as well. Early steam driven tractors were hardly more efficient than horses, but they did not need fodder. As a

Fordson Model F Tractor

consequence, land used to produce food for horses could be used to produce food for humans and a small gain in productivity resulted. Henry Ford manufactured the first mass produced gasoline powered tractor in 1917; the Fordson tractor constituted more than three-quarters of the U.S. tractor market by 1925. A 50 horse power tractor could pull 16 plows; harrows and seed drills could follow and plant acres in a day.

As farms became more productive, fewer hands were required to produce increasing amounts of food. In 1910, the average American farm had approximately 2.2 farm workers. By the year 2000, that figure had dropped to below 1.2 farm workers per farm. The hours of labor required to produce a bushel of wheat dropped dramatically from 1890 to 1930 and to 1950. In 1890 it took approximately 45 hours of labor to produce 100 bushels of wheat on five acres. By 1930, that number had decreased to approximately 15 hours, and by 1950, 100 bushels of wheat could be produced on five acres in about 5 hours of labor. By century's end, 3 out of every 4 Americans lived in urban areas (see Exhibit 3.3).

This trend toward urbanization is not unique to the U.S., obviously. Sociologists and demographers Ron Wimberley, Libby Morris, and Gregory Fulkerson, of North Carolina State University and the University of Georgia interpolated from United Nations projections to the year 2010 and designated May 23, 2007, as the day on which the world's population became more urban than rural for the first time in history.

Nature also played an important role in spurring on the great rural to urban migration. In the mid-1930s, years of drought and misguided federal agriculture policy conspired to produce one of history's worst climate disasters: the great American Dust Bowl. The Homestead Act of 1862 granted freehold title to 160 acres of land in the Great Plains and West.

Exhibit 3.3. Percentage of U.S. Population in Urban Centers

Year	Number	% Urban (not Suburban)
1790	3.90 million	5%
1860	31.43 million	20%
1870	39.81 million	25%
1880	50.15 million	28%
1890	62.94 million	35%
1900	75.99 million	40%
1910	91.97 million	45%
1920	105.71 million	51%
1990	277.89 million	75%
2004	293.63 million	80%

Source: Based on http://www.census.gov/population/censusdata/table-4.pdf

That much land in Illinois or even Iowa was enough to sustain a family of six or eight at a relatively comfortable level. However, a parcel of land no bigger than 160 acres in the semiarid High Plains of Nebraska, Colorado, Kansas, and down to the Panhandle of Texas virtually guaranteed poverty to its recipients at the first appearance of drought. Too small for ranching and too dry for farming, the land was plowed mercilessly to grow wheat that was heavily subsidized by the federal government during and immediately after World War I. As drought gripped the Great Plains in the late 1920s and early 1930s, once temporarily fertile farm land dried, turned to dust, and blew into lethal storms that devastated homes, towns, and tens of thousands of individual lives. Those who abandoned the denuded farmlands of Western Kansas and Oklahoma, of Eastern Colorado and New Mexico, and particularly from the once thriving Texas Panhandle, headed west to California, where, unwelcome and branded "Okies," they often gravitated to towns and cities in search of unfamiliar work. By 1938, one third of all families in the Oklahoma Panhandle had left their farms.[6]

As families left farms in the early 20th century and relocated in cities, factory work began to replace farm work. The unfamiliar skills required in manufacture began to be taught in secondary school. Labor unions were desirous of restricting entry of young people into the trades thus maintaining higher wage levels. Young men and women began to stay in school well into their teens.

Until child labor laws were instituted in the second decade of the 20th century, young children were significant contributors to the family income. Approximately 2 million children worked in factories in the U.S. in 1900. In families where children under the age of 16 were working prior to 1916, nearly a quarter of the family's income was earned by children. Earlier attempts to enact restrictions on child labor were struck

6.   Egan, Timothy. (2006). *The worst hard time: The untold story of those who survived the Great American Dust Bowl*. Boston: Houghton Mifflin.

down by the U.S. Supreme Court because they interfered with a child's right to contract with an employer. An attempt to pass a constitutional amendment controlling child labor failed in the 1920s. The fact that compulsory school attendance laws required attendance to age 16 and not older was the result of a compromise between the desire to educate children to the limit of their potential and the desire not to deprive families of a source of income. The Great Depression was a major influence limiting employment of children who would, if employed, contribute to even higher adult unemployment. Not until 1938 did the Fair Labor Standards Act impose meaningful restrictions on the employment of children younger than 16.[7] Today, few laws apply to the work of children on their family's farm.

The nation began to view education as closely connected to the economy in manifold ways. As Thomas F. Green and his colleagues (1980) showed, the comprehensive high school began to assume its modern form in 1910, precisely at the point at which fertilizers and tractors began to transform agricultural productivity. In Exhibit 3.4, the percentage of children enrolled in elementary and secondary school is displayed from 1870 to 1990. Although education was nearly universal at the elementary school level as early as the late decades of the 19th century, secondary school attendance is a phenomenon of the early decades of the 20th century. Adolescent boys and girls were no longer needed as extra hands on the farms.

High schools were formerly elite academies educating the children of the wealthy in the classics so that they could take their rightful place in the professions of law and medicine. The comprehensive high school that emerged in the early decades of the 20th century sought to train children from the middle and lower economic classes in how to be factory workers. Schools began to teach industrial education, a type

---

7.   The Fair Wage and Hours Law, as the act was widely known, established a work week as 40 hours at a wage of no less than 40 cents an hour. The law, vigorously opposed by the businesses and industries, was upheld by the U.S. Supreme Court in 1941.

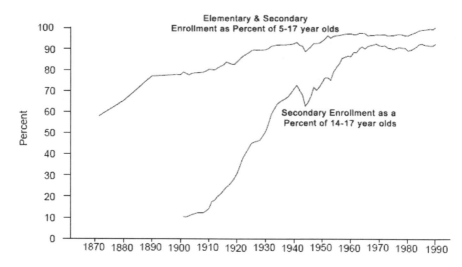

Exhibit 3.4.   Based on Figure 7, p. 27, in Snyder, Thomas D. (1993). *120 years of American education: A statistical portrait.* Washington, DC: U.S. Department of Education, National Center for Education Statistics.

of training that provided factories with pretrained workers at public expense. During this period and subsequently, the National Association of Manufacturers became a powerful player in setting education policy. Much education history of the late 19th century focused on the role of immigrants from Europe and how the U.S. school system changed to address the issue of assimilation. But the migrants from farms to cities in America between 1910 and 1930 were far more numerous and influential in shaping the nature of public education.

In 1914, Edwin G. Cooley, former Superintendent of Schools for the city of Chicago, proposed a dual system of secondary education in America. Students would be tracked at age 14 into either a college preparatory system or a system of training for an industrial job (a system of tracking that exists even in this day in some countries):

> Separate schools are necessary whose equipment, corps of teachers, and board of administration must be in the closest possible relation to the occupations. In such schools the applications of general edu-

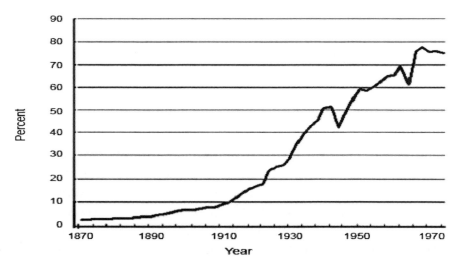

Exhibit 3.5.   High school graduates as a percentage of the 17 year-old U.S. population, 1871-1970. Based on Green et al. (1980).

cation to vocational work can be made only by men who know the vocations. The boards of education administering such institutions must give them far greater attention on the practical side than the ordinary boards of education need to do in the case of academic schools.[8]

Thomas Green placed the creation of the comprehensive secondary school in America in the second decade of the last century:

the claim is advanced that the system in the American case does not much predate 1910.... [The graph in Exhibit 3.5] shows that the remarkably regular and unyielding rise in the high school attendance rate that continued until 1965 began about 1910. [An accompanying table] shows that the ratio of B.A. or First Professional Degree to high school graduates of four years earlier drops precipitously from the late nineteenth century until about 1920, and then it slowly rises some 10 to 15 percent to its present fairly stable level.

8.   Quoted on page 2 in Wraga, William G. (2000). *The comprehensive high school in the United States: A historical perspective.* Paper presented at the meeting of the John Dewey Society, New Orleans, Louisiana. ERIC Document # ED443170.

These two facts, taken together, constitute evidence that the high school was transformed from an essentially college preparatory institution to a comprehensive secondary school in the second decade of the [twentieth] century.[9]

Urban Life and Desirable Family Size

In rural cultures, each live birth promises to ease the burden of work on the other family members some 10 years later. More pairs of hands to help with planting, cultivating, and harvesting are welcome additions. The work life of children in early 20th century rural societies is scarcely imaginable by today's youth. Tona Drbohlavová's recollection of her childhood in 1916 rural Bohemia provides a glimpse into the hard life of children (and, incidentally and far less significantly, the importance of fertilizers):

> I started helping my father with this work when I was about twelve. In the spring, we hauled manure to the field on the hill. My father loaded a wheelbarrow, tied a loop of rope around me, and I pulled. My shoulders got all bruised from the rope. Harvest work was not as bad.[10]

As was seen in Exhibit 3.2, the typical farm in America in 1910 was worked by two persons, often a father and a son, sometimes by both husband and wife. As fertilizers changed the amount of corn and vegetables that could be grown on an acre of ground and as tractors and other farm implements greatly increased the number of acres that could be worked by one person, the one-laborer farm became the standard. Additional children no longer contributed needed labor to work on the farm. In fact, additional children began to constitute an economic drain on the family.

9.   Green, Thomas F. with Ericson, David P. & Seidman, Robert H. (1980). *Predicting the behavior of the educational system*. Syracuse, NY: Syracuse University Press. (p. 178)

10.   Welner, Sylvia, & Welner, Kevin G. *(2005). Small doses of arsenic: A Bohemian woman's story of survival*. Lanham, MD: Hamilton Books. (p. 13)

The following equations are perhaps among the most important in explaining the shape of contemporary life in the U.S. although they still do not apply in many poor nations around the world:

In Rural societies: More babies = Higher Living Standard

In Urban societies: More babies = Lower Living Standard

There are exceptions to the equations, of course; welfare policies can distort their function among the abject poor. And modern rural societies in which children contribute almost no labor to the highly automated enterprise also see a declining standard of living as family size increases. But for the vast majority of those modern urban economic classes between the very poor and the very rich, the implications of the equations are inescapable.[11]

In cities, large families exert economic stress on a family. Visitors to large modern urban cities like San Francisco or New York often ask the inhabitants the same question: How would you raise a child in a place like this? Not, how would you raise four siblings in a city like this? Small living spaces, the lack of convenient open spaces for play, the need for constant supervision of very young children make child rearing in cities a daunting challenge irrespective of the cost. Espenshade[12] estimated that American families spent approximately one third of their entire disposable income on their children during the 1970s. That proportion is likely higher today.

---

11. The determinants of fertility are several and their interrelationships the subject of extensive research by economists, sociologists, and anthropologists, to name just a few disciplines. Foremost among the economists whose work has cast real light on the relationships of fertility to economic conditions is Richard A. Easterlin, (2004). *The reluctant economist: Perspectives on economics, economic history, and demography.* Cambridge, UK: Cambridge University Press.
12. Espenshade, Thomas J. (1984). *Investment in children.* Washington, DC: Urban Institute Press.

Opinions about the ideal number of children in a family have shown a decline in desirable family size throughout the 20th century (see Exhibit 3.6). The "ideal number of children" has decreased from about three during the Great Depression (itself a strong inducement not to have large families) to replacement level, slightly above two, in 2004. The actual number of children born to women in the U.S. fell below replacement level for the first time in 1973. Highly industrialized and urban nations such as those in Western Europe have very low fertility rates. For Germany, to take one example, the average number of children per family is well below 1.5.

In the 1980s and 1990s, young urbanites began to talk about the ideal family configuration, which they abbreviated with the acronym DINKS: Double Income No Kids.

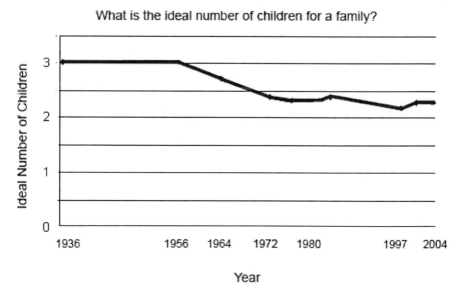

Exhibit 3.6.   Opinions about the ideal number of children per family, 1936-2004. From various sources including Hagewen, Kellie J., & Morgan, S. Philip. (2005). Intended and ideal family size in the United States, 1970-2002. *Population and Development Review, 31*(3), 507–527.

As children came to be viewed as economic liabilities, they came to be seen in a less favorable light more generally. Nichols and Good[13] have written on the devaluing of children in U.S. culture, focusing on adolescence and how myths and stereotypes are invented to justify this depreciation of youth. When a 1989 survey of adults eliciting their attitudes toward teenagers was compared with survey results from the late 1960s, more adults viewed teens as selfish (1969 = 6% vs. 1989 = 81%), materialistic (1969 = 15% vs. 1989 = 79%), and reckless (1969 = 14% vs. 1989 = 73%). Fewer adults in the later survey viewed teenagers as being patriotic (1969 = 65% vs. 1989 = 24%). Youngsters today appear to be valued less than when they had meaningful work to contribute to the family. Or, perhaps, other people's children are valued less while one's own are overvalued, out of some guilt about not spending as much time with them or depriving them of siblings.

---

13.   Nichols, Sharon L., & Good, Thomas. (2004). *America's teenagers myths and realities: Media images, schooling, and the social costs of indifference.* Mahwah, NJ: Erlbaum.

Chapter Four

Pills … That Prevent Conception or Extend Life

"Pills" is used here as a metonym for pharmaceuticals, other medical and surgical treatments of disease and pathologic conditions, as well as health sustaining practices such as diet, exercise, and the like. The pharmaceuticals discussed here are of two types: (1) the birth control pill, and (2) all those drugs that are increasingly extending life expectancy. Both types have had profound effects on the nature of the U.S. population in the last 50 years and promise to have an even greater impact in the next 50.

Birth Control Pills

The birth control pill (technically, "oral contraceptives" comprising various combinations of steroidal hormones, specifically estrogen and progestin) grew out of research on infertility that was being pursued by a number of investigators during the first half of the 1950s. The pharmaceutical company Searle applied for Food and Drug Administration

Fertilizers, Pills, and Magnetic Strips: The Fate of Education in America
pp. 75–83
Copyright © 2008 by Information Age Publishing
All rights of reproduction in any form reserved.

(FDA) approval of their trademarked drug Enovid in 1957 as a treatment for menstrual disorders. It was approved. By July 1959, Searle had completed trials that indicated that Enovid was an effective contraceptive drug. By the time FDA approval was granted, it is estimated that Enovid had already been in use for a few years by over a half million women. The FDA approved the drug for use on June 23, 1960, and thus the fabled 60s received a huge boost toward the lifestyle that would come to characterize them ever after. Condoms could be abandoned and were, until the emergence of AIDS decades later. Intercourse and contraception could now be separated, and vigorously were.

A small drop in the birth rate in the U.S. is apparent starting in the mid-1950s; the decline becomes more obvious in the 1960s as states began to legalize the sale of the contraceptive pill[1] (see Exhibit 4.1). The crude birth rate (live births per 1,000 population) dropped from about 25 in the decade after WWII to about 15 by the end of the 1960s, a decline of 40%. The fertility rate for U.S. women fell below replacement level (2.1) for the first time in history in 1973. Roe vs. Wade was first decided in a Texas court in about 1971 and finally upheld by the U.S. Supreme Court on January 22, 1973. The impact of the decision on the birth rate graphed in Exhibit 4.1 is not apparent. The pill had already done its work.

The number of children ever born to 1,000 women ages 40-44, at the virtual end of their childbearing years, fell below 2 in the early 1990s.

As the U.S. population redistributed itself from farms to cities and suburbs, it changed from a *pronatal* (favoring the birth of children) society to an *antinatal* (disfavoring the birth of children) society. Hoping to preserve their standard of living

1.   The birth control pill was not available to married women in all states until 1965 when the U.S. Supreme Court ruled in Griswold vs. Connecticut that the Constitutional right to privacy extended to a "right of marital privacy" as it struck down a Connecticut law that prohibited the sale of the oral contraceptive. Not until 1972 was this particular "right of privacy" extended to unmarried women (*Eisenstadt vs. Baird*).

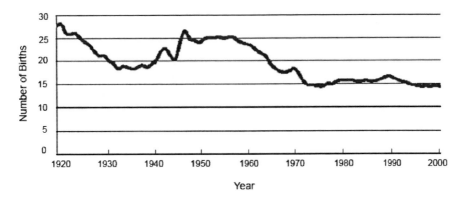

Exhibit 4.1.   Births per 1,000 persons in the U.S., 1920-2001. From National
Center for Health Statistics.

**Exhibit 4.2.   Number of Children Ever Born to
1,000 U.S. Women Ages 40-44, 1976-2002**

1976	3,091
1980	2,988
1985	2,147
1990	2,045
1995	1,961
1998	1,877
2000	1,913
2002	1,930

and free women to enter the job market, couples elected to
decrease the size of their families. For the first time in history,
an effective means of choosing not to have children became
available. Oral contraceptives needed no marketing campaign to become one of the most often prescribed drugs of
the 1960s and 1970s. As with so many other things, these
innovations affected different social and racial groups differ-
entially. The fertility gap between rich and poor and between
White and ethnic minorities widened both for economic and
religious reasons.

"Pills" That Extend Life

Pharmaceuticals and medical technology in general are extending life expectancy beyond anything imagined a century ago. It is easy to forget or never have known that the leading causes of death in the U.S. in 1900 were pneumonia, influenza, tuberculosis, and diarrhea, all of which today are far down the list of causes of death. The "elderly" (age 65 and older) constituted only 1 in every 25 Americans in 1900; in the year 1995, approximately 1 in every 8 Americans is elderly, and in a few years, 1 in every 5 Americans will be classified as elderly. Between 2010 and 2050, the percentage of the U.S. population older than 85 will quadruple.

A recent RAND study estimates that approximately 40% of adults can be expected to die of Alzheimer's disease (dementia, organic brain syndrome, or whatever it will be called). The cost of maintaining elderly persons in this state will surely burden the health-care system at the expense of other, less critical sectors of the economy.[2]

Between 1996 and 2006, the FDA approved 39 new drugs for the treatment of cancer. To be sure, some of these drugs are merely palliative, but no one would gainsay the tremendous strides made in the treatment of many different types of cancer in the last 25 years. Pharmaceuticals, surgical techniques, and diagnostic techniques for early detection are having a revolutionary impact on death rates from cancer. The development of the prostate specific antigen (PSA) test in the 1980s has resulted in earlier detection of prostate cancer and led to a 4% annual decline in the prostate cancer mortality rate in the U.S. in the past decade. From 1993 to 2001, the death rate in the U.S. from cancers of all types dropped an average of 1.1% per year. Compounded over 9 years, this reduction amounted to approximately a 13% reduction in the cancer death rate. In 2002, this reduction increased to better

2.   RAND. (2005). *Future health and medical care spending of the elderly.* Washington, DC: Author. Retrieved October 5, 2005, from http://www.rand.org/publications/RB/RB9146/

**Exhibit 4.3.   Common Medical Conditions With a
Sample of Associated Drug Treatments**

Medical Condition	*Drug Treatment*
Stroke	tPA (tissue plasminogen activators)
Heart Disease	Warfarin (Coumadin); Statins (Zocor, Lipitor)
Hypertension	ACE (angiotensin converting enzyme) inhibitors
Diabetes	Sulfonylureas
Cancer	Gleevec, Xeloda, Efudex

than 2%, with the most dramatic reduction for colorectal cancer. The death rate from colorectal cancer is currently falling
at a rate of nearly 5% per annum. From 2001 to 2004, the incidence of breast cancer diagnoses in women declined by more
than 3% yearly. [3] These statistics will eventually be reflected
in significantly increasing life expectancy figures, since the
diseases in question are typically not progressive and once
cured are unlikely to reoccur. Survivors may live into their
mid-80s as a routine matter, where the eventual deterioration
of their immune systems is likely to subject them to different
diseases. Added to these advances are new surgical techniques that sometimes greatly increase the odds of curing a
particular carcinoma and other times greatly reduce the risk
of life threatening complications from loss of blood, infection,
and trauma.[4]

---

3.   Epsey, David K. (2007). *Annual report to the nation on the status of cancer, 1975-
2004, featuring cancer in American Indians and Alaska Natives*. Retrieved Oct. 15, 2007,
from http://www.cancer.org/docroot/NWS/content/
NWS_1_1x_Decline_in_Cancer_Deaths_Doubles.asp.
4.   On December 14, 2005, the author underwent a prostatectomy for a malig-
nancy by means of the *da Vinci Surgical System* (a registered trademark of Intuitive
Surgical, Inc.). The operation lasted less than an hour and was performed by a sur-
geon sitting at a console several feet removed from the operating table. It is con-
ceivable that with reliable telecommunications, that he could have been a
continent away from the site of the operation. No transfusions were needed, and
the hospital stay was less than 24 hours. Traditional prostatectomies lasted four
hours and involved long hospital stays. This experience, revolutionary in the early
21st century, is likely to become commonplace within a few years. The company's
stock (ISRG) tripled in 2007.

Life Expectancy

Life expectancy (estimated years of life remaining) for newborns increased nearly 60% during the 20th century from approximately 49 years to about 77 years. Baby Boomers who will attain the age of 65 in 2012 can expect to live another 18 years on average (20 more years for women, 17 more years for men). The life expectancy of a newborn in 2005 was approximately 78 years, and that figure continues to rise each year as new pills and treatments for disease are developed (see Exhibits 4.4 and 4.5).

Life expectancy has risen gradually since as long as any believable data can be arrayed to answer the question. Life expectancy from classical Greece to medieval Europe rose barely 5 years, from 28 years into the early 30s. The gradual introduction of sewers in medieval Europe and more generally in the 18th and 19th centuries greatly increased life expectancy by reducing the infant mortality rate. Increases in the life expectancy of newborns rose steadily during the 20th century. But with low infant mortality rates being attained in the U.S. by mid-20th century, subsequent gains in life expectancy are credited to advances in medicine: the introduction of antibiotics (arsphenamine in 1909, penicillin in 1928, and the like); blood pressure monitoring and controls for strokes and blood clotting (warfarin in 1940); and virtually countless advances in pharmaceuticals and treatment methods that emerge almost weekly.

The impact of the effect of pills is more evident in the data on life expectancy ("years of life remaining") for persons who have attained the age of 65 years (see Exhibit 4.4). In 1900, a person who had attained the age of 65 years could be expected to live 12 more years, until age 77. That figure changed little until about 1940 when each subsequent decade added a year to a 65 year-old's life expectancy. Currently, a person who has survived to the age of 65 has a life expectancy of slightly greater than 83 years.

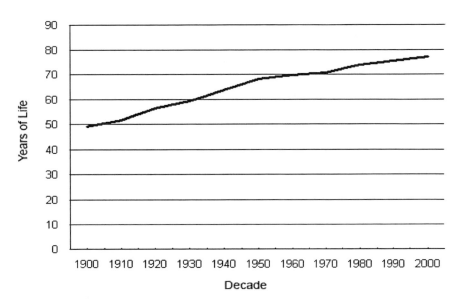

Exhibit 4.4.   Estimated years of life remaining for ncwborns, 1900-2000. From *National Vital Statistics Reports*, Vol. 54, No. 14, April 19, 2006, p. 30 Washington, DC: National Center for Health Statistics.

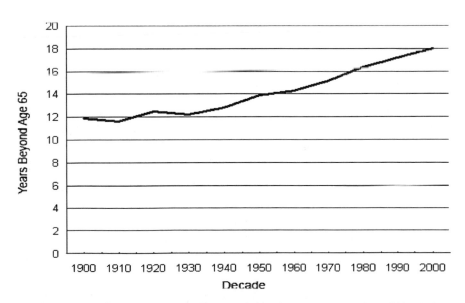

Exhibit 4.5.   Estimated Years of Life Remaining for Persons Age 65, 1900-2000. From *National Vital Statistics Reports*, Vol. 54, No. 14, April 19, 2006, p. 30 Washington, D.C.: National Center for Health Statistics.

The single sour note in this song concerns lifestyle changes that produce chronic conditions that shorten life. Lack of exercise and diets of fast food lead to heart disease, diabetes, and high blood pressure that together account for almost 40% of all deaths from disease among persons 65 years or older. The most popular pharmaceuticals are prescribed for these conditions: Atorvastatin (brand name Lipitor for heart disease), Amlodipine (brand name Norvast for blood pressure), Rosiglitazone (brand name Avandia for diabetes). It is difficult to predict if the nation will reverse the trend toward increasing lifestyle mortality.

Pills and Public Life

No society can expect to go unchanged by such profound shifts in the fertility and age of its population as those afforded by the advances in medical technology of the last 60 years. This amazing evolution is apparent even in the nature of the drugs that are commonly prescribed today in contrast to earlier times. Whereas oral contraceptives were one of the most prescribed drugs in the 1960s and 1970s, today such drugs stand in the low 20s in a ranking of most prescribed drugs. Far ahead of them in the rankings are drugs to treat acid reflux, osteoporosis, hypertension, inflammation of various types, and, at the top, excess levels of low density lipoproteins ("bad" cholesterol).

As will be seen in subsequent chapters, America in the 21st century will reflect the changing age demographics in manifold ways. What will concern us here is how attitudes toward publicly financed institutions, principally public education, can be expected to change. The aging of the U.S. population can be expected to impact public education through competition for funds between medical care and other sectors of the public economy. Moreover, older voters appear less willing to support the education of fewer and fewer grandchildren, or more precisely, other people's grandchildren. We shall return to the subject of the aging U.S. population when we examine how the particular character of population growth is affecting education policy.

Chapter Five

Magnetic Strips: Easy Credit and the American Economy

Credit cards first changed America's spending and saving habits. Now they are beginning to shape public life; generations saddled with personal debt are unlikely to vote for taxes to build libraries, parks, museums, and schools.

How Big Banking Came to Sioux Falls

In the early 1970s, several of the nation's largest banking corporations opened major facilities in Sioux Falls, South Dakota. The population of the town has grown little since then. Its current size is about 130,000 inhabitants, roughly the population of a couple of square blocks of Manhattan. Today, Sioux Falls is home to more than a half dozen major credit card companies (BankFirst, Capital Card Services, Citibank, HSBC, PREMIER Bankcard, The Total Card Inc., Wells Fargo) and several other smaller companies. Combined, these companies are by far the major employer in the city. What accounts for the interest of these financial institutions in this little town on the banks of the Big Sioux River?

Fertilizers, Pills, and Magnetic Strips: The Fate of Education in America
pp. 85–94
Copyright © 2008 by Information Age Publishing

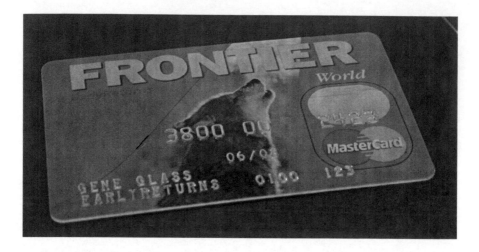

The business of making small unsecured loans to millions and millions of individuals had to wait for the invention of the technology that would make possible the transfer and storage of the attendant information. If banks had to keep track on paper and by telephone of millions of loans of a few hundred dollars, the overhead cost (person hours and postage) of handling the information would wipe out any profits even with high interest charges. All this changed in about 1960.

An obscure IBM engineer named Forrest Parry, working on a contract to develop a security system between his employer and the CIA, had the idea of attaching a piece of magnetic tape to a plastic card to form a type of gate card. Magnetic tape was the principal data storage medium for the computers of that day. Parry, an alumnus of a tiny university in southern Utah, grew frustrated with his inability to get the tape strip to stick to the small plastic card. As the story goes, Parry arrived home one evening carrying a collection of cards and pieces of magnetic tape to find his wife in the middle of doing the family ironing. Sensing his frustration and wishing to help, his wife placed a card on her ironing board, laid a strip of tape across the card, and with her clothes iron solved his problem. The banking industry soon realized the possibilities.

During the winter holidays in 1966,[1] Diner's Club mailed 6 million credit cards with a $1,000 limit to inhabitants of metropolitan Chicago. Family pets, toddlers, and felons all received a thousand dollars of instant credit for the holidays. The effect of this marketing campaign was controversial; it later became known as the "Chicago Debacle." Critics speaking in Congressional hearings demanded that credit cards be outlawed. But critics were powerless to loosen the historically close ties between politicians and the banking industry. Congress banned the mass mailing of credit cards in the mid-1970s, but once the industry acquired the resources to tell Congress what to do, such restrictions disappeared, never to return.[2] However, the industry had to wait for a favorable economic and legal climate before it began to revolutionize the very relationship between people and their money.

The U.S. economy suffered unprecedented inflation of its currency during the 1970s. The prime interest rate soared above 15% and banks were paying 20% interest to borrow money to lend to their customers. In states like New York with strict usury[3] laws, banks were restricted to charging as little as 12% interest on money that cost them 15% and more. Something had to give, and it gave first in South Dakota.

South Dakota banks were suffering the same effects of rampant inflation, only South Dakota had a legislature that could act more quickly than the law-making bodies of larger states. Although South Dakota has a history of tight usury laws, the pressure of expensive money prompted the legislature to eliminate the interest rate cap on loans. The impact was

---

1.   Diners Club and American Express introduced their charge card systems in the 1950s. In 1951, Diners Club issued credit cards to a couple hundred customers; these cards could only be used at a couple dozen New York city restaurants. This rudimentary technology had to await the invention of the requisite computer and telecommunications infra-structure to reach profitability.

2.   The relationship between Congress and financial institutions has always been close, and even reasonable restrictions seldom stand a chance of passage. When Congress attempted to force mutual funds to disclose fully their fees to share holders, the funds' lobbyists successfully argued that so much information would merely confuse investors and limit their ability to make rational decisions.

immediate on the tiny banking industry of South Dakota, but its extension beyond the state's borders was threatened by a law suit in the mid-1970s.[4] The ruling, known as the Marquette Bank decision that came down from the U.S. Supreme Court in December 1978, allowed banks to charge the rate of interest prevailing in the state in which the bank is incorporated regardless of the location of the borrower. So if a card holder in Massachusetts where usury laws prohibited interest charges above 15% has credit card debt to a bank in South Dakota, the South Dakota bank may charge 25% interest without regard to Massachusetts law.

This opportunity did not go unnoticed by Citibank 1,300 miles to the east. Citibank had been struggling under the usury laws of the state of New York. But when the Supreme Court decision opened the door to South Dakota, the corporation moved its credit card headquarters to Sioux Falls within months. By 1981, Citibank's credit card business was completely transacted from the small town on the Big Sioux. Not to be outdone, the state of Delaware soon eliminated its interest cap and became the credit card capital of the East. (The 10 largest credit card companies in the U.S. today are incorporated in states with virtually no usury laws.) Banking industry lobbyists quickly succeeded in influencing a number of federal laws that protected the booming credit card business and allowed the large corporations to circumvent any future state or local usury laws. By the early 1980s, the indus-

---

3. "Usury" is the sin of charging excessive interest on loans. The negative commandment against usury is as old as the Torah, where prohibitions against taking more for loans appear in several places. Exodus 22:25: "If you lend money to any of my people with you who is poor, you shall not be like a moneylender to him, and you shall not exact interest from him." The commandment has been the subject of various interpretations over the centuries, at times interpreted as meaning that Jews may not charge interest on loans to other Jews, but Gentiles may be charged interest for loans. A common understanding eventually emerged that the prohibitions were against charging "excessive" interest on loans. Or from the Koran: "O you who believe, you shall not take usury, compounded over and over. Observe God, that you may succeed." (Al-'Imran 3:130)

4. *Marquette vs. First Omaha Service Corporation.*

try was set to do business on an unprecedented scale. America's attitudes toward debt and consumption were in for a profound change.[5]

A Nation's Changing Attitude Toward Money

Before small unsecured loans were possible on a mass scale, people saved cash to make purchases of furniture, jewelry, fancy clothing, stereos, or television receivers. A few dollars from each paycheck accumulating in a savings account over months eventually built up to where a purchase could be made. This scenario, common two generations ago, must seem quaint to today's young consumers. Now, purchases are made on credit cards almost as soon as the impulse takes hold in the mind of the buyer. Unpaid balances grow and are paid off gradually with interest in the future. The feeding of these appetites for instant gratification brings massive profits to the credit card industry. The scale of the credit card industry in the U.S. today is astounding. The industry reported more than $30 billion in *profits* in 2005—greater than McDonalds; greater than Microsoft. Today, credit cards are ubiquitous.[6]

More than three quarters of American households have credit cards; and of those who do not have them, most wish they did. The average family owns eight credit cards. More than 700 million credit cards were in use in 2005, 2.3 cards for each man, woman, and child in the country. But the ubiquity of credit cards is not the story of how small, unsecured (non-collateralized) credit is changing America. The unpaid bal-

---

5.   Much of this history of the credit card industry is available for viewing online; the award winning Frontline documentary, Secret History of the Credit Card, can be accessed at http://www.pbs.org/wgbh/pages/frontline/shows/credit/view/, last retrieved on December 28, 2007. The documentary won the 2004-05 Emmy for investigative journalism and the 2005 Alfred I. duPont-Columbia University award.

6.   Bertola, Giuseppe; Disney, Richard; & Grant, Charles. (Eds.) (2006). *The economics of consumer credit*. Boston: MIT Press.

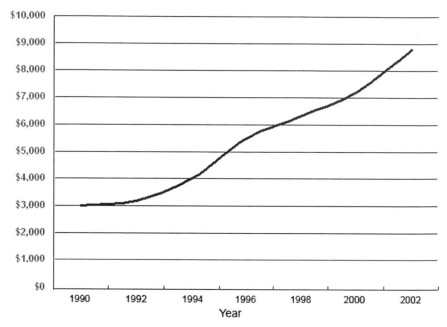

Exhibit 5.1.   Average credit card debt per household (1991-2003). Based on http://moneycentral.msn.com/content/Banking/creditcardsmarts/P74808.asp

ances, the debt, owed the industry by the credit card users is altering how Americans buy, save, and vote.

In 2005, total credit card debt in America exceeded $800 billion, more than $2,500 for every person in the country. This level of debt nearly tripled from 1991 to 2002 (see Exhibit 5.1). The data in Exhibit 5.1 include those who pay off their debt each month, so the debt carried by those who do not is roughly double the average figure for the nation as a whole. Nearly three quarters of the industry's profit comes from interest charges. Less than one third of credit card holders pay off their most recent credit card bill. The rest carry debt forward at annualized interest rates topping 15 and 20%. And the debt is not being carried by the rich, who became rich by lending money instead of borrowing at exorbitant interest rates. One third of households with credit card debt exceeding $10,000 have household incomes under $50,000. Millions of Americans now carry medical debt on their credit cards, compounding a situation reaching tragic proportions. Credit card interest rates merely exacerbate the situation for millions of Americans.

College students are prime targets for credit card marketing. The University of Oklahoma signed a $1 million contract with Bank of America to provide exclusive marketing rights to their students. One study revealed that 80% of college students have two or more credit cards and enter the workplace after graduation with an average of $3,500 in credit card debt. By 2007, seven states had proposed laws banning or restricting credit card marketing on campus. Typically these bills are killed by legislators, who happen to be subject to the pressure as well as the beneficence of the banking lobby.[7]

In a telephone survey of more than 1,100 middle- and low-income persons age 18 or older who reported having carried credit card debt at least for the previous 3 months, the distribution of credit card debt was as depicted in Exhibit 5.2. In 2006, the average credit card balance was more than $4,250 with the average household owing more than $9,000 on credit cards.[8]

Exhibit 5.2 Household Credit Card Debt for Persons Age 18 and Older Who Carried Some Debt During the Previous 3 Months

Amount of Credit Card Debt	Percent of Households
More than $7,500	35
$5,001—$7,500	10
$2,501—$5,000	24
Less than $2,500	31

Source: Data based on Draut, Tamara. (2005). *The plastic safety net: The reality behind debt in America.* New York: Demos. A Network for Ideas & Action. http://www.demos.org

---

7.   "Debtor Nation," aired on CNN, April 9, 2007; http://transcripts.cnn.com/TRANSCRIPTS/0704/09/pzn.01.html
8.   Claritas, demographic and marketing research company. http://www.claritas.com/

In March 2007, Bank of America announced that it would begin to issue credit cards to individuals who have no Social Security number, most of whom would be foreigners living in the U.S. Apparently, Bank of America is desirous of competing with the strip mall check cashing companies for the business of undocumented Mexican laborers. Not surprisingly, the corporation casts its new marketing campaign as an effort to help people establish a credit history.

The fine print in credit card contracts warns that the lender may change the rate of interest charged at any point for any reason, such as, a late mortgage payment or a missed car loan payment.[9] Known as "universal default," this provision gives credit card companies prerogatives virtually unheard of in any other sector of business. The company can triple rates from 8%, say, to 25% and higher. At 25% interest, a debt would double in 3 years (from $1,000 to $1,953). It is as though a vendor having sold a customer a product for $100 comes back later and demands more money claiming that the price has changed. Contracts generally include provisions for "retroactive billing"; attracted to a contract by the promise of some number of months of no interest charges, customers who are late on a monthly payment can find themselves charged interest retroactively back to the point at which the card was first issued. In 2006, the U.S. Senate rejected by a vote of 74 to 24 an amendment to a bill that would have capped credit card interest rates at 30%. In 2007, the credit card industry settled a law suit out of court in which they were accused of concealing fees of as much as 3% on pur-

---

9.   The fine print on the application for one of the most popular cards runs to over 1,600 words. Typical terms and conditions take forms such as the following: "We reserve the right to change the account terms (including the APRs) at any time for any reason, in addition to APR increases that may occur for failure to comply with the terms of your account. For example, we may change the terms based on information in your credit report, such as the number of other credit card accounts you have and their balances. The APRs for this offer are not guaranteed; APRs may change to higher APRs, fixed APRs may change to variable APRs, or variable APRs may change to fixed APRs. Any changes will be in accordance with your account agreement."

chases made outside the U.S. The industry never admitted guilt but agreed to reimburse card holders in amounts that could total more than $1 billion. One would think that an industry with such generous profit margins would not have to resort to duplicity. Each year politicians pledge to do something to curb the enormous power of the credit card industry, but seldom does anything happen. After the fall election of 2006 where Democrats took control of the House and Senate, hearings on the credit card industry were scheduled and actually took place in March 2007. CEOs of the major credit card companies apologized for some questionable practices.

> The indebtedness of U.S. households, after adjusting for inflation, has risen 42.0% over the last five years.

> The level of debt as a percent of after-tax income is the highest ever measured in our history. Mortgage and consumer debt is now 120% of after-tax income, more than twice the level of 30 years ago.

> The debt-service ratio (the percent of after-tax income that goes to pay off debts) is at an all-time high of 13.9%.

> The personal savings rate is negative for the first time since the Depression.[10]

Personal Debt and Public Expenditures

When medical debt is added to the nation's appetite for consumption, the burden becomes overwhelming for many. Americans are now a nation averse to saving and in love with spending on personal goods and services. In 2006, net savings in the U.S. was negative for the first time since the Great Depression. Whether the desire to consume was latent in the populace and could only be expressed when the technology

10.   Mishel, Lawrence, & Eisenbrey, Ross. (2006). *What's wrong with the economy?* Memorandum of the Economic Policy Institute. http://www.epi.org/content.cfm/pm110

permitting small unsecured loans became available, or whether the affordances of the technologies created the appetite is debatable and irrelevant. Americans now spend beyond their means and mortgage their own and their children's future. In the first 5 years of the 21st century, inflated home prices allowed many Americans to refinance their mortgages and "cash out" some of the equity in their homes to pay off credit card debt, tuition for children going to college, medical debt, and to satisfy growing appetites for goods. Many soon held mortgages for greater than the market value of their homes. The questionable lending practices of the financial industry made "subprime" loans to unqualified buyers with provisions for interest rates ballooning to 11 and 12 percent. Mortgage defaults and home foreclosures began to rise ominously in 2007. The implications for the health of public institutions, public infrastructure, and public services are profound. Who will vote for higher taxes to support libraries, parks, recreation centers, senior centers, and, yes, public schools, when personal debt swells, equity shrinks, and savings vanish?

Chapter Six

America is Growing Browner, Older, and Deeper in Debt

It is obvious, perhaps, from the preceding chapters that America as a demographic entity is growing older and deeper in debt. Both characteristics bear on how the majority will view such policy questions as support for public education. The country is gradually changing in one other respect that can be expected to influence how pubic institutions will fare in future competitions for resources. The population of the U.S. would have grown substantially less over the past 30 years if it were not for the rapidly increasing Hispanic share of the population. In a real sense, America is growing browner, older, and deeper in debt.

The United States is Becoming Browner

The most noteworthy demographic shift in the U.S. population in the past 50 years has been in the representation of Hispanics.[1] While the share of the U.S. population for Blacks has remained constant over the past 50 years and the

Fertilizers, Pills, and Magnetic Strips: The Fate of Education in America
pp. 95–116
Copyright © 2008 by Information Age Publishing

non-Hispanic White share has decreased from approximately 90 to 75%, the most remarkable change has been in the Hispanic share. The percentage of the U.S. population identified as Hispanic has nearly tripled in since 1970, from about 4% to about 15%. Hispanics are currently the largest minority in the U.S. The eighth and ninth most popular surnames in the 2000 U.S. Census were "Garcia" and "Rodriguez," respectively; "Martinez" surpassed "Wilson" for the first time in popularity; 6 of the 25 most frequently recorded surnames are Hispanic.

Since 1970, the contribution to U.S. population growth due to the fertility of what demographers call the "population stock" (i.e., the population present in the country in 1970) has been equaled by the growth due to immigration. Prior to 1965, an average of approximately 175,000 persons immigrated to the U.S. each year. Currently, the annual rate of immigration is about 1 million persons. If U.S. population growth were from the 1970 population stock alone (i.e., if there had been no immigration since 1970), the 2030 population of the country would be about 250 million persons; at present, it is over 300 million. It is projected that Hispanics will constitute one quarter of the U.S. population by the year 2050. The number of Hispanics under age 20 in the U.S. is expected to double by 2050, from about 14 million in 2005 to nearly 33 million in 2050.

Even more significant for schools than mere headcounts are the numbers of persons who speak primarily Spanish in

---

1.   Prior to 1980, the U.S. Census did not even classify Hispanics as a separate ethnic or racial group. Beginning in 1980, the Census began to count Hispanics but had difficulty with the fact that Hispanics as an ethnic group are represented by more than one race. In 2000, the Census asked the recorder to classify the person counted by the following rubric: "Is the person Spanish/Hispanic/Latino? a) Mexican, Mexican-American, Chicano; b) Puerto Rican; c) Cuban; d) Other Spanish/Hispanic/Latino?" The Census Bureau warns that population figures for Hispanics are not comparable from 2000 to previous censuses. But the regular progression of the curves in Exhibit 6.1 appears to indicate that the slightly changing questions posed by the census takers over the decades do not confound any inference likely to be drawn here.

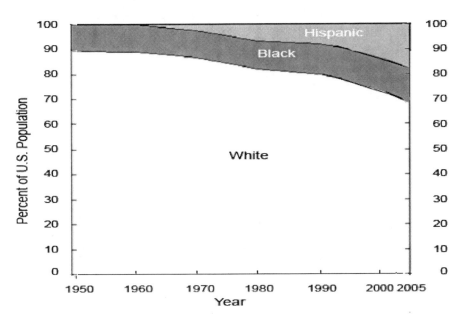

Exhibit 6.1.   U.S. population by race/ethnicity, 1950-2005. From various sources at http://www.census.gov.

their home. Data from the 1980 through 2000 Censuses show remarkable increases in these numbers (see Exhibit 6.2).

Two thirds of U.S. Hispanics are identified as Mexican or Mexican-American. Those who identify as Puerto Rican or Cuban constitute 10% and 4% of the Hispanic population, respectively. Nearly one quarter of Hispanics claim ancestry from other countries: South America, Caribbean, Central America. Not surprisingly, the majority of Hispanics are located in the Southwestern states. The percentage of Hispanics is displayed in Exhibit 6.3 for four regions of the country from reports of the 1980, 1990, and 2000 Census.[2]

There has, in fact, been little growth in the White population in the U.S. in the past 30 to 35 years. Exhibit 6.4 shows the percentage increase in three ethnic/racial categories for the three decennial Censuses beginning with 1970. The White

---

2.   Tienda, Marta, & Mitchell, Faith. (Eds). (2006). *Hispanics and the future of America*. Washington, DC: National Academies Press.

Exhibit 6.2.   Spanish Spoken at Home, U.S. Residents, Age 5 and Older

	1980	1990	Change 1980-1990	2000	Change 1980-2000
Speakers of Spanish at home, ages 5+	11,116,200	17,339,200	+ 56%	28,101,100	+ 153%

From Crawford, James. (2002). Census 2000: A guide for the perplexed. Retrieved November 16, 2007, from http://ourworld.compuserve.com/homepages/jWCRAWFORD/census02.htm

racial group has grown minimally as a share of the U.S. population since 1970, and were it not for immigration, probably would have declined. There were 190,000,000 persons listed as White in the 1980 Census; the corresponding figure for 2000 was 211,000,000. The percentage growth in the category "Hispanic Origin" is greatest, increasing more than 50% in each decade since 1970.[3]

This remarkable shift in the nature of the U.S. population arises from two sources: the greater fertility rate of Hispanic women and immigration to the U.S. from Mexico and Central America. Immigration in turn is due to the addiction of American business to low cost labor and its eagerness to employ workers from Mexico and Central America.

In the early 1970s, the White non-Hispanic birth rate fell below the "replacement rate" of 2.1 live births per woman. The total fertility rate is the average number of babies born

---

3.   The Hispanic Origin category was defined three different ways in the 1970 Census special reports on which Exhibit 6.4 is based. The first and second criteria were applied in a 15% sample and the third in a 5% sample; the two estimates agreed closely: (1) as the Spanish language population (the population of Spanish mother tongue plus all other individuals in families in which the head or wife reported Spanish mother tongue); (2) as the Spanish heritage population (the population of Spanish language and/or Spanish surname in the five Southwestern states of Arizona, California, Colorado, New Mexico, and Texas, the population of Puerto Rican birth or parentage in New York, New Jersey, and Pennsylvania, and the population of Spanish language elsewhere; and (3) as the population of Spanish origin or descent based on self-identification.

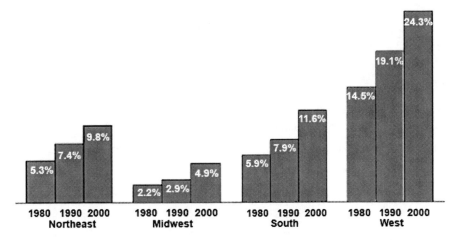

Exhibit 6.3.   Percentage Hispanic of regional population, 1980, 1990, and 2000. From U.S. Census Bureau.

Exhibit 6.4.   Percent Growth in Two Racial/Ethnic Categories in the Decennial Census, 1970-1990

Racial/Ethnic Group	1970-1980	1980-1990	1990 2000
White	6.4%	4.3%	5.5%
Hispanic origin	52.3%	50.0%	59.0%

From Gibson, Campbell & Jung, Kay. (2002). Historical census statistics on population totals by race, 1790 to 1990, and by Hispanic origin, 1970 to 1990, for the United States, regions, divisions, and states. Working Paper Series No. 56. Washington, DC: Population Division, U.S. Census Bureau

to women during their reproductive years. A rate of 2.1 is generally considered to be "replacement" level. Pending some unforeseen developments, future population growth in the U.S. is likely to come from immigration or an increase in live births among higher fertility groups (e.g., Hispanic women).

While the fertility rate in the U.S. for non-Hispanic Whites has remained below replacement level (2.1) in recent years and the rate for non-Hispanic Blacks has fallen gradually to about replacement level (2.26), the fertility rate for Hispanics is by far the highest of the three groups. Between 1995 and

**Exhibit 6.5.   Live Births and Fertility Rates by
Race/Ethnicity of Mother, 1990 to 2000**

Race/ Ethnicity		1990	1995	2000
White	Number of live births	2,626,500	2,382,640	2,362,970
	Total fertility rate	1.85	1.79	1.88
	Percent of total live births	63.2	61.3	58.2
Black	Number of live births	661,700	587,780	604,350
	Total fertility rate	2.55	2.25	2.26
	Percent of total live births	15.9%	15.1%	14.9%
Hispanic	Number of live births	595,070	679,770	815,870
	Total fertility rate	2.96	3.02	3.11
	Percent of total live births	14.3%	17.5%	20.1%
Asian/Pacific Islander	Number of live births	141,640	160,290	200,540
	Total fertility rate	2.003	1.924	2.073
	Percent of total live births	3.4%	4.1%	4.9%

2000, the number of live births to Hispanic mothers exceeded the corresponding number for Black mothers. Live births to Hispanic mothers constituted one of every five births in the nation in 2000 (see Exhibit 6.5).

The total fertility rate for Hispanic immigrants to the U.S. is 3.51, compared to the fertility rate of 2.40 for women who remain in Mexico. It has been estimated that 1 in every 10 babies born in the U.S. in 2002 was the child of a mother whose place of birth was Mexico or Central America and who did not hold U.S. citizenship.[4] In the year 2000 for Hispanic

---

4.   The Mexican-American Legal Defense Fund disputes this claim of the Center for Immigration studies; MALDEF officials question whether Camarota was able accurately to determine the legal status of the mothers and relied instead on the birth certificate report of the mother's place of birth. Camarota, Steven A. (2005a). *Birth rates among immigrants in America comparing fertility in the U.S. and home countries.* Washington, D. C.: Center for Immigration Studies. Retrieved November 28, 2005, from http://www.cis.org/articles/2005/back1105.html.

girls age 19 or younger in the state of Arizona, for example, the annual rate of pregnancy was 60 per 1,000; the rate for Anglos was 15 per 1,000.[5]

The U.S. fertility rate is significantly higher than fertility rates of other industrialized nations, exceeding the average of the other nations by 32% (2.05 vs. 1.55). However, this superiority is due almost entirely by the greater Hispanic fertility rate in the U.S. The U.S. non-Hispanic White fertility rate of approximately 1.8 roughly matches that of other industrialized European nations (see Exhibit 6.6).

In 1965, the Hart-Cellar Act (also known as the Immigration Act of 1965) was passed by Congress and signed into law on October 3rd by President Lyndon Johnson. Policies that had governed immigration into the U.S. since the third decade of the 20th century were dramatically changed almost overnight. The provisions of the act allowed for greatly increased immigration from poor countries of both the Eastern and Western Hemispheres; such immigration had been severely restricted in the past. An annual quota of 170,000 immigrants from the Eastern Hemisphere was adopted, with no more than 20,000 permitted to immigrate from any one country. A yearly limit of 120,000 was placed on immigration from Western Hemisphere nations, but without a quota by nations.[6] The impact of the law on immigration rates was immediate. Exhibit 6.7 shows the number and percentage of foreign born persons counted in the decennial U.S. Census by decade from 1900 to 2000.

Immigration in the early decades of the 20th century was largely from Southern Europe, Russia, Poland, and the British Isles. Over 2 million Italians immigrated to the U.S. between 1910 and 1920. Total immigration from Mexico in the decade of the 1930s numbered fewer than 25,000 persons.

---

5.   Arizona Department of Health Services.
6.   Reimers, David M. (1985). *Still the golden door: The Third World comes to America.* New York: Columbia University Press.

**Exhibit 6.6.   International Fertility Rates of
Selected Nations 1995-2005**

Nation	1995	2000	2005
United States	1.98	2.06	2.05
France	1.71	1.87	1.92
Ireland	1.85	1.90	1.88
Norway	1.87	1.85	1.84
Australia	1.83	1.76	1.81
Denmark	1.81	1.77	1.80
Finland	1.81	1.73	1.80
United Kingdom	1.71	1.64	1.79
Sweden	1.74	1.55	1.77
Netherlands	1.53	1.72	1.71
Canada	1.66	1.49	1.52
Austria	1.42	1.36	1.41
Spain	1.17	1.23	1.34
Germany	1.25	1.38	1.34
Greece	1.31	1.27	1.33
Italy	1.19	1.26	1.32
Russia	1.34	1.19	1.29
Japan	1.42	1.36	1.25
Poland	1.55	1.37	1.24
South Korea	1.65	1.47	1.08

Adapted from Population Reference Bureau, http://
www.prb.org/pdf07/TFRTable.pdf

Immigration declined substantially as a proportion of the
nation's population in midcentury—fewer than 5% of the
population was foreign born in 1970—only to accelerate
rapidly after 1970. Between 1901 and 1920, 86% of all
immigrants to the U.S. were from Europe with only 3% from
Latin America. Between 1980 and 1993, the percentage of
European immigrants to the U.S. dropped to 13% while the
percentage of immigrants from Latin America rose to 43%.[7]
More than 30 million persons, some 14% of the total

7.   *Immigration and Naturalization Service Yearbooks of Immigration Statistics.*
Retrieved March 23, 2007, from http://www.dhs.gov/ximgtn/statistics/publications/
yearbook.shtm.

Exhibit 6.7.   Number of immigrants (foreign born) to the U.S., 1900-2000. From Decennial Census of the United States; http://www.census.gov.

population, were classified as "foreign born" in 2000. Of these 30 million persons who immigrated with authorization to the U.S., approximately one third indicated that Mexico or Central America was their place of birth.

The Immigration Act of 1965 was cast primarily as a civil rights issue by its framers and proponents. Old quotas in effect since 1921 on individual nationalities were wiped out. Motivated by a flood of immigrants in the decades leading up to 1920 that had a depressing effect on wages of native-born Americans, Congress passed the Johnson Quota Act on May 19, 1921. The Act limited the yearly number of immigrants from any single country to 3% of the number of persons from that country who were counted as residing in the U.S. in the 1910 Census. The quotas thus imposed allocated half the number of possible immigrants to northern and western European nations and half to eastern and southern Europe. The political power of immigrant groups decreased as a result of the 1921 law.[8]

Opponents of the Immigration Act of 1965 who feared a heavy influx of immigrants from non-European cultures were assured by the bill's backers that American culture was not endangered. Senator Edward Kennedy of Massachusetts spoke to the Senate Subcommittee on Immigration and Naturalization:

> Our cities will not be flooded with a million immigrants annually. Under the proposed bill, the present level of immigration remains substantially the same.... Secondly, the ethnic mix of this country will not be upset.... Contrary to the charges in some quarters, [the bill] will not inundate America with immigrants from any one country or area, or the most populated and deprived nations of Africa and Asia.... In the final analysis, the ethnic pattern of immigration under the proposed measure is not expected to change as sharply as the critics seem to think.... The bill will not flood our cities with immigrants. It will not upset the ethnic mix of our society. It will not relax the standards of admission. It will not cause American workers to lose their jobs.[9]

Officially recorded immigration statistics tell only part of the story. Obviously, accurate counts of the persons residing in the U.S. without proper authorization are difficult to obtain. Estimates of unauthorized persons who have entered the country vary between 5 or 6 million and 20 million. Such figures are hardly useful. The highly credible Pew Hispanic Center estimates that more than four-fifths of unauthorized immigrants to the U.S. come from Mexico, or Central and South America.[10] Various U.S. administrations appear to see little advantage to the nation's economy in stemming what continues to be a flow of cheap labor across the Mexico-U.S. border. And Mexico itself pressures the U.S. not to restrict unauthorized immigration, arguing that it is a human rights

---

8.   Higham, John. (1955). *Strangers in the land: Patterns of American nativism, 1860-1925*. New Brunswick, NJ: Rutgers University Press.

9.   U.S. Senate, Subcommittee on Immigration and Naturalization of the Committee on the Judiciary, Washington, DC, Feb. 10, 1965 (pp. 1-3)

10.   Pew Hispanic Center. (2006). *Modes of entry for the unauthorized migrant population*. Retrieved February 26, 2007, from http://pewhispanic.org/files/factsheets/19.pdf.

issue. Mexico is exporting some of its most impoverished citizens who then send money home to relatives in amounts that exceeded $15 billion in 2007. Surely this arrangement is not incidental to the Mexican government's position on undocumented immigration into the U.S. At the same time that it argues for a porous border to the north, Mexico assiduously guards its southern border against what it considers illegal immigration from Guatemala. The causes of this massive immigration from the South are not simple, although they are routinely oversimplified in heated debates. The myth that a corrupt Mexican government has impoverished its own people who now seek employment north of the border is a gross exaggeration, though it may contain a grain of truth. The causes are both political and economic, and they have as much to do with U.S. policy as they do with Mexican politics.

The Free Trade Agreement of 1994 and U.S. subsidies to its own giant agricultural corporations have combined nearly to destroy the profitability of Mexican corn farming. The central role of corn in the average Mexican's diet can not be overstated. The average citizen of Mexico eats about 10 corn tortillas a day, more in rural areas. After 1994, when U.S. corporations enjoying significant economies of large-scale and government subsidies began selling their cheaper corn in Mexico, the Mexican corn market was significantly negatively impacted. Poverty in rural areas worsened. Without subsidies from the Mexican government and with a tradition of small independent farms resulting from the 1910 Revolution that split up large plantations into *ejidos*, the Mexican farmer could not compete with U.S. agri-business in the production of the staple crop of the Mexican diet. Attempts in the U.S. to promote the production of ethanol from corn have recently resulted in increased prices for corn exported to Mexico, exacerbating poverty in the country's rural areas. When the tariffs on corn are finally eliminated completely in 2008 as part of the North American Free Trade Agreement, and given the transition in U.S. corn production to ethanol rather than as a food crop that is driving up the price of corn on the world market, the economic circumstances that are driving rural Mexicans north in search of work are likely to become even worse.

> More than half of all migrants leaving Mexican villages go to destinations in Mexico; however, villagers' propensity to migrate to U.S. jobs more than doubled from 1990 to 2002. This surge in migration mirrors an unexpectedly large increase in the number of Mexico-born people living in the United States revealed by the U.S. 2000 Census.... [M]igrants from Mexico represented 77 percent of the U.S. farm workforce in 1997–98, up from 57 percent in 1990. [11]

Approximately 15% of the village population of Mexico was estimated to be working in the U.S. in the first few years of the 21st century. Add to this the fact that many *maquiladoras* along the U.S.-Mexico border are being dismantled because Mexican workers are becoming more expensive than workers in China and India, and the problems of immigration are further exacerbated.

Public attitudes toward immigration from Latin America are negative and growing stronger. For a few moments, at least, a strident, one-issue anti-immigration politician (Representative Tom Tancredo, R-Colorado) could be taken seriously as a presidential candidate during the early stages of the 2008 presidential campaign.[12]

---

11.   Mora, Jorge, & Taylor, J. Edward. (2006). Determinants of migration, destination, and sector choice: Disentangling individual, household, and community effects. In Maurice Schiff & Çaglar Özden (Eds.), *International migration, remittances and the brain drain* (pp. 21-51). Washington, DC: World Bank and Palgrave Macmillan. (pp. 22-23)

12.   By November 2007, undocumented immigration from Latin America had become a "hot button" issue among the Republican candidates vying for the support of their White majority base. It occupied a good deal of the debate during the campaign leading to the Iowa caucuses even though Iowa has fewer than 5% immigrant population. In a CNN (Cable News Network) debate among the candidates televised on November 28th, former Governor of Arkansas Mike Huckabee was criticized by former Governor of Massachusetts Mitt Romney for having given college scholarships to the children of illegal immigrants while governor. Huckabee spoke more aspiration than reality when he replied that American citizens are better people than to punish children for the actions of their parents.

The Public Schools Grow Browner Too

The population growth numbers reported earlier are matched by the large growth in the percentage of Hispanic students in K-12 public schools in the U.S., as shown in Exhibit 6.8. The percentage of public school students who are Hispanic tripled between 1972 and 2004 (from 6 to 18%),[13] while the White K-12 proportion declined from 78 to 61%. When this growth in the public school population is broken out by region of the country, it can be seen that approximately one third of the public school students in the Western U.S. were Hispanic in the year 2000 (see Exhibit 6.9). While the percentage of K-12 pupils classified as White in each region remained fairly constant from 1972 to 2000, the percentage of Hispanic pupils increased substantially in each region. The increase is particularly marked in the Western U.S. Whereas about 15% of K-12 pupils were Hispanic in the Western U.S. in 1972, that figure rose to about 30% in 2000. The concentration of Hispanic students in the Southwest is even more noticeable when one focuses on individual states; for example, the K-12 population of California is 46% (vs. 32% in the general population), Arizona, 37% (vs. 25%, general population), New Mexico, 52% (vs. 42%), and Texas, 44% (vs. 32% in the general population).[14] A recent report from the Pew Hispanic Center documents that Hispanic students are concentrated in very large high schools with high student-teacher ratios and high incidence of poverty.[15] The state of California must construct a new school at a rate of nearly one per day to accommodate the explosive growth in its school age population. Representation of Hispanics in the school attending population after Grade 12 is small, however. Fewer than one quarter of Hispanics ages 18

---

13.   U.S. Department of Education, National Center for Education Statistics, Common Core of Data.

14.   U.S. Department of Education, National Center for Education Statistics, Common Core of Data.

15.   Fry, R. (2005). *The high schools Hispanics attend: Size and other key characteristics.* Washington: Pew Hispanic Center. Retrieved November 8, 2005, from http://pewhispanic.org/reports/report.php?ReportID=54.

Exhibit 6.8.   Percentage of Public School Students Enrolled in Grades K–12 Who Were Minorities: October 1972-2000

	White	Total Minority	Black	Hispanic	Other Minority
1972	77.8%	22.2%	14.8%	6.0%	1.4%
1975	76.2	23.8	15.4	6.7	1.7
1980	72.8	27.2	16.2	8.6	2.4
1985	69.6	30.4	16.8	10.1	3.5
1990	67.6	32.4	16.5	11.7	4.2
1995	65.5	34.5	16.9	14.1	3.5
2000	61.3	38.7	16.6	16.6	5.4

From U.S. Department of Commerce, Bureau of the Census. October Current Population Surveys, 1972–2000.

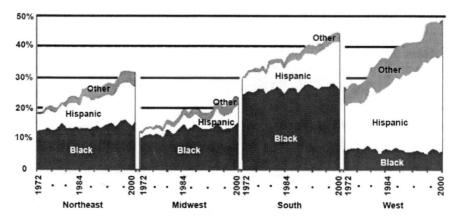

Exhibit 6.9.   Percentage of public school students K-12 who are minorities by region, 1972-2000. Based on Wirt, John et al. (2002). *The condition of education, 2002,* p. 45.

to 24 were enrolled in college or universities in 2000. Approximately 6% of the bachelor's degrees conferred in 1999-2000 were earned by Hispanics.

Projections of numbers of children of various races and ethnicities by the U.S. Census Bureau place the proportion of Hispanic children between the ages of 0 and 17 years at a quarter of the population by 2020 (see Exhibit 6.10).

Exhibit 6.10.   Percentage of U.S. Children Ages 0-17 by Race and Hispanic Origin, Selected Years 1980-2004 and Projected 2005-2020

Race and Hispanic Origin	1980	1985	1990	1995	2000	2005	2010	2015	2020
White, Non-Hispanic	74%	72%	69%	66%	61%	58%	56%	54%	53%
Black	15	15	15	15	16	16	15	15	15
Hispanic	9	10	12	14	17	19	21	23	24

The U.S. is Growing Older

America is graying. As recently as 1960, children under the age of 18 constituted more than one third of the U.S. population. In 20 more years, the percentage of children in the U.S. is expected to drop under one quarter, and they will be outnumbered by persons age 65 and older.[16]

> The demographic facts are familiar, but quite dramatic: While life expectancy in the United States in 1900 was a mere 47 years, people in the 21st century are expected to live to be almost 90, a whopping extra 40 years of life. Hardly any facet of our existence will be unaffected by that sweeping change.[17]

Prominent among the facets of American life that will be changed by the aging of the populace are the nation's economic circumstances. Excluding defense and debt interest, more than half of federal spending supports retired persons in their 60s or older. Social Security and Medicare are the obvious expenditures, but there are also veterans' benefits and pensions for civil service employees, retired military, and elected officials. Medicaid, originally conceived of as public assistance for poor people, is increasingly used

16.   Nichols, Sharon L., & Good, Thomas. (2004). *America's teenagersmyths and realities: Media images, schooling, and the social costs of indifference.* Mahwah, NJ: Erlbaum.
17.   Yankelovich, Daniel. (2005). Ferment and change: Higher education in 2015. *The Chronicle of Higher Education.* November 25. Retrieved December 7, 2005. from http://chronicle.com/weekly/v52/i14/14b00601.htm.

as aid for elderly. Nursing homes are increasingly the recipients of Medicaid funds. In 1995, the cost of Social Security and Medicare was 17% as a share of workers' taxable payroll; that figure is projected to rise by 2040 to between 35 and 55 %.[18] Veterans' benefits resulting from the Iraq War could push the figure nearer the larger figure. The chances are slim that some change in the political winds will shift power toward younger people or minorities. The most powerful political group in the nation today is the American Association of Retired Persons (AARP).[19] Its power is likely to grow along with the median age of the nation's populace; it expects to have 70 million members by 2015. Information on the rate of minority membership in AARP is not readily available.

As the population as a whole ages, fewer and fewer families have children of school age. In 1970, half of the married couples in the U.S. had one or more children under 18 in their household. By 2005, that percentage had dropped to 34%; in other words, the percentage was cut by nearly one third. Interest in the fate of public education would be expected to wane as fewer families send their children to school.[20]

Ethnicity and Age

When the aging U.S. population is categorized by ethnicity, the appearance of change in the composition of the U.S. population is remarkable. Quite clearly, the Hispanic population is much younger than the non-Hispanic (largely White) population. Exhibit 6.12 shows age pyramids for the Hispanic and

---

18.   Peterson, Peter G. (2000). *Gray dawn: How the coming age wave will transform Americaand the world.* New York: Three Rivers Press.
19.   Morris, Charles R. (1996). *The AARP: America's most powerful lobby and the clash of generations.* New York: Times Books/Random House.
20.   U.S. Census Bureau, *Current population reports;* and *America's families and living arrangements: 2000, 2003, 2004, and 2005.*

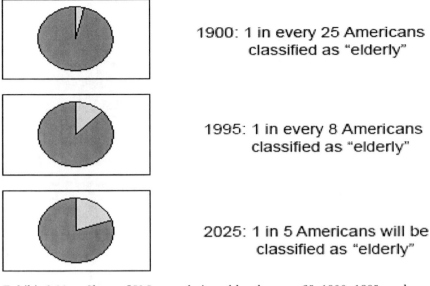

1900: 1 in every 25 Americans classified as "elderly"

1995: 1 in every 8 Americans classified as "elderly"

2025: 1 in 5 Americans will be classified as "elderly"

Exhibit 6.11.   Share of U.S. population older than age 65, 1900, 1995, and 2025 (projected).

non-Hispanic populations of the U.S. from the 1980 and the 2000 Censuses. As an example of how the graphs in Exhibit 6.12 are read, note that in the 1980 Census, approximately 5.8% of all persons classified as Hispanic were males under the age of 5 years, and approximately 2% were females between the ages of 50 and 54.

The age pyramids show that the Hispanic population of the U.S. is proportionally much more heavily represented among the younger ages than the non-Hispanic. This feature is even more pronounced in the 2000 Census than in the 1980 Census. More precise figures comparing the non-Hispanic White and Hispanic populations for particular age groups appear as Exhibit 6.13. What is particularly noteworthy in Exhibit 6.13 is that whereas non-Hispanic Whites constitute only about half of the school age population in the country, they constitute more than 75% of the persons over age 50. It is naïve to think that disparities like these will not play out with obvious political consequences.

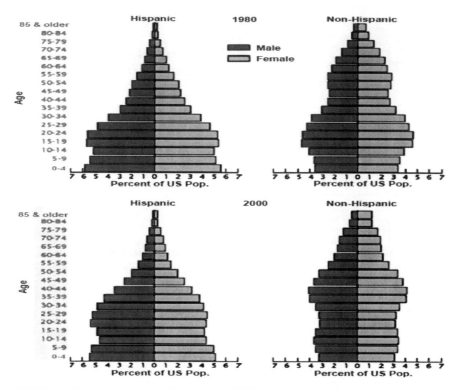

Exhibit 6.12.   Age and sex distribution of U.S. population by Hispanic and non-Hispanic origin, 1980 and 2000. Based on Hobbs, F. and Stoops, N. (2002). *Demographic trends in the 20th century.* Washington, DC: U.S. Census Bureau, 2000 Special Reports, Series CENSR-4, U.S. Government Printing Office.

"... Another Day Older and Deeper in Debt"[21]

America's "baby boomers"—the product of the post-WWII surge in the birth rate starting in 1946 and continuing for 15 to 20 years—must be feeling like the miners in the Merle Travis song from the 1950s: "Another day older and deeper

---

21.   The song "Sixteen Tons" (sung by Tennessee Ernie Ford) was popular in the mid-1950s; it described the plight of the American miner, who lived in the company town and traded at the company store. The company charged the miners whatever the company wished and the miners never escaped from poverty and debt. The credit card companies may be the modern equivalent of the mining companies.

Exhibit 6.13.   U.S. 2000 Population Classified by Selected Ages and Race/Ethnicity

Ages	Hispanic	Non-Hispanic White	Other	% Hispanic	% Non-Hispanic White	% Other Races
0 to 4	3,717,975	11,194,346	7,981,452	16.2	48.9	34.9
5 to 9	3,623,680	12,303,903	8,245,602	15.0	50.9	34.1
10 to 14	3,163,412	12,882,540	7,645,532	13.4	54.4	32.3
15 to 19	3,171,646	12,759,934	7,459,956	13.6	54.5	31.9
50 & older	4,804,966	61,751,490	15,100,500	5.9	75.6	18.5

From http://www.census.gov/population/cen2000/phc-t08/tab08.pdf

in debt." A survey of 1,000 adults in 2004, reported that "get out of debt" led "lose weight" as the most frequent New Year's resolution.[22] More Americans are sinking deeper in debt.

- The level of debt as a percent of after-tax income is the highest ever measured in our history. In 2006, mortgage and consumer debt was greater than after-tax income on average.[23]
- Personal savings in the U.S. was negative in 2005 for the first time since 1933 during the Great Depression.[24]
- The indebtedness of U.S. households rose over 40% in real dollars (inflation adjusted) in the first 6 years of the 21st century.[25]
- The debt-service ratio (the percent of after-tax income that goes to pay off debts) is at an all-time high of

22. *Forbes Magazine*, March 16, 2005. Retrieved February 27, 2007, from http://www.forbes.com/business/2005/03/16/cz_0316findsvpdebt.html
23. For disposable income: Bureau of Economic Analysis, NIPA Table 2.1. 2006. For mortgage and consumer debt: Federal Reserve Flow of Funds Accounts, balance sheet tables. 2006. http://www.federalreserve.gov/releases/z1/.
24. Bureau of Economic Analysis. (2006). NIPA Table 2.1. http://www.bea.gov/bea/dn/nipaweb/index.asp.
25. Federal Reserve. (2006). *Flow of funds accounts, balance sheet tables: Total household liabilities.* http://www.federalreserve.gov/releases/z1/. Deflated using CPI-U from the Bureau of Labor Statistics.

13.9%.[26] (From Economic Policy Institute; http://www.epi.org)

The average "baby boomer" (a person born between 1946 and 1964), the earliest of whom became 60 years old in 2006, had total net worth—assets, including real estate equity, minus liabilities—of $110,000. Economists are beginning to speak of the 50-50-50 problem: half of the people over age 50 in the U.S. have total savings (including 401K and retirement) under $50,000. The average baby boomer can expect to inherit from his or her parents less than $50,000. This "silver tsunami," as some have named it, will exert unprecedented pressures on the political and economic systems of the country. I will return to the question of the bleak financial outlook for the American middle-class and what it means for public education in the next chapter.

The "sub-prime" mortgage crisis that became evident in 2006 and 2007 placed greatly increased pressure on the finances of millions of families. Predatory lending practices resulted in home equity loans with complex and often unexplained provisions for resetting rates from 6 and 7% to 11 and 12% within 2 to 3 years. Loans were given based on scant documentation of a borrower's ability to pay. Mortgage brokers were rewarded with high fees for any loan made no matter how risky. Many borrowers who could have qualified for long-term fixed interest rate loans were steered instead toward adjustable rate mortgages that would quickly balloon to well over 10%. Soon, payments escalated from $800 to $1,200 in many instances. Payments were missed. Home foreclosures became commonplace. The effects of this financial disaster for hundreds of thousands of families will reverberate in the nation's economy for years.

It is clear that the typical American entering what was once thought to be the relaxed and restful retirement years now

---

26. Federal Reserve. (2006). http://www.federalreserve.gov/releases/housedebt/default.htm

faces many years—thanks to medical advances—of marginal financial subsistence. There are basically only four sources of income during retirement: continued employment, government benefits, private pensions, and personal savings. The outlook for all of these four is increasingly bleak. For many, the golden retirement years are more likely to be spent greeting customers at a Wal-Mart than in a beach chair on the coast of Florida or in an RV in Yuma. A recent survey of 2,500 adults between the ages of 45 and 64 asked respondents to name income sources other than Social Security that they expected to draw upon when they retired.[27] Their responses are tallied in Exhibit 6.14. Nearly half of all persons surveyed expected to supplement savings, pensions, and Social Security income by continuing to work.

Conclusion

The demographic stage is set for a few decades of public policy making. Currently, about 40% of the non-Hispanic population is at or above the age of 45. Approximately 81% of the Hispanic population is younger than 45. The median age of the Hispanic population in the U.S. in 2000 was 26 years, and it will decline over the next 20 years, while at the same time the median age of the non-Hispanic White population was 38 years and is increasing.[28] Older, White Americans entering their retirement years with diminishing assets and the prospect of continued work will be asked to support the public institutions that increasingly will be serving a younger, browner clientele. One may hope for a generous spirit among

---

27. From the Thrivent Financial Retirement Survey reported in *USA Today*, April 19, 2007, p. 1.
28. For most of the figures given here, the African American population of the U.S. stands midway between the non-Hispanic White and the Hispanic population; median age in the 2000 Census was 30 years; approximately 73% are under age 45; and so forth.

Exhibit 6.14.   Percentages of Persons Ages 45-64 With Expected Sources of Income Other Than Social Security After Retirement

Savings and Investments	Employment	Employer Pension	IRA	Inheritance
52%	43%	39%	36%	16%

these older Americans; however, no one should be surprised if they demur.

Peter G. Peterson observed in *Will America Grow Up Before It Grows Old?* that by 2025, "the proportion of all Americans who are elderly will be the same as the proportion in Florida today. America, in effect, will become a nation of Floridas."[29] Perhaps, it is more accurate to say that taking ethnicity and age into account together, America is becoming a nation of Arizonas. Later we shall see how the demographics, politics, and education policy of Arizona may portend the fate of public education in America.

---

29.   Peterson, Peter G. (1996). *Will America grow up before it grows old: How the coming Social Security crisis threatens you, your family and your country.* New Yoek: Random House.

Part III.
What
Accountability
Means

Chapter Seven

Robots, Cars, and 4BR/2.5BA

The forces of fertilizers, pills, and magnetic strips, joined by the transformative power of industrial robotics in the manufacturing sector, have fundamentally changed the place of human services in the American economy. As manufacture becomes cheaper through robotics or "outsourcing," greater percentages of the nation's economy are spent on services—medical care, fire and police protection, and, of course, education. Consequently, these services attract more cost-cutting attention. The middle class in America—traditionally the supporter of public institutions—is not only disappearing; it is being strangled by increasing consumption and debt. More and bigger cars and larger houses—four bedrooms and two-and-a-half bathrooms—necessitate two-income families, who increasingly succumb financially under mounting debt. Often they are forced to file for bankruptcy. The effects of these changing economic conditions has only begun to be seen. Public education, as one of the largest public expenditures outside of national defense and health care, is under tremendous pressure to change. The crisis in elementary and secondary education is not a crisis in achievement, but rather

Fertilizers, Pills, and Magnetic Strips: The Fate of Education in America
pp. 119–144

a crisis in cost, or more properly, a crisis in the willingness of the middle class to support a long-standing institution.[1] The reforms proposed in the name of making education better and the nation's children more competitive internationally are in reality proposals to cheapen education for the poor and privatize it for the White middle class.

Robots: Manufacture Versus Service

There exists a syllogism that governs a large part of modern macroeconomic life:

- Each year, Product X can be manufactured to the same level of performance at less cost.
- Each year, Human Service X can not be provided at the same level at reduced cost.
- Therefore, each year a greater percentage of the gross domestic product is taken up by Human Service X.

The increasing productivity of manufacturing originally owed its existence to British invention during the Industrial Revolution; it got a boost from Henry Ford in the early 20th century, and it now surpasses all comprehension due to the wonders of computers and industrial robotics. Fifty years ago, roughly half of the U.S. workforce was engaged in manufacture; today that figure is dropping to the vicinity of 10%. This remarkable transformation of the economy is due in part to technological invention and in part to corporations chasing after cheap labor in poor countries, "outsourcing" as it has come

---

1.   I deal in this book only with public education from kindergarten through Grade 12. Postsecondary education presents its own problems of cost and accountability. Indeed, the rise in the cost of college—in 2007, tuition, fees, board, and room at the average U.S. 4-year public university exceeded $13,000—has been enormous, roughly twice the rate of inflation since 1960. Although the parallels between K-12 and 13-16 education are many, they are subjected to substantially different economic and political influences. See Baum, Sandy, & Ma, Jennifer. (2007). *Trends in college pricing*. New Yok: College Board.

to be called.[2] The future of this division between manufacture and service economies for the U.S. will likely see an even greater skewing toward service industries. Manufacturing that is labor intensive has no durable competitive advantage for the U.S. in a global economy. Clearly, labor is cheaper elsewhere in the world, and only that manufacture that can not be outsourced will remain an important part of the U.S. economy.

The first patents for industrial robots were issued in the early 1950s to George Devol, founder of the company Unimation. Applications were limited in the early years. It was not until 1969 that the first articulated robot mimicking the movements of the human arm appeared, the invention of industrial engineer Victor Scheinman of Stanford University. Applications of industrial robots grew rapidly in the 1970s when several Japanese firms began using robots in the manufacturing process. The Japanese refused to honor international patent laws and copied several U.S. designs. As much as any influence, the introduction of industrial robots spurred the growth of the Japanese economy in the 1970s and 1980s. Only a few non-Japanese producers of robots survived during the 1980s and early 1990s. Costs of industrial robots vary from about $10,000 to as much as $100,000. By 2007, all welding on vehicles at Chrysler was done by robots. The number of auto workers in Detroit dropped from about a half million in 1980 to about a quarter million in 2005. Of course, not all this decline was due to automation, but a good bit of it was. Modern developments in manufacturing robotics include the introduction of "vision guided" robots. For less than the cost of a half dozen employees, a company can purchase a robot that far exceeds the productivity of human beings—and never asks for a holiday.

---

2. How technology has enabled the outsourcing of manufacture to third world countries in the race for greater profits was explained in detail in Thomas L. Friedman (2005), *The world is flat: A brief history of the twenty-first century.* New York: Farrar, Straus & Giroux. Whether a similar outsourcing of professional services (medical, legal, accountancy, and the like) will succeed to the same degree remains to be seen.

There are no parallel increases in productivity in the area of human services, and it is my contention that to expect such increases is naïve. Such naiveté is distressingly often exhibited by those who feel that their success in the business of manufacture gives them special insights into how to reform service institutions. There does not exist the equivalent of Moore's Law[3] (that data density—computer storage—doubles every 18 months) in the field of human services. In 1960, funds for the U.S. Department of Health, Education and Welfare amounted to 6% of the federal budget. Today the Department of Health and Human Services funds amount to nearly one quarter of the total federal budget. Each year, tax payers see larger and larger proportions of their income spent on services. Why do school costs rise each year when a personal computer costs a fourth as much today as it did in 1985 and is many times more powerful? The public's anxiety and displeasure are expressed in manifold ways. Human relationships of the type seen in the interactions between teachers and their students, nurses and their patients, social workers and their clients, police officers and those whom they encounter, are not subject to significant technological improvements on a par with the increases in productivity of manufacture. This is in itself a complex and lengthy argument to detail, and I won't attempt to do so here.

Year after year, political pressure will be exerted on the human services sector because it consumes larger and larger portions of the cost of living. Since that sector is primarily public, the pressure is exerted on taxes and, hence, the issue becomes hyperpoliticized. This pressure to make services cheaper and more productive—generally misguided and clumsy as it is—is what is observed today in the accountability movement in many areas of human services. In the early decades of the 20th century, the likes of Frederick Winslow Taylor and Henry Ford implemented their ideas of scientific management and mass production to improve industrial effi-

---

3.   Gordon Moore, cofounder of Intel.

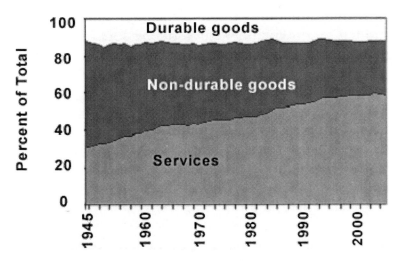

Exhibit 7.1.   Distribution of personal consumption expenditures, 1945-2004. Based on data from U.S. Department of Commerce, Bureau of Economic Analysis. http://www.bea.gov/

ciency. These ideas enjoyed success in the manufacturing of products; but their modern day equivalents for service industries are considerably less successful.[4] Industrial manufacturing output could be counted in terms of numbers such as how many cars roll off an assembly line per day. But a service industry may be accountable for curing a neurosis or instilling a love of learning in a young child; simple numbers can not capture the successes and failures of these endeavors. And the ritualistic activities of modern accountability methods—goal stating, performance targets, and the seemingly endless recording of numbers of little value—merely burden service providers with bureaucratic requirements.

In Exhibit 7.1, the distribution of personal consumption expenditures in the U.S. among durable goods, nondurable goods,[5] and services is graphed across 60 years from 1945 to 2004. The share was split 35% and 65% between services and

4. Callahan, Raymond E. (1962). *Education and the cult of efficiency.* Chicago: University of Chicago Press.
5. Durable goods include such things as motor vehicles, furniture, and major appliances. Nondurable goods include food, clothing, fuel and the like.

goods, respectively, at the end of WWII. By 2004, services constituted approximately 60% of personal consumption, nearly reversing the distribution of the late 1940s. Consumption of services in the U.S., indexed to the year 2000 to correct for inflation, has risen more than tenfold since 1930 (see Exhibit 7.2). These expenditures include, of course, the cost of both K-12 and postsecondary education.

The rise of the service economy has not only had profound effects on the nation's institutions, particularly, its public institutions; it is changing the very behavior of the total economy as well. Historic patterns of boom and bust, typical of manufacturing economies that overproduce then retrench, are disappearing from the U.S. economy. The three longest periods of economic growth—save for mobilizations for war in the 20th century—occurred in the decades of the 1980s, the 1990s, and the first decade of the 21st century. Economists attribute this largely to the changing character of the economy from manufacture to services.

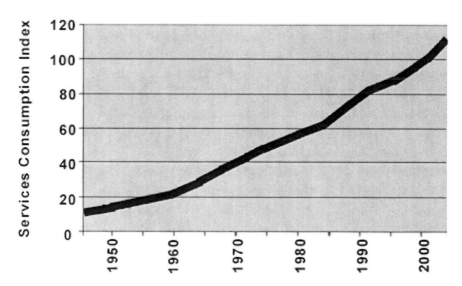

Exhibit 7.2.   Selected services—medical and dental care, hospital and nursing homes, and education at all levels—consumption index. Index created to equal 100 in 2000. Based on data from U.S. Department of Commerce, Bureau of Economic Analysis, http://www.bea.gov/

Expenditures for Health Services

Medical expenses are a big part of this steep rise in consumption of services. In 1960, the average U.S. family spent $71 on health insurance premiums; 12 years later this figure increased almost threefold to $196. By 1984 they were paying $370 in health insurance premiums. The figure for 1996 was $854, and in 2003, the average American family paid health insurance premiums totaling more than $1,200.[6] This increase is roughly 1,700% while the dollar inflated over that same interval from 1960 to 2003 by approximately 600%. Family health expenditures rose almost by half in 3 years from 2000 to 2003. Many employers are cutting back on health insurance offered to their employees. The percentage of workers with employer-provided health insurance is steadily falling. "Nearly 3.7 million fewer people had employer-provided insurance in 2004 than in 2000."[7]

Escalating medical costs are increasingly straining the finances of middle class and poor families. Sixteen percent of American households reported having had problems paying medical bills in the 12 months preceding January 2004. Families are going into debt to meet medical expenses, and often into bankruptcy as a result. A survey published in 2007 revealed that patients without health insurance were charged two and a half times more for equivalent hospital services. There are about 50 million uninsured Americans. The gap between the charges of the insured and uninsured more than doubled between 1985 and 2005.[8]

---

6.   U.S. Department of Labor. (2006). *100 years of U.S. consumer spending: Data for the nation, New York City, and Boston* (Report 991). Washington, DC: Author.

7.   Mishel, Lawrence; Ettlinger, Michael; & Gould, Elise. (2004). *Less cash in their pockets: Trends in incomes, wages, taxes, and health spending of middle-income families.* Washington, DC: Economic Policy Institute. Retrieved February 13, 2006, from http://www.epi.org/content.cfm/bp154

8.   Anderson, Gerard F. (2007). From "soak the rich" to "soak the poor": Recent trends in hospital pricing. *Health Affairs, 26*(3), 780-789.

Elizabeth Warren, a professor of contracts law at the Harvard Law School and the nation's leading expert on bankruptcy, has conducted extensive research on families who declare bankruptcy. Warren and her colleagues, reporting in 2000 on findings from Phase III of the Consumer Bankruptcy Project, wrote: "One out of four debtors, or an estimated 326,441 families in 1999, identified an illness or injury as a reason for filing for bankruptcy. One third of the debtors said that they had substantial medical bills, that is, that they had incurred $1,000 or more in medical bills not covered by insurance. Combining those identifying medical reasons with those indicating substantial medical debts (an overlapping but not perfectly coextensive group), the financial consequences of medical problems were a factor in the bankruptcy cases of an estimated 596,198 families in 1999."[9] These figures echo the findings of the medical debt and credit study performed by the Demos organization in 2007.[10]

- Twenty-nine percent of low- and middle-income households with credit card debt reported that medical expenses contributed to their current balances; almost 70% reported having had major medical expenses in the previous 36 months;
- Low- and middle-income medically indebted households were carrying one and a half times as much credit card debt as those without medical debt ($11.5 thousand versus $8 thousand).

The Center for Studying Health System Change, a nonpartisan Washington, D.C. policy research organization, reported that for low income, chronically ill patients on some

9. Warren, Elizabeth; Sullivan, Teresa A.; & Jacoby, Melissa B. (2000). Medical problems and bankruptcy filings. Retrieved March 5, 2007, from the Social Science Research Network: http://papers.ssrn.com/sol3/papers.cfm?abstract_id=224581
10. Draut, Tamara. (2007). Borrowing to stay healthy. New York: Demos: A Network for Ideas & Action. Retrieved March 6, 2007, from http://demos.org/page495.cfm

**Exhibit 7.3. Percentage of Persons Younger Than Age 65
with No Medical Insurance for Selected Years (1997-2003)**

Race/Ethnicity	1997	1999	2001	2003
White	13%	12%	11%	11%
Black	20%	18%	18%	19%
Hispanic	34%	32%	32%	33%

Source: Based on data from Hargraves, J. Lee. (2004). *Trends in health insurance coverage and access among Black, Latino and White Americans, 2001-2003.* Tracking Report No. 11. Washington, DC: Center for Studying Health System Change.

form of health insurance, 42% spent more than 5% of their income on health costs in 2003. The comparable figure in 2001 was only 28% of a comparable group of persons. And as always, the tragedy of unequal medical care falls more heavily on racial and ethnic minorities. As Exhibit 7.3 shows, a fifth of all Blacks and a third of all Hispanics have no health insurance. Medical care is delayed until illness overtakes its victims, and then expensive help is sought in hospital emergency rooms.

Medical advances will probably succeed more in increasing the average lifespan than in eradicating illness among the elderly. The vast majority of money spent on one's health care is expended in the last few years of one's life. As people live longer and have fewer children to contribute to their care as they age, the burden of health care costs will fall increasingly on public funding through such programs as Medicare and Medicaid.[11] A 65-year-old couple retiring in 2007 will expend more than $200,000 in health care services during the remainder of their lifetime, assuming current life expectancy

11. These estimates are based on a model that assumes that individuals are not covered by an employer-sponsored retiree health plan; furthermore, it is assumed that expenses associated with Medicare Parts B and D, Medicare cost-sharing provisions, and prescription drug costs are included. Costs of other health-related services or products (e.g., over-the-counter medications, dentistry services, long-term care, and the like) are not included. Based on a study by Fidelity Employer Services Company, and employee benefits consulting firm. Retrieved April 10, 2007, from http://content.members.fidelity.com/Inside_Fidelity/fullStory/1,,7448,00.html

estimates. As medical advances increase the length of life for these retirees, the expected costs of health services for the remainder of their life can be expected to rise to closer to a quarter million dollars. Total remaining lifetime expenditures for a couple retiring in 2008 can be expected to rise by approximately 6 percent over the $200,000 figure. It is estimated that the average retiree will spend approximately half of his or her Social Security benefits on health care services in the next 15 years. In the competition for public monies, health care for the elderly can be expected to do very well, at the expense of other public services.

Expenditures for Education

One area of the service sector where rising costs are continually decried by politicians and conservative critics is K-12 public education. John Chubb and Eric Hanushek, long-time critics of public education, pointed out that inflation corrected expenditures on public K-12 education rose nearly 4% annually in the 3 decades from 1960 to 1990.[12] These critics' hard data on costs are usually coupled with naïve assertions about the effectiveness or "productivity" of public education in a way that invites readers to accept the myth that while expenditures have risen faster than inflation, children are learning less than in the past. Allan Odden claimed that in spite of huge increases in the cost of public education since Sputnik, "student performance—and thus education productivity—have [sic] not improved that much."[13] The facts are that education spending increased far less in the last half of the 20th century than expenditures for all health related services. Richard Rothstein and Karen Hawley Mills

12. Chubb, John E., & Hanushek, Eric A. (1990). Reforming educational reform. In Henry J. Aaron (Ed.), *Setting national priorities: Policy for the nineties*. Washington, DC: Brookings Institution.
13. Odden, Allan R. (Ed.) (1992). *Rethinking school finance: An agenda for the 1990s*. San Francisco: Jossey-Bass. (p. 11)

have effectively refuted the most outlandish claims of the education cost critics.[14] Only by using dubious inflation measures and ignoring the substantial increase in services expected of the public schools in the last fifty years were the critics able to paint their gloomy portrait of a system gobbling up tax dollars while sinking into mediocrity. Rothstein and Mills showed that inflation corrected per pupil expenditures rose about 60% from 1967 to 1991, far less than the doubling claimed by many critics. More significantly, perhaps, is that schools were called on to provide a much broader set of services—for handicapped students, non-English-speaking students, health and nutritional services, counseling, crisis management, security, and the like. Parents continue to demand more transportation and food services. The percentage of school budgets devoted to regular instruction actually dropped from about 80% in the late 1960s to around 60% in 1990. A third of the increase in per pupil expenditures supported services to special-education students, 8% went to improved lunch programs; about 10% went to counseling and dropout prevention programs. Teacher salaries grew modestly, averaging approximately 1% annually in inflation corrected dollars, due to the increasing age and stronger credentials of the teacher force. The federal government and states have imposed unfunded mandates on public schools— one of the most severe being the recent No Child Left Behind Act—leaving the expense to municipalities that levy property taxes.

Rothstein and Mills concluded that "Our findings suggest only that reforms are not likely to be well designed if reformers, failing to examine the varied rates of spending growth in education's many programs, assume an unproven collapse in school productivity."[15] Not unexpectedly, the critics' claims were not muted by Rothstein and Miles's warning. In 2006,

14.   Rothstein, Richard, & Miles, Karen Hawley. (1995). *Where's the money gone? Changes in the level and composition of education spending.* Washington, DC: Economic Policy Institute.
15.   Rothstein & Mills, *op cit.*, p. 2.

Greene and Winters could actually claim, using data unsuited to any valid comparison of professional compensation, that public school teachers were overpaid. These authors actually argued that public school teachers make higher hourly wages than architects and economists.[16]

In 2006, President George W. Bush recommended cutting over $700 million from federal special education programs in order to offset more tax cuts. In 2008, the first of the 78-million-person baby boomer generation will begin to draw Social Security benefits. The pressure to further reduce federal expenditures for services to children will intensify. I do not wish to add fuel to the current (Republican) Administration's cries of "crisis" in federal entitlement programs. Social Security solvency is far from being an unsolvable economic problem. Modest increases in the amount of such benefits subject to income tax, small increases in age eligibility, and reduced benefits to rich retirees could keep the program viable at near current levels for decades. The political determination to oppose the American Association of Retired Persons is lacking. Federal spending on services to children has declined since 1960, from 20% to about 15% in 2006, as "non-child" spending on Social Security, Medicare and Medicaid has risen, from about 20% to above 45% in 2006. The lines of Exhibit 7.4 will most certainly grow further apart as the retired, largely White, middle-class baby boomer generation continues to age.

The Weakened American Middle Class

The American middle class[17] through its taxes and its patronage has been the supporter of public institutions for at least a century. That is beginning to change as the wealth distribution in the U.S. separates into the wealthy and the poor.

---

16. See Bracey, Gerald. (2007). *Get rich: Be a school teacher.* Retrieved March 19, 2007, from http://www.huffingtonpost.com/gerald-bracey/get-rich-be-a-school-tea_b_40506.html

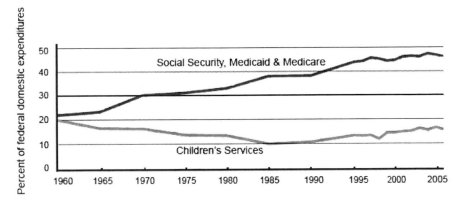

Exhibit 7.4. Percent of Federal expenditures to children's services and major entitlements, 1960-2006. Based on data in Carasso, Adam, Steuerle, C. Eugene, & Reynolds, Gillian. (2007). *Kids' share 2007: How children fare in the federal budget.* Washington, DC: Urban Institute. Retrieved March 19, 2007, from http://www.urban.org/UploadedPDF/411432_Kids_Share_2007.pdf

The assault on labor unions dating from the 1970s, tax laws that began to be rewritten with the Republican victories in the general elections of 1980,[18] free-trade agreements under neoliberals in the 1990s, and legislation continuing to today are gutting the middle class and creating a bimodal distribution of wealth: the very rich at one end and the borderline poor at the other. One wonders whether the U.S. is becoming another Hong Kong on a national scale, with ostentatious and conspicuous wealth on the one hand, massive abject poverty on the other, and little in between. With these changes comes

17. The term "middle class" has no simple definition, or rather, has several similar working definitions. No more precision than ordinary usage is necessary for the arguments made here. Like pornography, most people know what the "middle class" is when they see it. Sociologists (e.g., Dennis Gilbert (1997), William Thompson and Joseph Hickey (2005) have taken quantitative approaches to defining the American middle class that result in designating roughly 50% of the center of an income distribution as the "middle class." For my purposes, that number is much too small and the middle class can be taken as nearly all but the very rich and the very poor.

18. In a 7-year period (1981-1988) under the Ronald Reagan administration, the highest personal income tax bracket was lowered from 70% to 28%, thus reaping a sizeable benefit for the rich.

weakened support for public education as just one of many institutions facing pressure to make do with less.

Beginning in the early 1970s, a combination of technological change, globalization, and hostile negotiations on the part of large corporations ushered in the doom of the labor unions in the U.S.[19] Fully one quarter of private company employees were union members in 1973; today the figure is 7% and it is not rising. My father began serving his apprenticeship as a printer in 1923. For nearly 40 years he was a member of one of the strongest labor unions in the nation, the International Typographical Union. His union struck against the introduction of computers into the composing room at the newspaper in 1963. He never worked another day as a printer, and when he retired from other work 10 years later, the ITU retirement fund was broke. His was the first, perhaps, but not the last trade to be wiped out by modern technology. As unions began to disappear, so did the American middle class.

Free-trade policies began to be enacted during the Reagan administration in the 1980s, specifically the U.S.-Canada Free Trade Agreement in 1988. Later, NAFTA in 1994 during the Clinton Administration threw middle-class workers in the U.S. auto industry and other manufacturing industries into competition with low-wage workers in Asia, Central and South America. At the same time, professionals were protected in such legislation, helping raise the upper middle class into a new wealthy class. In Thomas Friedman's "flat world," it is the American middle class that gets crushed. Free trade wipes out middle and lower middle class manufacturing jobs, but protects professionals. Over 3 million manufacturing jobs were lost in the American economy in the first 5 years of the 21st century.[20] At about the time that the country starts to see legal services and medical

---

19.   "We're going to crush labor as a political entity" and ultimately "break unions." Grover Norquist, right-wing anti-tax activist, quoted in Lilly, Scott. (2007). *Beyond justice: Bush administration's Labor Department abuses labor union regulatory authorities.* Washington, DC: Center for American Progress. (p. 4)

services "outsourced," one can expect to see Congress act to protect professional, white collar jobs.

From the mid-1970s to 2000, the income from salary and wages of Americans at the 90th percentile rose by more than one third, roughly 1% a year. Consequently, the 10% highest income earners barely managed to stay even with inflation in the last 30 years of the 20th century. But consider the 1% highest income earners; their income from salary and wages over the same period increased by 87%. The 1 in 1,000 highest earner saw a gain in income of 181%; and the 1 in 10,000—the top .01%—highest earner's income rose approximately 500%.[21] While economic productivity rose impressively in the U.S. in the latter half of the 20th century, only the highest earners in the income distribution benefited. The principal researchers studying this phenomenon did not mince words in their description of what has happened to the American middle class as the rich prospered from increasing productivity:

> over the entire period 1966-2001, as well as over 1997-2001, only the top 10 percent of the income distribution enjoyed a growth rate of real wage and salary income equal to or above the average rate of economy-wide productivity growth. Growth in median real wage and salary income barely grew at all while average wage and salary income kept pace with productivity growth, because half of the income gains went to the top 10 percent of the income distribution, leaving little left over for the bottom 90 percent. Half of this inequality effect is attributable to gains of the 90th percentile over the 10th percentile; the other half is due to increased skewness within the top 10 percent.[22]

Dew-Becker and Gordon had advice for their colleagues who study the rising income inequality of the past 50 years:

20.   Bureau of Labor Statistics, Current Employment Statistics Survey. (2006). http://www.bls.gov/ces/home.htm. See also Bivens, Josh. (2005). Trade deficits and manufacturing employment. *Economic Snapshot.* November, 20, 2005. http://www.epi.org/content.cfm/webfeatures_snapshots_20051130

21.   Dew-Becker, Ian, & Gordon, Robert J. (2005). *Where did the productivity growth go? Inflation dynamics and the distribution of income* (Working Paper No. 11842). New York: National Bureau of Economic Research.

22.   Dew-Becker, Ian, & Gordon, Robert J., *op. cit.*, p. 1.

Economists have placed too much emphasis on "skill-biased technical change" and too little attention to the sources of increased skew-
ness at the very top, within the top 1 percent of the income
distribution. We distinguish two complementary explanations, the
"economics of superstars," i.e., the pure rents earned by sports and
entertainment stars, and the escalating compensation premia of
CEOs and other top corporate officers. These sources of divergence
at the top, combined with the role of deunionization, immigration,
and free trade in pushing down incomes at the bottom, have led to
the wide divergence between the growth rates of productivity, average compensation, and median compensation.[23]

Nor have the economic circumstances of the middle class
improved since Dew-Becker and Gordon completed their
analysis in 2001. Lawrence Mishel and Ross Eisenbrey studied
the declining fortunes of the middle class from the beginning
of the George W. Bush Administration to 2005.[24] Although corporate profits were increasing to record levels, the wages and
incomes of average Americans were declining. In 2005, infla-
tion-adjusted wages were below where they were at the start
of the recovery in November 2001, but productivity was up by
15%. From 2001 to 2006, the median household income in
inflation adjusted dollars fell from $46,000 to $44,400.[25] Wage
growth in real dollars stagnates while corporate income
growth is distributed as corporate profits benefiting stock
holders and management. As was pointed out in Chapter 6,
debt for the average U.S. household rose dramatically in the
first 5 years of the 21st century. In real dollars, debt rose more
than 40% between 2001 and 2006.[26] And in 2005, personal sav-

---

23. Dew-Becker, Ian, & Gordon, Robert J., *op. cit.*, p. 1.
24. Mishel, Lawrence, & Eisenbrey, Ross. (2006). *What's wrong with the economy.*
Washington, DC: Economic Policy Institute. Retrieved March 7, 2007, from http://
www.epi.org/content.cfm/pm110
25. U.S. Census Bureau. (2004). *Income, poverty, and health insurance coverage in the
United States.* Retrieved November 10, 2007, from http://www.census.gov/hhes/
www/income/income.html. Median household income for Hispanics was 25%
lower.
26. Federal Reserve. (2006). *Flow of funds accounts, balance sheet tables: Total household liabilities.* http://www.federalreserve.gov/releases/z1/

ings was negative for the first time since 1933, while corporation profits were setting record highs.

It has been estimated by the Tax Policy Center[27] that in 2006, the income earner at the 99th percentile in the nation's income distribution will receive salary and wages in excess of $400,000; the 1 in 1,000 highest earner—the top tenth of 1%—will take in more than $1,500,000 in wages and salaries. While federal tax reform is touted as bringing tax relief to the middle class, it nearly always is regressive, favoring the wealthy over the middle class and poor. Various tax reforms at the federal level in the past 7 years have saved far more on a percentage basis for the upper income earners than for the middle class. If tax cuts made by Congress in 2005 are eventually made permanent, by 2011 the top 1% will receive an average cut equal to 6.5% of after-tax income or $60,000, and the top one tenth of 1% of income earners will receive an average tax cut of 7.5% or $300,000. Those in the middle fifth of the income distribution will receive an average cut of 2.3%, amounting to $836. As Warren Buffett has pointed out, he will pay income tax at a lesser rate than his secretary.

What happened to the American middle-class dream? More couples are employed than ever before in the history of the nation, but seldom has the middle class felt more economically pressured. At the same time that the American middle class has been victimized by a ruling oligopoly of corporations buying off politicians—government by and for the corporations—they have been inflicting additional harm on themselves through their rapidly changing habits of consumption. It is tempting at this point to explore the sidebar issue of how the nation's appetite for consumption is linked to corporate interests through the mechanism of advertising. There is definitely some truth to this position, but it is so obvi-

---

27.   The Tax Policy Center, a Joint Venture of the Urban Institute and Brookings Institution. http://www.taxpolicycenter.org/home/

ous and has been so well documented for decades that it doesn't require further mention.[28]

Elizabeth Warren, Leo Gottlieb Professor of Law at the Harvard Law School, and her daughter, Amelia Warren Tyagi, published their analysis of the declining American middle class in 2001 under the title *The Two Income-Trap: Why Middle-Class Mothers and Fathers Are Going Broke.* Working off of surveys of persons who had declared bankruptcy[29] and Bureau of Labor statistical surveys, Warren and Tyagi sought to account for the rising bankruptcy and debt rates among modern middle class families with two employed parents. The authors worked vigorously to dispel the "over-consumption myth" as an explanation of middle class economic woes, spending a good deal of space in an attempt to refute the arguments advanced by John de Graaf, David Waan, and Thomas Naylor in *Affluenza: The All-Consuming Epidemic,*[30] and by the economist Juliet B. Schor in *The Overspent American: Upscaling, Downshifting, and the New Consumer.*[31] Warren and Tyagi's counterarguments depend a good deal on arbitrary distinctions between "necessities" (housing and transportation foremost among them) and luxuries (expensive vacations, fancy clothes, jewelry, and other things one can only imagine). In truth, no clear line can be drawn between many middle-class expenditures. How many "extras" must be added to a new automobile before it is classified as a luxury instead of a necessity?

Warren and Tyagi's counterarguments fail to dispel the so-called myth of a two-income middle-class family caught in a trap of steeply rising appetite for consumption, in my opinon. They cite convincing statistics on the *decreased* expenditures of

28. Packard, Vance. (1957). *The hidden persuaders.* New York: David McKay.
29. Sullivan, Teresa A.; Warren, Elizabeth; & Westbrook, Jay Lawrence. (2000). *The fragile middle class: Americans in debt.* New Haven, CT: Yale University Press.
30. de Graaf, John; Waan, David; & Naylor, Thomas H. (2001). *Affluenza: The all-consuming epidemic.* San Francisco: Barrett-Koehler.
31. Schor, Juliet B. (1998). *The overspent American: Upscaling, downshifting, and the new consumer.* New York: Basic Books.

the average family in such areas as clothing (21% less in infla-
tion-corrected dollars than in the 1970s), food (more than 20%
less in real dollars both at home and in restaurants than in the
1970s), and major appliances (nearly half as much as was spent
25 years ago). Expenditures are up only marginally for "entertainment" and "computers." They point out that the cost "per
car" of owning and operating a vehicle is less today than in the
past; but they neglect to point out at the same time that two and
three-car families are becoming the norm. So where is the cul-
prit? Housing is a major source of increased costs, they believe.
The average size of homes has increased significantly in the
past 50 years. Indeed, a trip through most American neighbor-
hoods built before the 1970s leaves the observer with one overwhelming impression: "How did people live in those little
things?" New homes built in the 1970s had average square
footage of about 1,600; but new homes built in 2005, averaged
more than 2,400 square feet with more than half having ceilings
higher than nine feet on the first floor.[32] Larger homes are
accompanied by higher property taxes; not insignificantly for
the purpose of the explanations being offered here is the fact
that most property taxes go to support public education.
Merely comparing house sizes across decades overlooks the
transition from apartments to single-family homes that took
place after WW II.[33] American families took up more living
space on average as the second half of the 20th century pro-
gressed, and they filled that space with more material goods. In
2006, the Austin Texas City Council passed a resolution limiting
new or remodeled homes in the central city to 2,300 square feet
because large homes were being built that crowded lots and
blocked neighbors' views. The county commissioners of Boulder County Colorado attempted to institute an ordinance that
would limit new house construction to less than 4,500 square
feet; the attempt failed. Municipal governments across the

32.   Joint Center for Housing Studies of Harvard University. (2006). *The state of the nation's housing 2006*. Cambridge, MA: Harvard University.
33.   Ford, Larry R. (1986). Multiunit housing in the American city. *Geographical Review, 76*(4), 390-407.

country have been alerted to the trend in swelling house sizes. Indeed, housing and automobiles represent the clearest expression of modern American overconsumption that is squeezing the middle class.

The rash of mortgage foreclosures that first appeared in 2006, particularly in states such as Nevada, Colorado, and Florida where mostly new homes were being mortgaged in the first few years after 2000, arose principally from middle class overconsumption in housing and the "subprime" lending policies of banks and other financial institutions. Middle-class families mortgaged larger homes than they could actually afford; foreclosures occurred disproportionately among houses in the range of a quarter million to three-quarter million dollars in market value. In a tally of foreclosures in a suburban Metropolitan Denver county in 2007, 41 of 90 foreclosures were on homes with market value above $300,000. Of course, it takes two to create a foreclosure in most instances: a naïve borrower and an equally naïve or subprime lender. The nation had no shortage of both in the Alan Greenspan era.

Greater housing costs and mortgage debt are strangling many American middle-class families. As Warren and Tyagi reported, the average American family with children in 1983 owned a home with market value of $98,000. By the year 1998, that same family would live in a home worth $175,000 in inflation corrected dollars. Oddly, Americans quest for bigger, fancier homes is not attributed to an increased appetite for consumption, according to Warren and Tyagi. The motive for bigger homes, they assert, lies elsewhere. Incredibly, they blame public education:

> In order to free families from the [two-income] trap, it is necessary to go to the heart of the problem: public education. Bad schools impose indirect—but huge—costs on millions of middle-class families. In their desperate rush to save their children from failing schools, families are literally spending themselves into bankruptcy. The only way to take the pressure off these families is to change the schools.[34]

34.   Warren, Elizabeth, & Tyagi, Amelia Warren. (2003). *The two-income trap: Why middle-class mothers and fathers are going broke*. New York: Basic Books. (p. 33)

This rather surprising interpretation is problematic on several grounds. Criticizing it here would be beside the point if it were not that Warren and Tyagi use it as the point of departure for a foray into education policy that is central to my own interpretations of what is happening in education today. The authors recommend a voucher program and free parental school choice as a solution for migration into expensive suburban housing that straps the middle class with debt and expenses beyond their means. Why a family would spend many times as much as the cost of a private education in the city in order to move to the suburbs is not addressed by the authors. To address this inconsistency might throw one back to a more serious consideration of the "overconsumption myth," as they call it. Public education is important, but it is doubtful that it can be blamed for the middle class exodus from inner cities to the suburbs. The latter has many motives, no doubt, and singling out one leaps over a host of motives to find a rationale for one's favored policy recommendations.

In 1955, my in-laws, Lorraine and Lawrence Rubin's life on the near northwest side of Chicago epitomized many of the economic forces to which millions of families were reacting at the same time. They asked themselves, "Should we have another baby or buy a car?" They settled on the car, bought it so that Lawrence would no longer have to take public transportation to his job sites as an electrician, and then Lorraine got pregnant with my sister-in-law, Janice. The pregnancy was unplanned and represented one of millions of failures of the "rhythm method" of birth control. Soon after, the family moved from the rapidly deteriorating urban area known as Logan Square, where they were renting an apartment, to Skokie in the Chicago suburbs where they purchased a four bedroom, two-and-a-half bath 1,900 square foot single-family home. Lorraine took a part-time job at the Bank of Lincolnwood to help pay the mortgage. The nature of the schools back then in downtown Chicago or in Skokie had nothing to do with these decisions.

In the first place, Warren and Tyagi produce no convincing evidence that the schools deserted by middle-class families were "failing." "It is time to sound the alarm that the crisis in education is not only a crisis of reading and arithmetic; it is also a crisis in middle-class family economics."[35] The facts are that even though middle-class economics are approaching a state of crisis, there never was a crisis in reading and arithmetic.[36] The old crisis bromide was used in the 1980s in specious explanations for the nation's economic problems; it can not be resurrected 25 years later to explain the dire economic straits in which American families find themselves. Increased expenditures for housing, vehicles, entertainment, and most significantly credit card debt, do indeed represent an increased appetite for consumption among the American middle class. To attempt to justify them as the regrettable consequence of seeking a better education for one's children may be putting a socially acceptable face on a less commendable motive. In the end, neither Warren and Tyagi nor I know much about the true motives of this mass of people called the middle class. That ignorance could prove far more damaging to the case I wish to make here about the support for public education than it proves to be damaging to the former authors' case. I will argue ultimately that the public's lack of support for public education arises in part from motives far more contemptible than their desire to acquire houses and cars beyond their means.

The Middle Class Concern With Money

The American middle-class has become increasingly focused on that which they are increasingly lacking: disposable income. Writers such as Warren and Tyagi have sought to put a more noble face on the portrait of avarice painted by

35.   Warren & Tyagi, *op. cit.*, p. 34
36.   Berliner, David C., & Biddle, Bruce J. (1995). *The manufactured crisis: Myth, fraud and attack on America's public schools*. New York: Addison-Wesley.

the likes of Schor and de Graaf. But to deny that the American economy has been built for the last 50 years on a culture of consumption is to deny an obvious reality.

Whereas in the past persons defined their personality by the work they did, today personalities are often defined by the manner in which persons consume, either goods or services. Mr. So-and-so is a sports fan; he saves up his vacation days and travels every March to watch Cactus League baseball. Ms. Such-and-such trades in her BMW every 2 years; she has resolved to all who will listen that she will never put more than 20,000 miles on a single car. It is not clear what work they do or how they earn a living; in fact, these circumstances change frequently. One can come to be identified primarily by which gym they attend or how many yoga classes a person takes in a week. Clothes no longer simply hide nakedness or retain body heat, they advertise social class: Under Armour; Aéropostale; Abercrombie & Fitch. The ethic of work has been replaced by hedonic consumption.

Alexander W. Astin surveyed college freshmen's attitudes toward a variety of issues each year.[37] Samples of as many as 250,000 freshmen from hundreds of public and private colleges across the country are surveyed and trends plotted across decades. When over 30 years 2,000 students were asked "How important is it to you to be very well off financially?" the results showed a remarkable trend. The percentage of students answering "Essential" or "Very important" nearly doubled from around 40% in 1970 to 75% in 1998 (see Exhibit 7.5). Astin's data show remarkable increases in students' materialistic attitudes, with an accompanying erosion of a valuing of community and family. Education is increas-

---

37.   Astin, Alexander W. (1998). The changing American college student: Thirty year trends, 1966-1996. *The Review of Higher Education, 21*(2), 115. Astin, Alexander W. (2000). The civic challenge of educating the underprepared. In Thomas Ehrlic (Ed.) *Civic responsibility and higher education* (pp. 124-146). Westport, CT: Oryx Press. Sax, L.J.; Astin, A.W.; Korn, W.S.; & Mahoney, K.M. (2000). *The American freshman: National norms for fall 2000*. Los Angeles: Higher Education Research Institute, UCLA. Astin, Alexander W. (1991). The changing American college student: Implications for educational policy and practice. *Higher Education, 22*(2), 129-143.

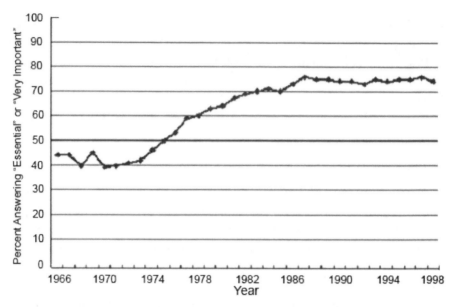

Exhibit 7.5.   Percentage of college freshmen answering "essential" or "very important" to the question "How important is it to you to be well off financially?" 1966-1988. From various publications by Alexander W. Astin.

ingly viewed by them as a means to achieve the good life defined primarily in terms of material goods and consumption.

Other surveys have corroborated this trend. "An independent annual nationwide survey of high school seniors by the University of Michigan confirms this trend toward growing materialism, as the fraction of students who rated 'having lots of money' as quite important burgeoned from 46 percent in 1976 to 70 percent in 1990, before drifting back to 60-65 percent in the mid-1990s."[38] During the past 30 years, the percentage of college freshmen who expect that a college education will bring them better jobs has risen from 20% to 80%.[39]

---

38.   Putnam, R. D. (2000). *Bowling alone: The collapse and revival of American community.* New York: Simon & Schuster. (p. 260, footnote 25)

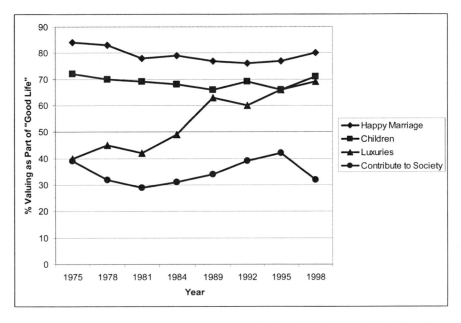

Exhibit 7.6.   Percent naming value as part of the "good life," 1975-1998. (After Putnam, 2000, p. 274)

When adults were asked "What is part of the good life?" from 1975 to 1998, the results in Exhibit 7.6 were obtained. "Luxuries" rose while "contribute to society" declined.

The Lost Supporters of Public Education

Industrial robots first began to radically reduce the cost of manufacturing in the U.S. after WW II. As a consequence, the share of the gross domestic product devoted to services rather than goods rose steadily throughout the 20th century. Medical advances of the last half of the 20th century yielded better and more costly means for preventing and curing disease. Increasing portions of the nation's expenditures for

39.   Kirp, D. (2005). This little student went to market. In R. H. Hersh, & J. Merrow (Eds.), *Declining by degrees: Higher education at risk* (pp. 116-124). New York: Palgrave Macmillan. (p. 116)

medical services mark the last 5 decades in our nation's history. As the federal budget share devoted to services to children dwindled, the share going to entitlements (Social Security, Medicare, and the like) for an aging population rose significantly, a trend certain to continue well into the 21st century. Concurrent with these trends, but greatly accelerating after 1980, the historic American middle class has been subjected to intense financial pressures by a series of events imposed upon them from without and willingly chosen from within: revised federal tax codes favoring the rich over the middle classes; free trade agreements leading to the outsourcing of industries to poor countries in search of low labor costs; increasing appetites of the middle class for larger domiciles and two automobiles; and others. With the middle class—the traditional partisans for public education—thus weakened, and with increasing pressure to contain the rising costs of public services, public education—never politically as strong as other interest groups—has been subjected to assaults on its autonomy and its professionalism in an attempt to reduce its cost. These assaults have assumed the form of reforms promising to avert the crisis toward which public education was alleged to be heading. That no such crisis ever existed was the subject of an earlier chapter. The promise of these proposed reforms is the subject of the next.

Chapter Eight

Reforming the Schools: Making Some Cheap and Others Private

The older, White voting public, facing their own financial exigencies in an uncertain retirement, is increasingly unwilling to shoulder the tax burden of educating "other" people's children, particularly when those children do not physically resemble or act like their own grandchildren.[1]

The dramatic changes in the nature of the school age population in the U.S. are spawning several changes in the nation's school system that are consistent with the interpretation that older, tax paying Americans wish to unburden themselves of the cost of supporting public education, and the majority of parents wish to secure some advantages for their school age children at public expense. These advantages

---

1. The reference to "other people's children" uses the language of Lisa Delpit (Delpit, Lisa D. (1996). *Other people's children: Cultural conflict in the classroom.* New York: The New Press) who clearly meant the children of ethnic and racial minorities, a usage also appropriate here. When interviewed by *USA Today* on the occasion of the release of a National Research Council report on the future of Hispanics in America, Roberto Suro, Director of the Pew Hispanic Center said, "[The challenge of meeting the needs of Hispanic students in the future] is getting mostly white voters to invest in the education of another group" (El Nassar, 2006).

Fertilizers, Pills, and Magnetic Strips: The Fate of Education in America
pp. 145–201

often entail isolation from minority children, who incidentally, then, are denied even the benefits of side effects from
attending the same schools as white middle class children.
This search for privilege and reduced costs has spawned most
of the education policy issues currently being debated:
vouchers, charter schools, tax credits, homeschooling and virtual schooling, English as second language (ESL) and bilingual education, the IB, alternative teacher certification, high
stakes testing, open enrollment. Many of these policies owe
their existence to the failure of voucher bills, a fact not irrelevant in the evaluation of the motives behind these "proxy"
policies.

The public, but professionals as well, are apt to ask one or
at most two questions of any proposed reform: Will it
improve students' academic achievement? What does it cost?
While important, these questions are secondary to questions
too seldom asked: Why *this* proposal and not others? *Who* is
proposing this reform? *Who wins* and *who loses* (money, pres-
tige, status, freedom) if we go down this path? Too often in
policy research, those who set the agenda win the debate.
When most things one might do will accomplish a little bit of
good and their bad side effects are harder to see or far in the
future, being in a position to ask the questions (Do charter
schools "work?" Is homeschooling successful?) guarantees
that other questions will be pushed into the background.
Most of the proposals to solve the "education crisis" in America have about them the character of cost reduction or
"choice." And "choice" is rationalized in terms of the motivat-
ing effects of competition or by appeals to personal freedoms.
These proposals come from politicians, doing the bidding of
the taxpayers—so be it in a representative democracy. But
what would the hot policy questions be if professional educators composed the agenda? Teacher sabbaticals? Home-based
discipline of disruptive students? Curriculum reform?
Teacher mentoring? Differentiated staffing with differentiated pay scales? The effects of adding teaching assistants to

regular classrooms? The impact of teacher aides on achievement?

Some act as if they are awaiting the definitive data that will resolve once and for all whether vouchers or charter schools or open enrollment are superior to the traditional way of doing things. Others claim that the data have arrived and they have them. The debates are decades old, and no data of any sort yet to be discovered can be imagined that would resolve them. The debates have all the characteristic of simple political debates, because that is precisely what they are.[2] They are debates about money, in the first place, and privilege in the second.

If there were clear and convincing evidence of substantial gains in academic performance resulting from instituting any one of these reforms, they would no longer be debatable policy issues. But such evidence is lacking, in spite of the protests of partisans who insist that their favorite solution to the crisis has been proven to be superior to all others. What drives the advocates? What is the source of their partisan energies? It is clearly not a case of having discovered, say, a miraculous cure for a virulent disease and wanting the world to benefit from it. One must look for the motives that drive the reformers. They are not hard to find. Reduce costs. Make schooling private at public expense for *my* children.

Ellen Brantlinger[3] has analyzed how well-educated middle class White parents use their knowledge of how to negotiate bureaucratic systems and secure privileged circumstances for their children in school. As Brantlinger explains, these circumstances are frequently more racially segregated. On a much broader scale, the White middle class as a whole negotiates the political process to achieve favorable school conditions for itself. These negotiated privileges take the form of the major education policy issues of the day.

2.   Glass, Gene V. (1987). What works: Politics and research. *Educational Researcher,* 16, 5-10.
3.   Brantlinger, Ellen. (2003). *Dividing classes: How the middle class negotiates and rationalizes school advantage.* New York: RoutledgeFalmer.

Vouchers: Competition for Public Education

When Milton Friedman died in 2006, it was reported in various media that his once radical ideas have now become an accepted part of American culture, for example, school vouchers. Obituaries often prompt understandable exaggeration. Friedman's school voucher idea—proposed in 1955 over half a century ago—was hardly new and certainly only accepted as a matter of debate, not as a part of American culture. In 1872, a French parliamentary commission recommended providing vouchers to citizens desiring to send their children to religious schools after the stunning defeat of the French in the Franco-Prussian War, a defeat that the French blamed on the "Prussian teacher [who has] won the war."[4] Crisis politics is not an invention of the 20th century. Friedman claimed that monopolistic public education is inefficient in terms of both consumption and production.[5] Consumers (parents) are limited, as a practical matter, to neighborhood schools that may not match the needs of their children, and the services produced by the monopolistic schools are both inefficient and overpriced.[6] For Friedman, education should be publicly financed but not exclusively provided by public schools. Education economists have found Friedman's ideas about education to be short on crucial specifics.[7] The economist Kenneth Boulding, whose wide ranging genius defied ideological boundaries, questioned the very basis of the

4.   Molnar, Alex. (2000). *Vouchers, class size reduction, and student achievement: Considering the evidence.* Bloomington, IN: Phi Delta Kappa. (p. 1)
5.   The author of a recent policy brief from the Milton and Rose Friedman Foundation (Aud, 2007) claims that voucher programs, of which there are very few, have saved taxpayers nearly $500 million in the past 15 years. In a critique of the Aud brief, Bruce Baker (2007), an education economist at the University of Kansas concluded that Aud failed to "make a sufficient case to informed policymakers for the positive fiscal impact of vouchers and tuition tax credits. In fact, it suggests quite the opposite—that fiscal gains are trivial at best."
6.   Friedman, Milton. (1955). The role of government in education. In R. A. Solo, (Ed.), *Economics and the public interest* (pp. 123-144). New Brunswick, NJ: Rutgers University Press.

voucher philosophy that competition would lead to better schools. Schooling, as Boulding reminded readers, is a special exchange in which those who pay for the service—parents and third party adults—are not the recipients of the service; children are.[8] As a consequence, the mechanisms of information flow that cause markets to work in more traditional relationships are missing in education. Indeed, the profit motive seems ill-suited to the business of public education.[9]

Bills to establish school voucher programs, or "opportunity scholarships" as they have been disingenuously called at various times, have failed in virtually every state legislature. Most recently in November 2007, the Utah voters went to the polls to soundly defeat a ballot proposition calling for what would have been the first universal voucher program in the nation. The voucher programs in Cleveland and Milwaukee—see immediately following—were sold to legislatures as trials or as experiments. The proposition that would have created Utah's Parent Choice in Education Program was fashioned to overcome previous objections based on loss of funding for public schools. For 5 years after a student left a public school to redeem a voucher at a private school, the public school that was left would continue to receive that child's state funding. Even with this stipulation,

7.   Levin, Henry M. (1990). The theory of choice applied to education. In W. H. Clune & J. F. Witte (Eds.), *Choice and control in American education: The theory of choice and control in education* (Vol. I, pp. 247-284). New York: Falmer Press. Murnane, Richard. (1986). Comparisons of private and public schools: The critical role of regulations. In D. Levy (Ed.), *Private education studies in choice and public policy* (pp. 153-169). New York: Oxford University Press.

8.   Boulding, Kenneth E. (1972). The schooling industry as a possible pathological section of the American economy. *Review of Educational Research, 42*(1), 129-143.

9.   "Whatever the flaws of the existing public school management and its poor performance in many urban areas, it does not appear that privatization via for-profit enterprises is the answer. EMOs [Education Management Organizations] have generally not been profitable, nor is there any evidence of any breakthroughs in educational results. And there is virtually no evidence that the quest for larger scale will address this critical feature." Belfield, C. R., & Levin, H. M. (2005). *Privatizing educational choice: Consequences for parents, schools, and public policy.* Boulder, CO: Paradigm. (p. 175)

the proposition was defeated by a vote of 62 to 38%. Even homeschooling parents motivated by religion opposed the proposition because it threatened to cross the line separating church and state.[10]

If there ever was an idea whose time refuses to come, it is school vouchers. Small pilot programs have been initiated infrequently—most notably in Milwaukee, Wisconsin—with the intent of trying out the idea and evaluating its effectiveness. Limited, experimental voucher programs have been adopted in a few instances; these are "means-tested," in the sense that only families below certain income levels may use them. However, the intention of voucher proponents is to make vouchers universal. But no state has implemented school vouchers on a wide scale. Indeed, one even wonders if the bills that are repeatedly introduced are merely stalking horses, setting up the opponents to compromise on "half-a-loaf" bills creating charter school programs or tuition tax credits, ideas that politicians have considered less radical and more acceptable. In fact, voucher opponents have settled for compromise legislation establishing charter schools in dozens of states in the U.S.

Currently, voucher programs of any significant size exist only in Milwaukee, Wisconsin, Cleveland, Ohio, and Washington, DC. The Milwaukee voucher program (Milwaukee Parental Choice), created in 1990, is the nation's oldest. More than 18,000 students were enrolled in the program during the 2007-2008 school year. Vouchers worth up to $6,500 per student were granted in that year. Half of the total funding of the program was taken from the state's allotment to the Milwaukee Public Schools. In 1996, a voucher program using primarily parochial schools as the voucher recipients was begun

---

10.   The CEO of Overstock.com, Mr. Patrick Byrne, contributed $6.2 million backing for the Utah provoucher campaign. When the proposition was overwhelmingly defeated, Byrne referred to the vote as a "statewide IQ test," and claimed that the citizens of Utah had failed it. Later he retracted the statement and called the vote a "sanity test" instead, which he also claimed they failed.

in Cleveland, Ohio. In 2002, the U.S. Supreme Court ruled that the Cleveland program was not unconstitutional.

The vigor with which voucher advocates argue for their proposals belies the utter absence of evaluation data that support claims of vouchers' benefits.[11] Wherever pilot programs have been evaluated, arguments over academic benefits, measured on standardized tests, have deteriorated into squabbles among statisticians over whether a few points on an achievement test can be attributed to the voucher program or uncontrolled factors (selectivity of the students, differential drop out rates between voucher students and nonvoucher students, and the like). The Wisconsin Legislature mandated an academic evaluation of the program; the evaluation was terminated in 1996 having shown no differences in achievement between voucher students in private schools and "comparable" public school students. "The [Voucher] vs. [Milwaukee Public Schools] comparison indicates absolutely no differences in math and a weak advantage in reading for [Milwaukee Public Schools] students. The latter effect becomes statistically insignificant once we correct for missing test data."[12] The verdict rendered by the most thorough analyses of the academic benefits of the Cleveland program mirrored that of the Milwaukee program:

> Overall, we find no academic advantages for voucher users; in fact, users appear to perform slightly worse in math. These results do not vary according to: adjustments for prior ability; intention-to-treat versus treatment effects; and dosage differences. Contrary to claims for other voucher programs, the CSTP is not differentially effective for African American students.[13]

---

11.   All attempts to assess the productivity of voucher programs have fallen far short of Levin's recommendations for evaluation: Levin, H. M. (2002) A comprehensive framework for evaluating education vouchers. *Educational Evaluation and Policy Analysis, 24*(3), 159-174.

12.   Witte, John. (1997). *Achievement effects of the Milwaukee Voucher Program.* Paper presented at the 1997 American Economics Association Annual Meeting, New Orleans, LA. Retrieved April 20, 2007, from http://www.disc.wisc.edu/choice/aea97.html

In spite of what must be considered the failure of the school voucher idea to take hold in the U.S., it continues to pop up in sometimes unexpected places. Elizabeth Warren, of the Harvard Law School, and her daughter, Amelia Warren Tyagi, published *The Two Income-Trap: Why Middle-Class Mothers and Fathers Are Going Broke* in 2001. Warren and Tyagi argued, contrary to conventional wisdom and a great deal of scholarship that they feel their data disproved, that "overconsumption" is not the reason for the strained economic condition of the American middle class. Conceding that Americans have in the last half century sought bigger, more expensive houses, Warren and Tyagi asserted that the motive for moving from smaller, older urban housing to larger suburban homes is to escape the failing public schools of the inner city. I repeat their advice already quoted in chapter 7:

> In order to free families from the [two-income] trap, it is necessary to go to the heart of the problem: public education. Bad schools impose indirect—but huge—costs on millions of middle-class families. In their desperate rush to save their children from failing schools, families are literally spending themselves into bankruptcy. The only way to take the pressure off these families is to change the schools.[14]

Warren and Tyagi recommend a voucher program and free parental school choice as a solution for migration into expensive suburban housing that traps the middle class in debt. Their proposal is naïve and unsupportable because it assumes the academic superiority of vouchers programs, and that has never been proven. If middle class families fled the inner cities in search of better education for their children, then why is the NAEP (National Assessment of Educational Progress) curve for Whites flat over that same period? And why is it that the only curve that shows significant improve-

13.   Belfield, Clive R. (2006). *The evidence on education vouchers: An application to the Cleveland Scholarship and Tutoring Program.* New York: National Center for the Study of Privatization in Education, Teachers College, Columbia University. (p. i)
14.   Warren, Elizabeth & Tyagi, Amelia Warren. (2003). *The two-income trap: Why middle-class mothers and fathers are going broke.* New York: Basic Books. (p. 33)

ment in NAEP scores is for young Blacks in the Southeast, who under court orders, were increasingly attending integrated schools over that same period? Their proposal is not unlike Herb Gintis's proposal[15] to introduce greater competition and choice into public education because it could not make racial segregation worse. Unfortunately, it can and it will. And it will not only be Whites segregating themselves off from Blacks, but from Blacks and Hispanics both, who will, of course, through regressive tax structures ultimately subsidize to a large measure the education of White pupils in suburban enclaves.

Robert Maynard Hutchins, at age 28, was named dean of the Yale Law School. At age 30, he was appointed chancellor of the University of Chicago. Hutchins was an intelligent man who saw far in both directions, to humanity's past, as in his Great Books project undertaken in the 1950s with Mortimer Adler, and to humanity's future, as in his founding of the Center for the Study of Democratic Institutions in 1959. Hutchins addressed the school vouchers issue in 1972:

> The support for the voucher plan in the country comes from those who do not want their children compelled to associate with those of other races and social status.[16]

James Bryant Conant, former president of Harvard University and prominent public education critic of the 1950s, wrote even more forcefully and with a greater sense of urgency than did Hutchins:

> The greater the proportion of our youth who attend independent schools, the greater the threat to our democratic unity. Therefore, to use taxpayers' money to assist such a move is, for me, to suggest that American society use its own hands to destroy itself.[17]

---

15.   Glass, G. V (Ed.). (1994). School choice: A discussion with Herbert Gintis. *Education Policy Analysis Archives, 2*(6). Retrieved April 21, 2007, from http://epaa.asu.edu/epaa/v2n6.html

16.   Hutchins, Robert Maynard. (1972). The great anti-school campaign. *The great ideas today.* Chicago: Encyclopedia Britannica. (p. 196)

17.   Conant, James B. (1970). *My several lives.* New York: Harper & Row. (p. 464)

The driving force behind the voucher movement—and its spin-offs into charter schools, tuition tax credits, and other similar policies—is the desire of the White voting public to create a "quasi-private" schooling experience for their own children; to wall off *their* school from the Brown invasion; to hold back the rising costs of public expenditures and provide what they see as a high quality education—the sort of education a child might receive in an expensive private school—but to have that cost subsidized by public tax monies.

Charter Schools: Making Public Schools Private

Historically, elite private schools were the refuge for the privileged classes seeking special treatment or escape from the public schools. Religious private schools have been a prominent feature of the American education landscape for well over a century. For many decades private school enrollments held steady, somewhere between 10% and 15% of all K-12 students. From 1900 to about 1920, roughly one tenth of children attending school in Grades K through 12 were enrolled in private schools. By mid-20th century, Catholic religious schools accounted for as high as 90% of the parochial school attendance in the U.S. But largely Catholic parochial schools waned as Protestant parochial and nonreligious private schools grew in size and number in the latter half of the 20th century.

In very recent years, the private school share of the student population has begun to drop; see Exhibit 8.1.[18] Noteworthy in the 10-year trend in private school enrollments is that the private school share has dropped in three regions of the

18.   Obtaining reliable counts of private school enrollments is quite difficult. Frequently data provided by the U.S. Department of Education (formerly U.S. Office of Education) are at odds with data from the decennial Census. Census figures on private versus public school attendance places the private school share at higher levels than other sources, but even these figures show a slight decline in private school share in the past 50 years from over 13% to around 11%.

Exhibit 8.1.   Private K-12 Enrollment as Percentages of all Students:
School Years 1989-90 Through 1999-2000

Year	% Private	Northeast % Private	Midwest % Private	South % Private	West % Private
1989–1990	10.4	15.4	12.0	7.8	8.5
1991–1992	10.2	14.7	11.7	7.8	8.6
1993–1994	9.8	13.9	11.2	8.0	7.9
1995–1996	9.9	13.6	11.2	8.1	8.3
1997–1998	9.7	13.3	11.0	8.2	7.8
1999–2000	9.8	13.3	11.0	8.4	7.8

From National Center for Education Statistics. (2006). *Digest of Education Statistics 2006.*
Washington, DC: U.S. Department of Education.

country but not in the South where post-1954 private schools sprang up as a means of avoiding court ordered segregation.

What is significant in contemporary U.S. education is that private school enrollments are declining slightly as a percentage of enrolled students. The White middle class is seeking to fund a disguised form of private (*quasi-private*) education within the public school system by means of vouchers, charter schools, tuition tax credits, open enrollment, homeschooling and the like. Although homeschooling is the fastest growing alternative to traditional public schools because of its smaller share of the population, charter school enrollments represent the largest alternative to the traditional public schools. At the beginning of the 2004-2005 school year, approximately 3,000 charter schools were in operation in 37 states. Approximately 1.5% (or more than 800,000) of public school students nationwide are enrolled in charter schools. The District of Columbia has the highest percentage of students enrolled in charter schools (11.35%), followed by Arizona (6.04%) and Delaware (4.35%).

Wherever charter school programs have been analyzed, the troubling specter of racial segregation has risen its ugly head. There is little question that to the person on the street, state funded charter schools are seen as "private" in spite of the fact that they are indeed public, that is, they are required to admit all students for whom there is space, adhere to federal laws governing special education and the like, and receive their funding from state revenues. "Charter school students across all racial groups in most of the sixteen states are more likely to attend intensely segregated minority schools than are public school students"[19] There is evidence that in such states as Arizona, charter schools are being used for "white flight" from high minority public schools.[20] In California, the same is true to a lesser extent, and some homeschoolers will cooperate to form a "charter school" in name only. Where "choice" is prominent, the resegregation of the American public school system is not far behind.[21]

In 1996-97, Arizona had nearly one in four of all charter schools in the U.S. My colleague Casey Cobb and I undertook an analysis that involved a series of comparisons between the ethnic compositions of adjacent charter and public schools in Arizona's most populated region and its rural towns. This method differed from the approach of many researchers studying ethnic segregation in charter schools in that it incorporated the use of maps to compare schools' ethnic make-ups (see Exhibit 8.2). The ethnic compositions of 55 urban and 57 rural charter schools were inspected in relation to their traditional public school neighbors. Nearly half of the charter schools exhibited evidence of substantial ethnic separation. Arizona charter schools not only contained a greater proportion of White students, but when comparable nearby tradi-

---

19.   Frankenberg, Erica, & Lee, Chungmei. (2003). Charter schools and race: A lost opportunity for integrated education. *Education Policy Analysis Archives, 11*(32). Retrieved November 15, 2005, from http://epaa.asu.edu/epaa/v11n32/.
20.   Cobb, Casey D. & Glass, Gene V. (1999). Ethnic segregation in Arizona charter schools. *Education Policy Analysis Archives, 7*(1). Retrieved November 15, 2005, from http://epaa.asu.edu/epaa/v7n1/
21.   Patricia Gándara has written eloquently on the effects of segregation on Hispanic students and how some have overcome these disadvantages. Gándara, Patricia. (1994). Choosing higher education: Educationally ambitious Chicanos and the path to social mobility. *Education Policy Analysis Archives, 2*(8). Retrieved June 19, 2005 from http://epaa.asu.edu/epaa/v2n8.html. Gándara, Patricia. (1995). *Over the ivy walls: The educational mobility of low-income Chicanos*. Albany: State University of New York Press.

tional public schools were used for comparison, the charters were typically 20 percentage points higher in White enrollment than the other publics. Fees Middle School in southern Tempe, Arizona (a suburb in the metropolitan Phoenix area) enrolled 50% minority pupils in 1996, while the Tempe Prep Academy, a charter school two blocks distant, enrolled only 17% ethnic minority students. Moreover, the charter schools that had a majority of ethnic minority students enrolled in them tended to be either vocational secondary schools that did not lead to college or "schools of last resort" for students being expelled from the traditional public schools. The degree of ethnic separation in Arizona schools was large and consistent; it has grown in succeeding years; and it is ignored by politicians and policymakers in the state.

In Exhibit 8.2 appears a map of charter and traditional public schools located in west Mesa, Arizona, with the proportions of White pupils enrolled in each school. Charter schools are indicated by triangles and traditional public schools by circles. For example, Holmes, a traditional public school in the lower right hand corner of the map, had 813 students enrolled, of which 46% were White. The adjacent Sequoia School, a K-12 charter school with 752 students, was 90% White. Two traditional public schools in Exhibit 8.2, Franklin West and Franklin 7&8, show very high percentages of White enrollment: 89% and 81%, respectively. The census tract which encompasses Franklin West, Franklin 7&8, and Mesa Arts Academy was 37% White in 1995. How could the Franklin traditional public schools be so White in an area that was predominantly ethnic minority? For one, the Mesa School District open enrollment policy allows parents to choose among public schools, and the prestigious Franklin schools are an especially popular choice. There is a distinctly lofty status attached to these schools, making them similar to private schools. At least in part, this explains how a public school that is 80-90% White is located in a neighborhood that is principally ethnic minority. In essence, the Franklin schools appear to contribute to separating students along ethnic lines. They are an aberration among the traditional public schools in that area, but as will be seen later, they illustrate still another form of quasi-privatizing public education—open enrollment.

In the most extensive and objective study of a state-wide charter school system published to date, Gary Miron and his colleagues at the Evaluation Center of Western Michigan University found convincing evidence that the charter schools of the state of Delaware were contributing to racial segregation.[22]

> The aggregate of charter schools does not differ greatly from the traditional public schools in the state. However, when we look at the data by schools, we find substantial differences in student demographics. Some charter schools primarily serve minority students, and others cater primarily to white students.

- This pattern of segregated charter schools based on race is also repeated in segregation by class and ability.
- On the whole, traditional public schools have higher percentages of low income students, students with special education needs, and students who have limited English proficiency.
- Some reasons that explain why the charter schools have become so segregated include the following:
  - The school may be located in a highly segregated housing market.
  - Parents choose these highly segregated environments for their child(ren) because of their desire for a homogeneous learning environment.
  - Targeted marketing and recruitment efforts by charter schools. For example, particular cultural profiles may attract a particular ethnic group; and specific offerings such as full day kindergarten may be more attractive to low-income families (Miron et al., 2007, p. 2).

Because individual charter schools enroll students that differ greatly from sending districts, one can argue that charter

---

22.   Miron, Gary; Cullen, Anne; Applegate, Brooks E.; & Farrell, Patricia. (2007). *Evaluation of the Delaware charter school reform: Final report.* Kalamazoo, MI: The Evaluation Center, Western Michigan University.

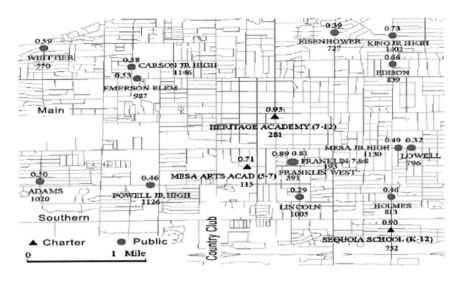

Exhibit 8.2.   Proportion of White students in charter (triangle) and traditional public (circle) schools located in West Mesa, Arizona, 1996.

schools may be accelerating the resegregation of public schools by leaving them more fragmented based on race, class, and ability.[23]

Like advocates for vouchers, researchers backing the charter school movement search for evidence of the superior academic performance of students in charter schools. None that stands up against the critique of neutral methodologists has been found.[24]

---

23.   Miron Cullen, Anne; Applegate, Brooks, E.; & Farrell, Patricia. (2007). *Op. cit.,* p. 3.

24.   "Unfortunately, despite claims by charter advocates, there is no systematic research or data that show that charter schools perform better than public schools. Since charter schools embody wildly different educational approaches and since charter and public schools obtain their enrollment in very different ways, evaluation and comparisons between the two require very careful analysis. At a minimum, it is certainly safe to say that there is little convincing evidence for the superiority of charter schools over public schools in the same areas. In fact, some of the studies suggest that charter schools are, on average, even weaker." Orfield, Gary. (2003). Foreword to Frankenberg, Erica & Lee, Chungmei. (2003). Charter schools and race: A lost opportunity for integrated education. *Education Policy Analysis Archives, 11*(32). Retrieved November 15, 2005, from http://epaa.asu.edu/epaa/v11n32/

Again, the best study addressing the question was that of Miron and his colleagues. They looked at the academic performance of charter school pupils in Delaware and compared it with the performance of students in the traditional public schools. The Evaluation Center's work on this topic benefited from one of the best data sets ever available to study the issue (compiled by the Delaware Department of Education) and from a level of sophistication in experimental design and analysis generally missing from other studies. Fifth grade reading and mathematics comparisons showed that:

> the 5th grade average math scale score for charter school students was significantly lower than the mean results for matched noncharter students. There is some indication of improvement in math scaled score since 2003-04. [For Grade 5 reading] the results suggest that, overall, charter school students are not performing at levels comparable to their noncharter peers in reading; and the gap appears to be widening.[25]

Test score comparisons in Grades 8 and 10 showed mixed results with the differences attributed to charter schools' selectivity in choice of students—"creaming" in some lexicons—in ways that could not be adequately controlled for in the statistical analyses. Although Miron and his colleagues took a rather benign view of the charter school situation in Delaware,[26] my own view is considerably less sanguine. It is true that Delaware, running a small and relatively tightly regulated charter school system, may have avoided many of the disasters that have plagues charter schools in other states; nonetheless, it is hard to credit the state with a success when the new system has contributed to racial segregation and done nothing to promote greater academic progress.

---

25.   Miron, Gary; Cullen, Anne; Applegate, Brooks E., & Farrell, Patricia. (2007). *Op. cit.*, p. vii.

26.   Miron, Gary, Cullen, Anne, Applegate, Brooks, E., & Farrell, Patricia. (2007). *Op. cit.* "On the whole, our findings indicate that the charter school reform in Delaware is rather successful" (p. xi).

Charter schools appear to be adopting one of four different characters: White academies run by individual experienced teachers; "drop-out" drill and kill factories run by large companies calling themselves Educational Management Organizations (EMOs); ethnic academies appealing to racial or ethnic loyalties for their clientele; and private/Montessori conversion schools.[27][28] Super Bowl XXX was played January 28, 1996, in Tempe, Arizona, a suburb of Phoenix. The National Football League donated $1 million to a newly opened charter school, Espiritu Charter School located in a poor section of Phoenix. Enrolling primarily Hispanic youngsters, Espiritu spent the money acquiring land, constructing a football field, a parking lot, and a classroom building. In 2007, Espiritu had an enrollment of 800 students. Its test scores had begun to slip. Fewer than one in five students passed the state's AIMS (Arizona Instrument to Measure Standards) reading test. The school expects a second windfall from the 2008 Super Bowl that will also be played in the Phoenix area. Espiritu Charter School is owned by brothers Armando and Fernando Ruiz. Armando

> theorizes that charter schools have evolved into two groups: those that take in kids who are behind in their academics and put them through weak courses to accumulate credits to graduate, and those that act as private, elite schools by taking only the brightest.[29]

The brief history of charter schools in America is replete with stories of theft, corruption, and ethical failure. The with-

---

27.   Carnoy, Martin; Jacobsen, R.; Mishel, L.; & Rothstein, Richard. (2005). *The charter school dust-up: Examining the evidence on enrollment and achievement*. Washington, DC: Economic Policy Institute and Teachers College Press. Renzulli, L., & Evans, L. (2005). School choice, charter schools, and white flight. *Social Problems, 52* (3), 398-418.

28.   Working with a distinction between *mission-oriented* and *profit-oriented* charter schools, Lubienski and Gulosino (2007) showed that profit-oriented EMOs located their charter schools so as to avoid concentrations of difficult and disadvantaged students.

29.   Kossan, Pat. (2007, March 24). Charter scores slide despite NFL funding. *Arizona Republic*, pp. A1 & A19.

drawal of strict government oversight of charter schools was supposed to unleash powers of creative innovation. It seems to have unleashed instead a torrent of greed and duplicity. Regulations governing charter schools in Arizona were egregiously lax. The lifting of bureaucratic burdens was an invitation to exploitation that some charter school organizers could not resist. It was possible within the letter of the enabling legislation to spend charter school funds to acquire property and then hold personal title to the property in the event the school failed, as many did.

Raymond Jackson founded ATOP Academy with two campuses—one in Phoenix and the other in Tempe—in 1997 as a K-8 charter school that was reported to have a combined enrollment in 1997-98 of more than 350 mostly poor African American students. Disinterested visitors to the school described a rigid, almost military style of "drill and kill" teaching. Textbooks were actually authored by Dr. Jackson himself and bought by the school. Within 5 years the ATOP Academy found itself at the center of a scandal over falsified reports and the school's charter was revoked. Jackson—who listed himself as Dr. Raymond Jackson, but even a Google search could find no evidence of his having earned a doctorate—later surfaced as principal of a K-8 school on the Hopi Indian Reservation in Northern Arizona for 1 year.

In the late 1990s, one of the earliest and largest charter schools in the nation, Citizen 2000 in Phoenix, Arizona, grew to more than 800 students in its second year of operation, largely by playing on the sympathies of its African American clientele. The school was closed suddenly in the spring semester of its second year. Students and teachers were abandoned by the school's founder without notice. It was later learned that the founder and principal, whose salary far exceeded that of any other principal in the state, had hired her sister as assistant principal, had used school funds to pay her divorce lawyer and her mother's mortgage on a condominium in the most exclusive area of town, and had left the state to relocate in Chicago. The Arizona Attorney General's office chose not to prosecute.

In 2004, auditors for the state of Arizona uncovered attendance counting problems at more than half of the 345 charter-school companies operating charter schools in the state. Attendance counts are the basis of state reimbursements to the charter schools. One company, Renaissance Educational Consortium operating several charter schools in the state, was discovered during the 2005-2006 school year, to be misreporting its enrollments by nearly 50%. Almost half of their student count was either not enrolled, regularly absent, or had dropped out of school altogether. The company received more than $100,000 from the state to which it was not entitled between June and October.[30] The Franklin Arts Academies, operator of three charter schools in the Phoenix suburbs, were notified in Match 2007 that their charter was about to be revoked for misreporting of student enrollment figures. Actual enrollment was fewer than 130 students, while 170 was the number reported to the Arizona Department of Education. Fraudulent reimbursements amounted to nearly a quarter million dollars a year.

Morningstar Academy principal Carolyn Kennedy managed to keep her job as principal of the Apache Junction Arizona charter school even though she failed to report an incident of a teacher molesting a girl in his class. The teacher, Bobby Kennedy, 28, was the principal's son. The decision to keep Ms. Kennedy in her position as principal was made by the charter school owner, C. Steven Cox. A reporter for the Arizona Republic discovered that Mr. Cox was under indictment on 112 counts of theft and misuse of charter school funds in California.[31]

---

30. Kossan, Pat. (2007, September 4). Arizona's charters overstate their enrollments, audits show. *Arizona Republic*, p. B1.
31. Kossan, Pat. (2007, September 12). Principal keeps job after failing to report molest. *Arizona Republic*, p. A1.

Charter school graft is not confined to the state of Arizona. Anne Lesley Kane was arrested on November 12, 2007, by the Boulder (CO) City Police. Ms Kane, founder and former lead teacher of the Horizons K-8 Charter School in Boulder, Colorado, was charged with four separate felonies: theft, attempting to influence a public servant, forgery, and embezzlement of public property. Approximately 90% of the students attending Horizons Charter School are White and from middle class families. Kane was alleged to have misrepresented her salary, allowing her to collect unwarranted retirement money from the state retirement fund.[32]

Ironically, when these schools collapse amid scandal and malfeasance, charter school proponents trumpet the failures as successes of the market at work. Jeanne Allen, head of the conservative Center for Education Reform, hailed the collapse of the ATOP Academy as a triumph of the free market:

> While Ray Jackson and ATOP have been a savior for hundreds of families, at no time should poor management be tolerated in any school. This case shows the power of the charter concept. If there are problems, these schools can be shut down. Such accountability is rarely seen in traditional Arizona public schools.[33]

The implication is that incompetence and duplicity exist in the traditional public schools but are never uncovered because of the public school monopoly. When a charter school fails, it is hailed as a triumph of the market place and presented as evidence of the superiority of those that remain open. When a public school runs into difficulties, it is cited as evidence of the failure of the entire public education "semi-monopoly." Poor performance and illegal behavior exist in the traditional public school sector, and they are frequently

---

32. Bounds, Amy. (2007, November 13). Horizons Charter founder facing theft, embezzlement charges. *Boulder Daily Camera*, p. A1.

33. Arizona puts school on notice to fish or cut bait; Phoenix case demonstrates power of charter school accountability. December 15, 1998. Retrieved July 14, 2007 from http://www.edreform.com/index.cfm?fuseAction= document&documentID=1525&sectionID=55

dealt with.[34] But they are usually dealt with in subtle ways that protect the dignity of the individuals involved while protecting the integrity of the school. Accurate figures do not exist on felonious and unethical behavior in the schools; however, the rate of felonious and unethical behavior certainly appears to greatly favor the charter school movement.

It is difficult to see that anything other than the White voting public's desire to simultaneously cheapen public education and create quasi-private schooling for their children is driving, in its larger part, the charter school movement. Private schools being increasingly outside the financial reach of all but the most well-to-do Americans, something akin to private schools but funded by public tax monies become the preferred alternative. Charter schools are evolving into the public version of the nonparochial private academies. That they symbolize to those parents who choose them a sanctuary from the menacing poly-cultural environments of the traditional public schools is an added attraction.

Tuition Tax Credits

The notion of tuition tax credits—not deductions for education costs but dollar-for-dollar forgiveness of tax indebtedness—has been championed by conservatives for some years. They argue that it is unfair to tax parents for public education when they choose to send their child to a private

---

34. Four school districts in rural Arizona were audited for special education expenditures and found that some fifth and sixth year high school students had sufficient credits to graduate but were kept on their books while the students were receiving vocational education. Some students were on campus less than five hours a week, which made them ineligible for state funding. In one case, state money was used to pay students' college tuition. The State Superintendent of Public Instruction, Tom Horne, recently increased the number of auditors in his department from one to nine. "If the Legislature wants to save money, all they have to do is give us more auditors" (see Kossan, Pat. (2007, December 21). Schools misused funding, state says. *Arizona Republic*, p. A1.

school and pay its tuition: The tuition tax credit "establishes basic fairness by allowing parents and others who choose an alternative school—public or private—to do so without being penalized."[35] Taxing persons to support public education when those persons send their children to private schools is said to deny parents freedom of choice. Without free choice, it is claimed, the monopolistic public education system can ignore its inefficiencies without penalty in the market place. When the regressive nature of this plan is pointed out, proponents are quick to argue that poor children who can not afford private school tuition will be the beneficiaries. The relationship of this argument to the arguments for vouchers and charter schools is obvious. Indeed, tuition tax credit bills tend to sprout up where proposed school voucher legislation fails. Some conservatives have moved education tax credits to the top of their agenda. After the repeated failure of voucher legislation and the problems in the charter school sector, tax credits impress them as being the only short-range viable step toward school choice.

Minnesota, Iowa, and Illinois permit state tax credits for K-12 school expenses (e.g., books, tuition, and various fees). Students may attend public, private, or religious schools. Iowa's tax credit plan became law in 1987; the credit is modest, amounting to only 25% of expenses up to the first $1,000 of expenditures, in other words, it is capped at $250. A Minnesota law since 1955 has permitted tax *deductions*, not credits, for taxpayers with pupils in public or private elementary and secondary schools. Expenses (e.g., private school tuition, tutoring, or books) not exceeding $1,625 for students in grades K-6 or $2,500 for students in Grades 7-12 may be claimed. The tax deduction currently costs the state of Minnesota more than $200 million annually. The Illinois education tax credit program became law in 1999. Parents can claim

---

35.   See http://www.mackinac.org/article.aspx?ID=362 from the Mackinac Center for Public Policy in Michigan: "The Mackinac Center for Public Policy is broadening the debate on issues that has [sic] for many years been dominated by the belief that government intervention should be the standard solution."

credits on tuition, books, and fees for public, private, and parochial education. Credits are limited to $500 per family. In the first 2 years of the program, approximately $130 million in credits were honored.

Florida and Pennsylvania join Arizona in allowing "tax credit vouchers" funded by forgiving state income tax. These instruments are distributed to individual schools—mostly private and religious—by intermediate organizations standing between the recipient school and the tax payer or corporation taking the credit. The money is then doled out to individual students in the form of scholarships. Corporate contributions in the Pennsylvania program are capped at $100,000 annually.

Glen Y. Wilson[36] examined the results from the first year (1998) of the Arizona Education Tax Credit[37] program, one of the first and largest programs in the nation. The tax credit law originally allowed individuals a dollar-for-dollar tax credit of $500 for donations to private schools and a dollar-for-dollar tax credit of $200 for donations to public schools, but only for extra-curricular activities in the latter case.[38] More than three-quarters of the private elementary and secondary schools in Arizona have religious affiliations. The statute was justified by its proponents on the grounds that it would help students from low income families attend private schools. However, the primary beneficiaries of the program turned out to be families who were relatively well off financially (see Exhibits 8.3 and 8.4). The per school donation to schools in the wealthiest quarter was nearly five times greater than that for schools in the poorest quarter. Per student donations in private

---

36.   Wilson, Glen Y. (2000). Effects on funding equity of the Arizona Tax Credit Law. *Education Policy Analysis Archives, 8*(38). Retrieved April 22, 2007 from http://epaa.asu.edu/epaa/v8n38.html

37.   Retrieved March 8, 2007, from http://www.azleg.state.us/arizonarevisedstatutes.asp. Law #43-1183.

38.   Upper middle class secondary schools have used their tax credit money for such things as band uniforms, trips to Europe, and cheerleading camps. A former Superintendent of Public Instruction used a $200 "scholarship" to recoup part of the expenses of sending her son on a vacation to Catalina Island.

Exhibit 8.3.   1998 Donations Under the
Arizona Tuition Tax Credit Program Related to School Wealth

	All Schools	Poorest Quarter	Second Poorest Quarter	Second Wealthiest Quarter	Wealthiest Quarter
Amount donated	$5,925,436	$663,272	$782,417	$1,359,790	$3,119,958
Percent	100%	11%	13%	23%	53%
Per school donation	$6,378	$2,858	$3,372	$5,836	$13,448

From Arizona Department of Education and Arizona Department of Revenue

Exhibit 8.4.   Estimated Per Student Basis Donation Data for
Public and Private Schools, 1998

	Public Schools	Private Schools
Per student donation	$8.81	$40.09
Number of students per donation	12.6	10.7

From *Digest of Education Statistics, 1999* and Arizona Department of Revenue

schools amounted to almost five times the amount per student in public schools.

Wilson concluded that Arizona's tax credit law increased educational funding inequity between rich and poor public schools in Arizona. Although it reduced costs of private education for some wealthy families, no evidence exists that poor students in any appreciable numbers used the funds to leave inadequate public schools and enroll in private schools. Indeed, recent studies showed that over 90% of the funds were used to defray tuition costs of students already enrolled in private schools.

The Arizona Tuition Tax Credit program has continued to expand. By the year 2006, a married couple filing a state tax return jointly could contribute a maximum of $625 to a private School Tuition Organization (STOs), which would then award scholarships to individual students to attend private or even religious schools. In 2006, the School Tuition Organizations received $51 million in tax-credit donations. They paid out $41 million to more than 350 private or religious schools. The Arizona Legislature passed a bill that permitted corporations to donate monies to STOs and take a dollar-for-dollar credit. The total amount contributed by corporations to all STOs in the first year of this program was $10,000,000. However, the corporate tax credit law allows for an increase in the cap of 20% each year until 2011, at which time the total allowable corporate contribution will approach $25,000,000. Some estimates put the total diversion of tax money from the state coffers to private schools above $300,000,000 for the first decade of the program.

The law appears to limit the award of scholarships to poor children, but setting the family income cap at 185% of income required to qualify for reduced cost school lunch only caps family income for a family with two children at about $70,000. Some have been highly critical of the Arizona Supreme Court's reasoning in upholding the education tax credit law. It was challenged in *Kotterman v. Killian* on the basis of a provision in the state's constitution that, nearly all had anticipated, should have disallowed government aid to private or religious schools.[39] The defense argued that the money is not going to private or religious schools but rather to intermediate School Tuition Organizations. Proponents of the tax credit program have also argued somewhat Jesuitically that the program does not violate the Constitution because it is parents, and not the state, who are choosing to enroll their children in religious schools.[40] To date, this argument has received a favorable hearing in the Arizona courts. Other states watch developments in the Arizona program with great interest.

A study by People for the American Way looked at the distribution of the education tax credits in Illinois and reported that nearly half were distributed to families with

39.   Welner, Kevin G. (2000). Taxing the establishment clause: The revolutionary decision of the Arizona Supreme Court in *Kotterman v. Killian. Education Policy Analysis Archives, 8*(36). Retrieved April 23, 2007, from http://epaa.asu.edu/epaa/v8n36.html

household income in 2000 of more than $80,000. Former Illinois superintendent of education Glenn McGee acknowledged that the tuition tax credit law "probably has not served its intended purpose. Maybe I was naïve. I said this was going to benefit poor kids."[41] In Pennsylvania, a newspaper reported that middle and upper-income families were receiving most of the tax credit vouchers that were redeemed at private schools, in spite of the fact that the program was initially sold politically as a benefit for poor families.[42] In Arizona, a newspaper writer confronted Darcy Olsen, a policy analyst at the conservative Goldwater Institute, with Wilson's data showing that the Arizona tuition tax credit monies were going largely to the children of well-to-do families. Her comment was uncharacteristically straightforward: "Has it only helped [the poor] more than moderate and wealthy families? Probably not. If it was sold that way, it's only an angle."[43]

Homeschooling and "Virtual" Schooling

Starting from a small base and in percentage terms, homeschooling is the fastest growing alternative to K-12 public education in the U.S. At the turn of the 21st century, approximately 800,000 children were being schooled at home

---

40.   The nation has come a long way indeed since presidential candidate John F. Kennedy spoke the following words to the Greater Houston (TX) Ministerial Association on September 12, 1960: "I believe in an America where the separation of church and state is absolute; where no Catholic prelate would tell the President should he be Catholic—how to act, and no Protestant minister would tell his parishioners for whom to vote; where no church or church school is granted any public funds or political preference."
41.   People for the American Way. (2003). *Who gets the credit? Who pays the consequences? The Illinois tuition tax credit.* Washington DC: People for the American Way. (p. 2)
42.   Averett, Nancy, & Wilkerson, James E. (2002, August 4). Tax law little aid to poor students. *The Morning Call*, p. A1.
43.   Kossan, Pat. (2002, March 23). School tax credits fail poor. *Arizona Republic*, p. A1.

(see Exhibit 8.5). Younger students are more likely to be homeschooled than secondary school students (see Exhibit 8.6). Apparently, and understandably, few parents care to brave the intricacies of teaching advanced algebra or fashioning a chemistry lab out of kitchen utensils. Homeschooled students are much more likely to be White than students attending the nation's public schools: 94% versus 67% (see Exhibit 8.7). Moreover, approximately 90% of the fathers of homeschooled children show academic achievement above the level of high school, whereas only 50% of males nationally have comparable achievement.

> A very large percentage of home school parents are certified to teach. Some 19.7 percent of the home school mothers are certified teachers, as are 7.1 percent of the fathers. Almost one out of every four homeschool students (23.6 percent) has at least one parent who is a certified teacher.[44]

A government survey in the late 1990s revealed that 33% of homeschooling parents cited religious reasons and 9% cited "morality" as the motivation for keeping their children out of the public schools.[45] Clearly, homeschooling is a White, middle-class movement with religious overtones that is growing rapidly.

State regulations governing homeschooling differ greatly. Some require that a certain curriculum be taught and that regular standardized tests be administered and the results reported to the state agency. Others, such as Texas, have almost no requirements at all.

Nearly 40 states have sanctioned *virtual schools* (online course taking) with an estimated enrollment in the early years of the 21st century of about 45,000 students (head

44.   Rudner, Lawrence M. (1999). Scholastic achievement and demographic characteristics of home school students in 1998. *Education Policy Analysis Archives, 7*(8). Retrieved November 26, 2005, from http://epaa.asu.edu/epaa/v7n8/
45.   Bauman, Kurt J. (2001). *Home schooling in the United States: Trends and characteristics* (Working Paper Series No. 53). Washington, DC: Population Division, U.S. Census Bureau.

Exhibit 8.5.   Estimates of the Number of U.S. Children
Schooled at Home: Current Population Survey and
National Household Education Surveys

	Number of U.S. Children Schooled at Home
CPS 1994[a]	356,000
NHES 1996[b]	636,000
NHES 1999	791,000

a. Current Population Survey of the U.S. Census Bureau
b. National Household Education Survey.
After Bauman, Table 1. From Bauman, K. J. (2002). Home schooling in the United States: Trends and characteristics. *Education Policy Analysis Archives*, *10*(26). Retrieved November 23, 2005, from
http://epaa.asu.edu/epaa/v10n26.html

count, not full time equivalents).[46] Arizona has allowed
schools to create virtual schools since 1998. Currently there
are 14 virtual schools being run by public school districts
and charter schools. The Arizona program operates under
the vague name of Technology Assisted Project-Based
Instruction. Few people know that this stands for online
schools; few even know that the program exists. An important player in the virtual school arena is an online learning
company known as K12, headed by former U.S. Education
Secretary William Bennett. These virtual schools expend little money for plant, utilities, and the like, and often spend
large amounts of money on software and other materials
produced by the very same companies operating the virtual schools. Like charter schools, virtual schools are not
bound by the procurement and bidding regulations that traditional public schools adhere to. Private companies are not
unaware of the fact that public education in the U.S. is a
trillion dollar industry representing almost 10% of the gross

46.   Clark, T. (2001). *Virtual schools: A study of virtual schools in the United States.*
Retrieved November 15, 2005, from http://www.wested.org/online_pubs/
virtualschools.pdf. Paulson, A. (2004, May 4). Virtual schools: Real concerns.
Christian Science Monitor. Retrieved November 15, 2005, from http://
www.csmonitor.com/2004/0504/p11s02-legn.html

Exhibit 8.6. Homeschool Students Classified by Grade With Percents and National School Percents

							Grade					
	1	2	3	4	5	6	7	8	9	10	11	12
Homeschool	7.4%	10.6%	14.1%	12.9%	12.6%	11.9%	10.3%	8.8%	5.7%	3.8%	1.6%	0.3%
Nation	9.1%	8.8%	8.9%	8.7%	8.6%	8.7%	8.7%	8.4%	9.0%	7.9%	7.1%	6.3%

After Rudner, Table 2.3. From Rudner, Lawrence M. (1999). *Op cit.*

Exhibit 8.7.   Racial Distribution of Homeschool Students and the Nation

	White (not Hispanic)	Black (not Hispanic)	Hispanic	Other
Homeschool	94%	1%	0%	5%
Nationwide	67%	16%	13%	4%

After Rudner Table 2.4. From Rudner, Lawrence M. (1999). *Op. cit.*

national product. Charter schools, and now virtual schools, present American business an opportunity for profits from one of the nation's biggest expenditures, K-12 education.

Virtual schools originally were developed to serve the needs of students who could not for one reason or another be physically present in a public school. More recently they have become alternatives to attendance in traditional public schools by persons seeking to educate their children at home. They are particularly popular at the secondary school level where homeschooling parents discover that their own competence to instruct their children in specialized subjects is lacking. Profit making companies and opportunistic school districts have discovered a market for virtual schooling among formerly homeschooled students.

One of the more bizarre cases of a virtual school concerns a tiny school district on the semiarid plains of southern Colorado, a third of a mile north of the New Mexico border. Branson, Colorado had no grocery store, no gas station and a population of fewer than 100 persons in the 2000 Census. Hardly visible in Google Earth, Branson is a most unlikely place to have received over $15,000,000 in state support for its 1,000 "virtual students" from around the state in the first 4 years (2001-2005) of its online school. "Cyberschools are the 800-pound gorilla of the choice movement, although vouchers and charter schools get a lot more attention," said William Moloney, education commissioner in Colorado, "where state financing for online schools has increased almost 20-fold in 5 years—to $20.2 million for 3,585 students today from $1.1 million for 166 full-time students in 2000."[47] In the fall of 2006, the State of Colorado was paying for the schooling of 8,236 online students.

More than 6,600 students are enrolled in 14 virtual schools operating in the State of Arizona for the 2006-2007 school year, an increase of more than 45% over the previous year. An interesting feature of Arizona virtual schooling is that most of the growth in student numbers is occurring in virtual schools operated by charter schools. Increasingly, the same interests driving virtual schooling are the interests that have driven the rapid expansion of charter schools and homeschooling. Parents wish to escape traditional public schools; commercial interests wish to make money off of public K-12 education; and the public in general represented by politicians wish to reduce the expense of another public institution. States are now witnessing the conjunction of homeschooling and charter schools. Homeschooling parents have organized into groups that then apply for a charter school license that entitles them to collect money from the state to educate their children at home, something they formerly did without being paid. California has seen several instances of this. The California Department of Education estimated that more than 90 homeschool charters with approximately 30,000 students were in operation in 2001.[48]

More than a hundred virtual schools now operate in the U.S., and both the size of these schools and their number are increasing dramatically. Legislatures learn that they can fund such schools at substantially lower per pupil costs. Companies have learned that they can operate them with large profit margins. Regulation of the virtual schools by state gov-

---

47. *New York Times*, February 9, 2005.

48. Huerta, Luis A.; Gonzalez, Maria-Fernanda; & d'Entremont, Chad (2006). Cyber and home school charter schools: Adopting policy to new forms of public schooling. *Peabody Journal of Education, 81*(1), 103-139. Huerta, Luis A. (2000). Losing public accountability: A home schooling charter. In Bruce Fuller (Ed.), *Inside charter schools: The paradox of radical decentralization* (pp. 177-202). Cambridge, MA: Harvard University Press.

ernments is often lax. One instance illustrates the potential for abuse. A high school senior taking an American History course from a commercial virtual school was contacted by the school on the last Friday of the month and told that he had to log 12 hours online before Saturday night, the last day of the month, or else his share of the state allocation for that month would be lost. He explained that he was working all day Saturday and that it would be impossible to put in that many hours. The company's representative told him to log his computer in to the school Friday night and simply leave it turned on all day Saturday, after which he could log off. The potential for abuse of public monies and of students' opportunity to acquire an education is obvious.[49]

Distance education specialists have noted strong interest in online instruction in Saudi Arabian universities. The driving force behind this interest appears to be primarily that of keeping men and women separated for instruction: men in one lecture hall with a live or televised instructor, women in a separate lecture hall. Whereas in Saudia Arabia there appears to be a fear of mixing with the opposite sex, in the U.S. some innovations appear to be motivated by a fear of mixing with the opposite class or race.

Open Enrollment

Open enrollment is built on the idea that public schools should not draw their students from fixed geographic "catchment areas," but that all families should be free to send their children to any school they choose within some particular jurisdiction, usually a school district. Among the alleged benefits of open enrollment is the expectation that all schools having to compete for students or else face "going out of business" will improve their operations and become better

---

49.   Reed, David. (2007, February 20). Personal communication. Mr. Reed was Administrator for Homebound Education for the Gilbert Public Schools, Gilbert, Arizona.

schools. Open enrollment arrangements are common, but studies of their impact on patterns of enrollment are rare. One of the few such studies is by Kenneth Howe, Margaret Eisenhart, and Damian Betebenner, professors at the University of Colorado, Boulder.[50]

The Boulder Valley (Colorado) Schools instituted an open enrollment policy in 1961, but it was never an important issue until the mid-1990s. Why it should lie fallow for so long and only rise to popular attention then is in itself further evidence of the shifting demographics of Colorado and the U.S. more generally. From 1980 to 2000, the Hispanic population of Colorado more than doubled from 340,000 to 735,000 persons. By the year 2001, more than one in five of the 28,000 students in the Boulder Valley Schools were exercising their option to attend a school outside their neighborhood school's boundaries. Howe and his colleagues graphed the median percentage of White pupils in the district's elementary schools for each year from 1994 to 2000 (Exhibit 8.8). The bottom fifth of elementary and middle schools in terms of percent White pupils—curve Q1 in the exhibit—dropped from 70% White to about 45% White in 6 years. In other words, a substantial number of White families exercised their choice by leaving the lowest fifth elementary schools in the district in terms of minority enrollments.

In a report to the district, Howe and his colleagues concluded:

> For their part, [Boulder Valley School Distirct] parents participating in open enrollment have what they perceive to be the best interests of their children in mind, across the array of groups participating. That no one or no group should be assigned responsibility, however, does not erase the fact that the current open enrollment system is riddled with inequities and has resulted in a disturbingly high

---

50. Howe, Kenneth; Eisenhart, Margaret; & Betebenner, Damian. (2001). School choice crucible: A case study of Boulder Valley. *Phi Delta KAPPAN, 83*(2), 137-146. (Condensed and reprinted, 2002, under the title "Research scotches school choice." *Education Digest,* 67(5), 10-17.) Retrieved November 27, 2005, from http://www.pdkintl.org/kappan/k0110how.htm

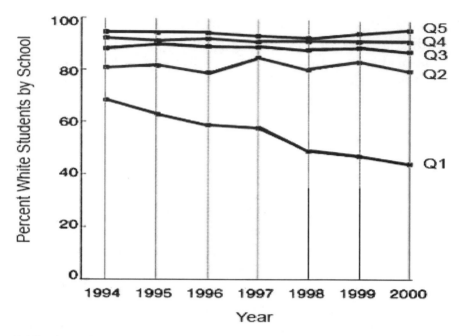

Exhibit 8.8.   Quintile medians of percentage of White students in BVSD elementary, middle, and K-8 Schools Fall 1994 to Fall 2000. Adapted from Howe, Eisenhart, & Betebenner, 2001.

degree of stratification among BVSD schools with respect to race/ethnicity and income.[51]

The measured and careful prose of the researchers was not matched by the impassioned opinions of both parents and educators who felt the effects of the open enrollment policy in their personal and work lives.

It doesn't take a rocket scientist to figure out that if you set up a program for school choice that requires research, an application process, the existence of a second car, and a schedule that permits chauffeuring kids across town every day for 12 years, that by and large, only affluent families will participate. Anyone who disagrees with this

51.   Howe, Kenneth, & Eisenhart, Margaret. (2000). *A study of Boulder Valley School District's open enrollment system.* Boulder, CO: Boulder Valley School District. (p. 14) Retrieved November 27, 2005, from http://www.bvsd.k12.co.us/downPdf/openenroll_report.pdf

statement does not understand the challenges many lower-income families face.[52]

We're on the bus from the movie Speed…. There's no mission, just more choices. [Choice is] smoke and mirrors. (Boulder, CO, middle school principal)[53]

And so, in this very liberal community where racism is anathema to the public consciousness, parents are abandoning racially mixed neighborhood schools in their search for a public school that mirrors the racially homogenous public and private schools of the past. The motivation may be what they perceive to be a better education for their children. The impact of their decisions may worsen education for all.

Advanced Placement

Advanced Placement (AP) courses are increasing rapidly in popularity. The AP program, organized in 1955 and since then administered by the college board[54], offers college level courses to high school students. The college board develops curricula in various subjects and administers AP examinations each year. The program is funded by the fees charged students who sit for the AP examinations. Currently, each exam fee is about $85. Many universities give credit toward graduation for passing each AP exam. Diligent students can accumulate nearly enough credits to begin college classified as Sophomores, thus saving their parents thousands and, in some circumstances, tens of thousands of dollars in higher

---

52. Streater, J. (2005, June 2). Stratification is inevitable result. *Boulder Daily Camera, 113*, 33.

53. Quoted in Howe et al. *Op cit.*

54. The college board, formerly known as the college entrance examination board, seems eager to expand its agenda from having originally been the policy body governing the Scholastic Aptitude Test to being an agent of reform of secondary education in America. Its evolving role probably accounts for its shortened name.

education costs. The AP program has expanded dramatically in recent decades as the cost of higher education has soared and middle class financial pressures have soared with them.

Enrollments nationwide in AP courses have risen approximately 140% in the past 10 years. In 1995, enrollments totaled 500,000 nationwide; 10 years later in 2005, 1.2 million students were enrolled in one or more AP course. The percentage of high school seniors taking AP exams nearly tripled in the 10-year period from 1985 to 1995, from 5% to around 15% (see Exhibit 8.9). The number of AP examinations administered more than doubled from 1990 (estimated 500,000) to 2000 (estimated 1,300,000).[55] During that same period, the number of high schools offering AP courses increased by 40%. Nearly one in four high school seniors nationwide took at least one AP exam in 2006. AP courses and exams are becoming a standard feature of American secondary education, at least in some places and for some students.

AP courses have become a means of tracking at the high school level. AP tracks provide a different, higher level of instruction than the regular high school curriculum and, at their best, resemble elite private school courses. Not surprisingly, minority students are disproportionately underrepresented in such classes and, indeed, attend schools that offer far fewer AP courses. AP courses are, therefore, less available to minority students than to White students. African American students make up 14% of the K-12 student population nationally, but only 7% of AP exam takers.[56] Hispanic students constitute 14% of AP exam takers, exactly the same percentage that they represent nationally in the K-12 population of students. However, Hispanic students receive college credit through AP

55. Lichten, W. (2000). Whither advanced placement? *Education Policy Analysis Archives, 8*(29). Retrieved December 2, 2005, from http://epaa.asu.edu/epaa/v8n29.html

56. Klopfenstein, K. (2004a). The advanced placement expansion of the 1990s: How did traditionally underserved students fare? *Education Policy Analysis Archives, 12*(68). Retrieved March 15, 2007, from http://epaa.asu.edu/epaa/v12n68/

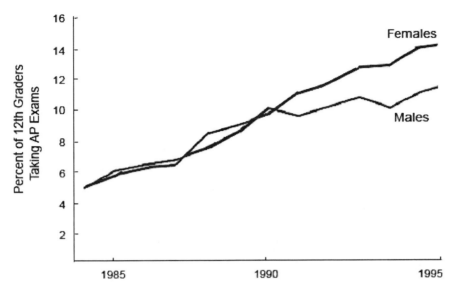

Exhibit 8.9.   Females and males taking advanced placement examinations as percentages of female and male 12th graders, 1984-1995. From U.S. Department of Education. (2000). *Trends in educational equity of girls and women.* Washington, DC: Office of Educational Research and Improvement. National Center for Education Statistics, 2000-030.

examinations at a far lesser rate than White students. Various programs have subsidized AP *test taking* for minority students in the past 20 years; but few programs subsidized the offering of AP courses that prepare students for the examinations. Klopfenstein wrote, "During the 1990s, AP incentive programs primarily subsidized test fees for low income students, but this provided no incentive for low income and rural schools to expand their AP course offerings." In spite of their low representation among students passing AP exams, minority students, and their teachers, make up about half of the photographs on the College Board Web site: http://www.collegeboard.com/

International Baccalaureate (IB) programs are increasingly popular for young people between the ages of 16 and 19. IB programs carry the concept of AP one step further. It is often said that the IB program creates a "school within a school," acknowledging the fact that IB students are segregated into a separate track that then has little to do with the conventional curriculum and its students. IB students study a 2-year intensive curriculum covering six subjects: mathematics and computer science, language, experimental science, individuals and societies, foreign language, and an elective in the arts (such as graphic art, music, or film studies). To be awarded the IB diploma, the student must pass an examination in each subject before completion of high school, much like with the AP exams. Unlike the AP system, assessment of students' performance is both internal (by the students' own instructors) and external from the organization's paper-and-pencil exams. "The grading system is criterion based (results are determined by performance against set standards, not by each student's position in the overall rank order)."[57] Various fees, training requirements, and accreditation procedures virtually require a sizeable investment of a school's resources in building and continuing to offer this program. Not surprisingly, the vast majority of IB programs are offered in upper-middle class schools.

Many school districts apply a different grading scale to AP, IB and honors classes in high school. The *honor point* is an extra point assigned in the conversion of letter grades (A-F) to numbers in the calculation of a grade point average (GPA). An A in an AP course receives a 5 in the calculating of the GPA; a B counts for 4 points instead of 3 as in regular courses. GPAs above 4.0 typically result. Thus do the students tracked into accelerated tracks enjoy an advantage in college admissions and other competitions over their peers in regular courses. This practice is widely regarded as legitimate and seldom questioned.

Arguably, the IB program receives its greatest impetus from the escalating costs of a college education. Far outstripping

---

57.   From the International Baccalaureate Organization Web site: http://www.ibo.org/diploma/slided.cfm

the rate of inflation, college tuition and fees and textbook costs are placing an increasing burden on middle class families. Several universities recognize the IB diploma as the equivalent of the freshman year of college. State legislators are being petitioned by parents to pass laws that will require public universities to admit IB graduates to the sophomore year. The savings to a family, as with the AP program, can total $10,000 or more.

Bilingual Education

In the 10 years of the last decade of the 20th century, the number of students K-12 classified as LEP (limited English proficient) rose by more than 100% while the overall school population grew by only 12%. Of the 5 million LEP students in U.S. public schools, 80% are Spanish speaking.

Whereas the most visible reform proposals have emanated from conservative quarters, bilingual education is a reform championed by liberal elites. Whatever its merits as an educational program,[58] its most obvious feature is that it has been overwhelmingly defeated when placed before the voting public as a referendum. To be more specific, anti-bilingual education propositions have, with one notable exception, passed with large majority votes. The "English only" Proposition 203 in Arizona, financed by California software entrepreneur Ron Unz, was approved by 63% of voters in a state-wide referendum. Proposition 227 in California, the "Anti-Bilingual Education Initiative," also financed largely by Unz, was passed by a 61 to 39% margin. Massachusetts similarly passed an anti-bilingual education referendum, Question 2, by a wide margin.

---

58.   The merits of bilingual education are the subject of a recently published meta-analysis: Rolstad, Kellie; Mahoney, Kate & Glass, Gene V. (2005). The big picture: A meta-analysis of program effectiveness research on English Language Learners. *Educational Policy, 19*(4), 1-23.

Amendment 31 in Colorado—Unz, again—was cast as the "Anti-Bilingual Education Initiative." It failed, that is, bilingual education was *not* outlawed in the public schools of Colorado, by a 44 to 55% margin in November 2002. The Colorado vote, which ran counter to the votes in California, Arizona, and Massachusetts, can hardly be counted as a victory for ethnic ecumenism. Ironically, it is widely believed that the anti-bilingual proposition was defeated by a starkly racist television advertisement funded by a liberal billionaire heiress, namely, Patricia Stryker[59] of Fort Collins, Colorado, which hinted that banning bilingual education would dump thousands of Brown children into formerly White classrooms slowing the progress of the White pupils. If this allegation is true, then the defeat of the Colorado proposition played on the very same motives among the White electorate that bilingual education opponents played on to defeat bilingual friendly propositions in other states.

A pervasive sense of ethnophobia is not the only motive working to ban the implementation of bilingual education. Bilingual education is set against *immersion* in the debate over the best way to educate English language learners. Bilingual education experts opine that as many as 4 or 5 years of balanced instruction in both languages (the child's native language and English) are needed for an optimal transition to fluency in English without loss of the opportunity to learn the full school curriculum while acquiring English.[60] Opponents of bilingual education, and there are many, argue that non-English-speaking students should be immediately immersed in English language classrooms. The immersion method (or less objectionable *structured immersion* method) is claimed to be superior on many grounds and the only practical way to deal with the large number of different native languages present in some classrooms. But the bilingual *versus*

---

59. Ms. Stryker was in favor of bilingual education and gave $3.3 million to defeat the anti-bilingual proposition. See Escamilla, K.; Shannon, S.; Carlos, S.; & Garcia, J. (2003). Breaking the code: Colorado's Defeat of the Anti-Bilingual Education Initiative (Amendment 31). *Bilingual Research Journal, 27*(3), 357-382.

immersion debate is only truly animated when the question is raised of what to do with millions of children entering U.S. schools who are fluent in Spanish and have no or limited fluency in English.

It should be obvious that certified teachers who are equally fluent in English and Spanish are rare. In 2000, there were 47 students in need of bilingual education for every certified bilingual education teacher. In certain states, the need was absurdly greater; Kansas and Mississippi had more than 1,000 students needing bilingual education for every certified bilingual teacher. The demand that would be created if classrooms of native Spanish speaking children were staffed with truly bilingual teachers would send the price of their services above the services of monolingual teachers. In short, staffing the necessary classrooms with genuinely bilingual certified teachers would incur a significant increase in the costs of public education. And that cost would rise each year as Hispanic children grow as a share of the K-12 public school population. The demand for bilingual teachers comes at a time when the country is ill disposed to pay for them. Under court orders for years to appropriate monies to provide instruction to monolingual Spanish speaking students in the state of Arizona, the legislature proposed to allocate $400 per child to teach them English.[61]

---

60.   "The one set of data that policy-makers want to hear nothing about is the fact that it typically takes immigrant children at least five years (often more) to catch up academically to native-speakers English…. Professor Elana Shohamy of Tel Aviv University in Israel reported that in the Israeli context, a period of 7-9 years is typically required for immigrant students to catch up, a figure consistent with the range found in North American data" (Cummins, Jim, 1999). *Language, Power and Pedagogy*. Retrieved April 25, 2007, from http://www.iteachilearn.com/cummins/lpp.html. See also Hakuta, K.; Butler, Y. G.; & Witt, D. (2000). *How long does it take English learners to attain proficiency?* Retrieved April 22, 2007 from http://www.stanford.edu/~hakuta/Docs/HowLong.pdf; Klesmer, H. (1994). Assessment and teacher perceptions of ESL student achievement. *English Quarterly*, 26(3), 5-7; and Thomas, W. P., & Collier, V. P. (2002). *A national study of school effectiveness for language minority students' long-term academic achievement*. Retrieved April 22, 2007 from http://www.crede.org/research/llaa/1.1es.html.

61.   The *Flores vs. Arizona* law suit is discussed later in this chapter.

Alternative Teacher Certification

Various alternatives to four-year university programs of initial teacher preparation and certification have existed for years, but in an age of escalating public expenditures (as a share of the gross domestic product) these alternatives are being addressed with a new sense of urgency. States are issuing emergency teaching certificates when school districts can document a shortage of staff in critical areas like science, math, or special education. Some states have developed short courses of a few weeks duration that lead to an alternative certificate, or a provisional certificate that might be made permanent after some probationary period. Teach for America (TFA) has become a visible effort to place teachers in distressed urban and rural environments. The intent of the TFA program is to place new bachelor's degree graduates with no university-based teacher training into schools for 2 years after a brief summer training experience. Few of the TFA teachers continue in the profession after their brief service. California granted more than 20,000 emergency permits or waivers of the certification requirements in the first 5 years of the 1990s,[62] and these alternatively certified and uncertified teachers tended to be placed in low achieving, high minority schools.[63] There is a positive correlation between a secondary school's drop out rate and its percentage of new teacher hires; the drop out rate is negatively correlated with the average level of teaching experience of the school.[64] To make matters worse, students of TFA teachers performed substantially more poorly on

62.   Fetler, Mark. (1997a). Where have all the teachers gone? *Education Policy Analysis Archives, 5*(2). Retrieved April 24, 2007, from http://epaa.asu.edu/epaa/v5n2.html
63.   Goe, L. (2002). Legislating equity: The distribution of emergency permit teachers in California, *Education Policy Analysis Archives, 10*(42). Retrieved April 23, 2007, from http://epaa.asu.edu/epaa/v10n42/
64.   Fetler, Mark. (1997b). Staffing up and dropping out: Unintended consequences of high demand for teachers. *Education Policy Analysis Archives, 5*(16). Retrieved April 24, 2007, from http://epaa.asu.edu/epaa/v5n16.htm.

standardized achievement tests than did the students of certified teachers.[65]

Charter schools often hire alternatively certified teachers or teachers lacking even emergency or provisional certification. Typically, a state's law creating charter schools will not require that the teachers be certified. As was noted earlier, charter school teachers are paid less on average than their counterparts in traditional public schools.

One of the engines driving the alternative certification movement is the desire to reduce the cost of public education. Traditionally uncertified teachers can not demand the same level of pay as certified teachers. Increasingly schools are turning to inexperienced teachers to fill the ranks of their teaching staff. Teachers with experience reentering the teaching force have always been a source of employees for the public schools. Compared with first-time teachers, the reentrants can command a higher salary. Reentering teachers made up 33% of all hires in 1988; just 3 years later that figure dropped to 24% and continues to drop.[66] In 1994, 57% of first-time teachers came from typical undergraduate teacher training colleges and universities, a decrease of about 10 percentage points from the figure 6 years earlier. A relatively new strategy on the scene is the rehiring of retired teachers on contracts with a commercial placement agency; the schools do not offer these retirees health or retirement benefits and they are paid at a level substantially below their last regular salary.

Some of this submarket hiring and provisional certification of teachers is taking place because of genuine teacher shortages. California, with a huge expansion of its

65. Laczko-Kerr, Ildi, & Berliner, David C. (2002). The effectiveness of "Teach for America" and other under-certified teachers on student academic achievement: A case of harmful public policy," *Education Policy Analysis Archives*, 10(37). Retrieved April 26, 2007, from http://epaa.asu.edu/epaa/v10n37/
66. National Center for Education Statistics. (1995). *America's teachers ten years after "A Nation at Risk."* Washington, DC: U.S. Department of Education Office of Educational Research and Improvement, NCES 95-766.

public education system in the past few decades, is a case in point. Significantly, that expansion has often been in areas enrolling disproportionately high numbers of Hispanic students. Schools with high incidence of poverty among their students have teacher turnover rates as much as 50% higher than more affluent schools.[67] However, rather than invest more in the preparation of regularly certified teachers, society has tended to circumvent more expensive avenues and purchase discounted services. It is well known that college graduates trained in science, mathematics, and technology would require significantly higher salaries to enter public school teaching than the market will bear. [68] Research shows that regularly certified and experienced teachers teach more effectively, that is, contribute more to their students' learning than uncertified, alternatively certified, or provisionally certifies teachers.[69] This research is all but ignored by policy analysts seeking ways of further reducing the cost of providing instruction in the nation's public schools.[70]

---

67.   Ingersoll, Richard. (2001). Teacher turnover and teacher shortages: An organizational analysis. *American Educational Research Journal, 38*(3), 499-534.

68.   Milanowski reported that nearly a 50% increase in starting salaries would be required to attract 40% of the math, science, and technology trained graduates into K-12 teaching. Milanowski, Anthony (2003, December 27). An exploration of the pay levels needed to attract students with mathematics, science and technology skills to a career in K-12 teaching. *Education Policy Analysis Archives, 11*(50). Retrieved April 25, 2007, from http://epaa.asu.edu/epaa/v11n50/

69.   See Darling-Hammond, Linda. (2000). Teacher quality and student achievement: A review of state policy evidence. *Education Policy Analysis Archives, 8*(1). Retrieved April 24, 2007, from http://epaa.asu.edu/epaa/v8n1/. Darling-Hammond, Linda; Holtzman, Deborah J.; Gatlin, Su Jin; & Heilig, Julian V. (2005). Does teacher preparation matter? Evidence about teacher certification, Teach for America, and teacher effectiveness. *Education Policy Analysis Archives, 13*(42). Retrieved April 26, 2007, from http://epaa.asu.edu/epaa/v13n42/. Laczko-Kerr, Ildi, & Berliner, David C. (2002). The effectiveness of "Teach for America" and other under-certified teachers on student academic achievement: A case of harmful public policy. *Education Policy Analysis Archives, 10*(37). Retrieved April 26, 2007, from http://epaa.asu.edu/epaa/v10n37/. Vandevoort, Leslie G.; Amrein-Beardsley, Audrey; & Berliner, David C. (2004). National board certified teachers and their students' achievement. *Education Policy Analysis Archives, 12*(46). Retrieved February 15, 2007, from http://epaa.asu.edu/epaa/v12n46/

High-Stakes Testing

The paper-and-pencil high stakes test is becoming a nearly ubiquitous feature of state education policy. What is "at stake" when the test is passed or failed is promotion from one grade to the next or graduation from Grade 12 for students, bonuses or mandatory retraining for teachers, and at times the threat of losing one's job for administrators. Negative sanctions are more prevalent than rewards. The incentive to perform well on these tests is high for students, teachers, and administrators. They typically cover only very limited parts of the curriculum: math, reading, writing. For the expenditure of only miniscule fractions of a state's investment in K-12 education, politicians, and various state boards can place themselves at the center of discussions of school curriculum. Their pronouncements fill newsprint and airways. Many of them consider it money well spent.

To most persons who are not experienced educators, high-stakes testing appears to have many benefits: the curriculum is focused more narrowly on the basic skills believed to be needed for success, somewhere, sometime; the curriculum becomes "aligned" (as with automobile tires, an "aligned" curriculum must be a good thing); teachers and students, thought to be complacent or lazy, are given incentives to produce, or suffer punishments and shame. High stakes

70.   Incredibly, one former member of a conservative think tank—whose mother just happens to have been a school teacher—argued that K-12 teachers are overpaid: Greene, Jay P., & Winters, Marcus A. (2007). How much are public school teachers paid? Civic Report No. 50. New York: Manhattan Institute for Policy Research. Retrieved April 1, 2007, from http://www.manhattan-institute.org/html/cr_50.htm. Lawrence Mishel argued that Greene and Winters supported their case by the disingenuous manipulation of flawed data to show, among other things, that K-12 teachers make more than architects, economists, and mechanical engineers: Mishel, Lawrence. (2007). Jay Greene's persistent misuse of data for teacher pay comparisons. Washington, DC: Economic Policy Institute. Retrieved April 5, 2007, from http://www.epi.org/content.cfm/webfeatures_viewpoints_teacher_pay_comparisons. Also see Bracey, Gerald W. (2007). *Get rich: Be a school teacher.* Retrieved March 19, 2007, http://www.huffingtonpost.com/gerald-bracey/get-rich-be-a-school-tea_b_40506.html

testing affords many noneducators the opportunity to work out a little hostility toward institutions that strike them as wasteful and inefficient. To researchers and most educators, high stakes testing looks quite different.

Paper-and-pencil tests capture little of the complexity of school learning. Few benefits in terms of academic achievement have been verified as resulting from the pressure that high stakes testing places on teachers, students, and their families. Small gains in very elementary arithmetic can be produced through drill and practice when teachers are pressured to prepare their students for such tests. Achievement gains in other academic areas appear not to result.[71]

The unintended consequences of imposing these sorts of reforms are negative and serious. Schools stop teaching what is not on the test. At the elementary school level, science, social studies, art, music, even, physical education are sacrificed so that more time can be spent in test preparation activities. Pushed to near the breaking point, teachers and administrators are tempted to bend the rules to avoid public shaming resulting from release of test scores to media. Some give in to temptation. Sharon Nichols and David Berliner have called these side effects "collateral damage" of the high stakes testing movement.[72] A single illustration from Nichols

71.   Nichols, Sharon L.; Glass, Gene V.; & Berliner, David C. (2006). High-stakes testing and student achievement: Does accountability pressure increase student learning? *Education Policy Analysis Archives, 14*(1). Retrieved January 15, 2007, from http://epaa.asu.edu/epaa/v14n1/. One might object to the generally negative tone of this treatment of the high-stakes testing issue and respond that if the increased accountability pressure results in better achievement among students, then it is not a bad thing. However, when the investigation is carried one more step to answer the question "What are the benefits of high accountability pressure?" the answers prove to be disappointing to those who hoped for good news. Nichols, Glass, and Berliner (2006) presented their analyses that led to the conclusion that only low-level math achievement is benefited by high accountability pressure. Reading achievement at both elementary and secondary school levels and secondary school math achievement are not improved when high stakes testing programs are instituted at state levels, much less, one would assume, at a national level
72.   Nichols, Sharon L., & Berliner, David C. (2007). *Collateral damage: How high-stakes testing corrupts America's schools.* Cambridge, MA: Harvard Education Press.

and Berliner's book makes palpable the chaos that results when the stakes on paper-and-pencil tests are raised too high. Texas has a long history of high-stakes testing; the following incident was reported to have taken place in the Houston public schools during the 1990s and early 2000s, when, incidentally, former U.S. Secretary of Education Roderick Paige was Superintendent:

> From 1994 to 2003, Wesley Elementary School in Houston won national accolades for teaching low-income students how to read and was featured in an Oprah segment on schools that "defy the odds." But it turned out that Wesley wasn't defying the odds at all: the school was simply cheating. The *Dallas Morning News* found that in 2003, Wesley's fifth-graders performed in the top 10 percent in the state on the Texas Assessment of Knowledge and Skills (TAKS) reading exams. The next year, however, as sixth-graders at the M. C. Williams Middle School, the same students fell to the bottom 10 percent in the state. Obviously, something was amiss! In the end, Wesley teachers admitted that cheating was standard operating procedure. But the school wasn't alone. The newspaper found several statistical anomalies in nearly 400 Texas schools in 2005.[73]

Houston Superintendent Paige took credit for the Houston Miracle—the near miraculous increase in test scores in unlikely places. Not until after he was chosen to lead the Bush administration's education reform efforts in 2001 was it revealed that the Houston Miracle was actually the result of fraud and gaming the system. Many students likely to score poorly on the state mandated tests were encouraged to leave school and others were held back from grades in which the testing took place and then advanced two grades to skip over the testing.

But the point here is not to recount these truly dreadful stories of the havoc wreaked by high-stakes testing. Rather, high-stakes testing must take its place along side the other contemporary movements that are understood here to

---

73.   Spencer, Jason. (2006, January 1). Schools accused of cheating: Three low-income Acres Homes elementaries had big TAKS gains. *Houston Chronicle*, p. 1

emanate from the unique economic and demographic circumstances toward which America has been moving over the past several decades.

High-stakes testing tends to inflict its sanctions at a much higher rate on poor children and ethnic minorities. At a state level, the severity of these testing programs and other accountability measures varies proportionally with the proportion of public school children who come from racial and ethnic minority groups.[74] This phenomenon is examined in detail in chapter 9.

The cost implications of reform by high-stakes testing are clear at one level and more subtle at a deeper level. It is indeed the cheapskate entry in the education reform debate. The tests can be built, printed, distributed, and later scored for an entire state for half the cost of building an elementary school. It is a reform much appreciated by tax conscious politicians. The less obvious long-range impact of high-stakes testing can be discerned in the questions that high school students immediately ask when confronted with the test. "If I pass this test, and this test is what I have to pass to graduate from high school, then why do I have to stay here after passing it?" To people whose understanding of all that an education confers upon a student is as benighted as the politicians who impose these tests, the question is taken seriously; and they and the larger public ask themselves, "Yes, why continue to pay from schooling when a student can show on a test that he or she knows what they need to know to succeed?" In the Spring of 2007, a bill passed quickly through both the Arizona House and Senate that authorizes the paying out of $1,500 in college scholarship money to high school seniors who complete required hours for graduation and pass the AIMS high school graduation test, provided that

---

74.   Madaus, George, & Clarke, Marguerite. (2001). The adverse impact of high-stakes testing on minority students: Evidence from one hundred years of test data. In Gary Orfield & Mindy L. Kornhaber (Eds.), *Raising standards or raising barriers? Inequality and high-stakes testing in public education* (pp. 85-106). New York: Century Foundation.

they leave school before the beginning of their final semester. The cost of maintaining a high school senior in school for a semester is about $3,500.

Arizona as a Microcosm of America 2025

In terms of demographics and economics, the state of Arizona now resembles what the U.S. population is likely to be in the year 2025. The population of Arizona in 2007 was approximately 6.5 million persons. Among states of any size, it ranks fourth behind California, Massachusetts, and New Jersey in the percentage of its population in urban centers: Phoenix and Tucson.[75] In 2006, its rate of growth, 3.6%, was the highest of any state, surpassing Nevada for the first time in over 15 years. Among the 150,000 persons relocating to the state of Arizona in 2006, 120,000 came from other states in the U.S. and 30,000 were immigrants to the U.S. Nearly 13% of its people are older than 65; by 2025 that figure will rise to over 20%. The Phoenix-Mesa-Scottsdale area was the sixth fastest growing metro area in the U.S. from 1990 to 2005 for persons over the age of 65.[76] Of the total Arizona population in 2000, one quarter was Hispanic. Approximately a third of the children speak a language other than English at home. In 2005, a Center for Immigration Studies analysis of new Census data revealed that 850,000 persons born outside the U.S. resided in

75.   The impression created by surveys that Arizona's schools are inferior is mistaken. It is based on such indicators as average class size and "percent of new teachers graduating from National Council for Accreditation of Teacher Education (NCATE) approved programs." Average class sizes in Arizona are larger than in most states because of the "urbanness" of the state. Concentration of population in metropolitan centers means that there are relatively few rural schools with their small classes to pull state averages down. Arizona has a pupil-teacher ratio of 21; North Dakota's ratio is 12. Moreover, the three public universities of Arizona joined such states as Wisconsin in opting out of NCATE in the 1980s, seeing it as a conservative drag on program innovation.

76.   Frey, William H. (2007). *Mapping the growth of older America: Seniors and boomers in the early 21st century.* Washington, DC: Brookings Institution.

the state, and of that number, approximately half were in the U.S. without proper authorization. Approximately one in every 12 persons in the state was an undocumented immigrant; approximately one in every 8 persons in the workforce is an undocumented immigrant. The differential between U.S. native and immigrant income in the state is two and a half times greater than the national average. In 2003, the most popular names for male babies were Jose (1st), Angel (5th) and Jesus (7th). If all the babies born in 2003 in Arizona (and no others) were to enter school in 2008, the kindergarten population would be 57% minority and 43% White.

In 2004, Arizona voters approved Proposition 200 which requires voters to show proof of U.S. citizenship and a photo ID to register to vote. The proposition also denies public benefits to undocumented immigrants. Although few immigrants ever

> You're at the forefront of growth in America in the 21st century, and you're getting huge diversity. It's the model for a new kind of global city.
>
> —William Frey, Brookings Institution demography on growth of the Phoenix metropolitan area

apply for such benefits, the proposition stands as a symbol of the hostility of the majority of citizens of the state toward Hispanics. In Maricopa County, where Phoenix resides, arrests of undocumented immigrants for being undocumented is a daily occurrence. In late 2007, the mayor of Phoenix, a Democrat, withdrew his support of a police department policy that prohibited officers from routinely asking persons about their immigration status, opening the door to racial profiling. In late 2007, the legislature adopted the Arizona Fair and Legal Employment Act. The law went into effect on January 1, 2008. Employers who twice knowingly employ (not just "hire") an undocumented immigrant can lose their license to conduct business in the state. Border agents noticed significant numbers of Mexican nationals leaving the state for good during the holidays leading up to the enforcement date for the law.

Many workers left the state to find work in neighboring states. Anti-immigrant sentiments are running deep in the state's psyche.

Arizona's Schools

Arizona's public schools are governed by policies that reflect the political and economic self-interests of an aging White middle class seeking to reduce its tax burden. The position of superintendent of public instruction is the third highest elected office in the state. As such, its incumbent, often an individual motivated to achieve higher office, is very responsive to the state's political climate. The state's education policy is characterized by conservative, market oriented, cost-cutting, and racially segregating programs. White, non Hispanic students constitute less than 50% of the K-12 Arizona public school population (see Exhibit 8.10).

Arizona has more charter schools, over 500, than any state in the nation. A record 93,210 students attended charter schools during the 2006-7 school year; this figure represents approximately 10% of all K-12 public school students in the state. The state has a tuition tax credit law that allows taxpayers to direct $625 annually of their state income tax to private school scholarships. Arizona has one of the most punitive and discriminatory high-school graduation exams (AIMS) in the nation. More than half of the high school seniors scheduled to graduate in 2006 were threatened with denial of a diploma unless they passed the AIMS test. In the end, few were denied graduation when it became clear to bureaucrats and State Board members that the state itself and its tax payers would ultimately be punished by the federal No Child Left Behind law if the graduation test failure rate remained high. By manipulating the cut-score for passing and changing the test questions, the failure rate was dramatically reduced. The state is fertile ground for profit-making companies open-

Exhibit 8.10. Composition of Arizona K-12 Student Enrollment by Ethnicity

Race/Ethnicity	2003-04
Non-Hispanic White	48.8%
Hispanic	37.7%
Native American	6.7%
Black (non-Hispanic)	4.7%
Pacific Islander or Asian	2.2%

From Arizona Department of Education. (2004). *Superintendent's annual report.* Available at: http://www.ade.az.gov/schoolfinance/Reports/

ing charter schools and virtual schools. Homeschooling is increasing rapidly in popularity in the state. Arizona is a crystal ball; it is as if one can look at the condition of education in the state today and see public education in the nation 15 or 20 years hence.

The creation of *traditional schools* aimed at attracting students under open enrollment policies is a growing feature of the education landscape. The Abraham Lincoln Traditional School, serving grades 3 through 8, is located in the Northwest section of Phoenix in an area that is majority Hispanic in ethnic composition. Only 15% of its students are Hispanic; 75% are White. Ward Traditional Academy in nearby Tempe is 65% White in an area that is less than 50% White. One parent explained why she and her husband chose Ward: "My husband and I were prepared to enroll my son in a private school but, we decided to give Ward a try since it was a brand new school, had uniforms, and the grades are K-8th." These traditional academies have been accused of contributing to segregation. "If it's segregation, it's segregation by work ethic and attitude," said Julie Boles, principal of Ward Traditional, which opened last school year with 300 students and expects 510 for this coming school year [2007-2008]. "Not every child is meant to be in a structured environment. We don't claim to serve everyone in the universe equally."[77]

The Arizona Legislature, dominated for decades by rural Republicans, has repeatedly attempted to pass school voucher laws. Few of these attempts have succeeded. More recent bills considered in the legislature have attempted to play on public sympathies; one bill that passed both houses and was signed by the governor created a $5 million voucher program that would send children with disabilities or in foster care to private schools and religious schools. An earlier bill that would have created vouchers for children of U.S. Armed Forces personnel was defeated in the legislature. The Arizona State Treasurer and a Republican, Dean Martin, sponsored a ballot proposition in 2006 while serving as a legislator that prohibits the state universities from offering in-state tuition to illegal immigrants. Such immigrants are also barred from receiving state financial aid and other social services. Anti-immigrant sentiment runs high.

The state has been embroiled in a bilingual education law suit for over 15 years. The *Flores vs. Arizona* case was originally decided in favor of the plaintiffs who claimed that the state failed to meet federal equal opportunity requirements for English instruction to non-English speaking students. The Arizona legislature was ordered by the court to fund such instruction adequately. A protracted battle over money has failed to produce a compromise between the legislature and the plaintiffs' lawyer, Tim Hogan of the Phoenix-based Arizona Center for Law in the Public Interest who represents the 140,000 non-English speaking students in the state. Currently, the state spends an additional $383 for each "English language learner." This amount would buy about 10 hours of instruction from a certified teacher. The courts have repeatedly ruled that the amount was inadequate. The legislature continues to stall. The state's superintendent of public

---

77.   Kossan, Pat. (2007, May 3). "Traditional" schools making a comeback. *Arizona Republic*, p. B1.

instruction claims that the issue is not about money; "leadership" is the key, in his opinion.

Troon is an unincorporated community 25 miles northeast of Phoenix. Its residents are upper-middle class and homes with appraised value under $1 million are rare. The preoccupation of Troon residents is, like its namesake in the U.K., golf. Troon has no schools for the nearly 500 school children who live there. Traditionally, students in unincorporated areas with no schools were assigned to schools in neighboring districts. The Arizona legislature enacted a law in 2005 that allows unincorporated areas with more than 150 students to create their own school district. So in November of 2006, the voters of Troon approved a ballot proposition that created the Christopher Verde School District. But the Christopher Verde School District has no intention of ever building schools. Instead, the district was created to exploit an open enrollment law that allows Troon parents to send their children to schools in neighboring districts and pay tuition that is far less than their property taxes would increase if they built their own schools. Property taxes at Troon will remain where they were before the Christopher Verde Schools were created: $1.80 per $100 of assessed valuation. The neighboring school district that will be educating Troon students will pay $2.50 per $100 of assessed value. "Arizona is seeing more of the traditional battle of the generations … between some retirees who want taxes—including school taxes—kept low, and most parents who want better support for the schools their kids attend."[78] Troon might more honestly rename its school district The Potemkin Village Schools.[79]

---

78.   Steinhauer, Jennifer. (2007, February 16). A school district with low taxes and no schools. *New York Times*. Retrieved February 20, 2007 from http://www.nytimes.com/2007/02/16/us/16scottsdale.html

79.   " 'Potemkin village' has come to mean, especially in a political context, any hollow or false construct, physical or figurative, meant to hide an undesirable or potentially damaging situation" (http://en.wikipedia.org/wiki/Potemkin_village).

In contrast to Arizona stands the neighboring state Utah, with only a moderately punitive high-stakes testing program, essentially no charter schools, and which voted in 2005 to drop out of the federal No Child Left Behind program, itself a punitive accountability invention. In 2007, the voters of Utah turned down a universal school voucher proposition by nearly a two-to-one margin. Utah is also one of the Whitest (only 10% Hispanic and African American in 2000), most pronatal states in America. Utah understands that its public schools are educating its *own* children.

Conclusion

The major education reform proposals debated today in the halls of legislatures, in the media, and in academic discourse arise from the circumstances of an aging, White middle class wishing to reduce the costs they bear for public education and secure some quasi-private school setting for their children and their children's children.

In writing about the No Child Left Behind (NCLB) program, which is essentially a federally mandated but unfunded high-stakes testing program, education researcher Gerald Bracey identified the motive behind many proposed education reforms: "I have never believed that this law is the idealistic, well-intentioned but poorly executed program that many claim it to be. NCLB aims to shrink the public sector, transfer large sums of public money to the private sector, weaken or destroy a Democratic power base— the teachers unions—and provide vouchers to let students attend private schools at public expense."[80] The motives behind conservative reform movements are no secret. They are publicly acknowledged by principals in the movement themselves. At a meeting of the Bradley Center for Philan-

---

80.   Bracey, Gerald W. (2006, July/August). Believing the worst. *Stanford Magazine.* Retrieved February 23, 2007, from http://www.stanfordalumni.org/news/ magazine/2006/julaug/features/nclb.html

Exhibit 8.11.   Characteristics of Major Education Reform Proposals

	Quasi-Privatize	Cut costs
Vouchers	✓	✓
Charter schools	✓	✓
Tuition tax credits	✓	✓
Home schooling	✓	✓
Virtual schools	✓	✓
Open enrollment	✓	
Advanced placement		✓
Immersion/Bilingual education		✓
Alternative certification		✓
High-stakes testing		✓

thropy and Civic Renewal of the conservative Hudson Institute, Chester Finn, former G. H. W. Bush administration education official, outlined his *theory of action* for reforming American education:

> What public education needs is to be forced to change. And in my experience, that force can best come from either or both of two sources:
>
> First, it can come from the state, through what's usually termed "standard spaced reform," a carefully aligned set of academic expectations and tests and consequences; now enshrined for better and for worse in the "No Child Left Behind Act."
>
> Second, that force can come from the marketplace; from the customer, via competition from private schools and charter schools and virtual schools and privately managed schools and homeschools and much more.[81]

The "much more" darkly hinted at by Mr. Finn surely includes the many policies discussed in this chapter and, conceivably, new inventions yet unimagined. The education

81.   Bradley Center for Philanthropy and Civic Renewal. (2003). *Giving better, giving smarter: Six years later* (discussion transcript.) Washington, DC: Hudson Institute. Retrieved January 15, 2008, from http://www.hudson.org/files/pdf_upload/Transcript_2003_05_15.pdf

debates that seem to many to be benign and well intentioned reveal depths of animosity and suspicion when exposed to light.

Chapter Nine

Accountability and Ethnicity

There exists an unmistakable and troubling connection between the accountability movement in public education and the changing ethnic composition of America's schools. Prior to the George W. Bush Administration's No Child Left Behind (NCLB) program, accountability measures were largely a matter of state-level education policy.[1] Indeed, Bush's NCLB program is largely based on programs he instituted in Texas as governor in the 1990s. Federal level accountability systems represent a mere continuation and centralizing of a state-level movement whose origins lie in the crisis politics of the conservative 1980s and the neoliberal education policies of the Clinton Administration. Contemporary accountability systems with their emphasis on high-stakes testing are not a more effective means of management or a more rational form of insuring quality in large organization performance. As many have observed, these systems have been installed in an attempt to embarrass educators and discredit public education.

1. The most insightful and critical analysis of the modern education accountability movement in America is due to Sherman Dorn (2007) in *Accountability Frankenstein: Understanding and taming the monster.* Charlotte, NC: Information Age.

Fertilizers, Pills, and Magnetic Strips: The Fate of Education in America
pp. 203–227
Copyright © 2008 by Information Age Publishing

Market accountability in a voucher or charter schools system is offered as an alternative to professional certification and accreditation. In the few instances where charter schools close their doors amid allegations or proof of incompetence or dishonesty, market accountability is said to be at work. Rather than a reflection on the broader market-driven education philosophy, these failures are taken as corroboration that the surviving charter schools must be excellent or else they would have similarly closed.

One of the least remarked upon features of these state accountability systems is why they differ so much from state to state in the severity of their consequences. Utah opts out of No Child Left Behind. Nebraska essentially finesses its more destructive effects. Colorado redefines "partially proficient" as "proficient"; Wyoming and Michigan discover that making gains on a test that nearly everyone passes the first time is nearly impossible. Why do some states embrace this federal intervention into the very curricula and employment practices of their schools while other states reject it? I contend that these various ways of dealing with accountability measures arise in part from the politics of race and privilege as these vary across the states.

Patterns of Racial and Ethnic Population

The nationwide trend toward increasing racial and ethnic minority population has been evident for many years. In 2006, the number of minorities (nearly all classified as Hispanic or Latino, Black, or American Indian by the U.S. Census Bureau) topped 100 million for the first time. The U.S. Census Bureau predicts that minorities will constitute more than half of the U.S. population by 2050.[2] However, the increase in racial and ethnic minority population has varied greatly from

2.   U.S. Census Bureau. (2007). http://www.census.gov/PressRelease/www/ releases/archives/population/010482.html

state to state over the past 50 years. These population increases have acted as a primary shaper of state accountability programs, especially high-stakes testing programs. Exhibit 9.1 is a map showing the concentration of the ethnic and racial minority population at three points in the last century: 1900, 1950, 2000. The pattern shows the well-known increase in percentage minority in the U.S. population with the concentration of this population in (Mexican) border states and the Southeast. Alaska is omitted only because they do not figure in later analyses in which accountability pressure is related to minority concentration at the state level. No data were reported for Alaska and Hawaii in the 1900 and 1950 Censuses. One can assume however that Hawaii had greater than 30% non-White population in each of those eras.

Of particular interest is the increase in the percentage of the Hispanic[3] population across the states. The percentage increases for Blacks are very small across states, most migration to the North having occurred long before 1980. In 2006, non-Hispanic Whites comprised less than half of the population in approximately 10% of all U.S. counties (303 out of 3,141 counties). In 1990, Whites were a minority in only 183 counties nationwide. Those counties in which Whites were in the minority are almost all in the Mexico border states of California, Arizona, New Mexico, and Texas, and the Southeastern U.S. states of Louisiana, Mississippi, Alabama, Georgia, the Carolinas, and Florida.

From Exhibit 9.2, it is obvious that very large increases in the concentration of Hispanic persons have occurred in the

---

3. "People who identify with the terms *Hispanic* or *Latino* are those who classify themselves in one of the specific Hispanic or Latino categories listed on the decennial census questionnaire—"Mexican, Mexican-Am., Chicano," "Puerto Rican," or "Cuban"—as well as those who indicate that they are "other Spanish, Hispanic, or Latino." Origin can be viewed as the heritage, nationality group, lineage, or country of birth of the person or the person's parents or ancestors before their arrival in the United States. People who identify their origin as Spanish, Hispanic, or Latino may be of any race." Hobbs, F., & Stoops, N. (2002). *Demographic trends in the 20th century.* Washington, DC: U.S. Census Bureau, Census 2000 Special Reports, Series CENSR-4, U.S. Government Printing Office. (p. B-3)

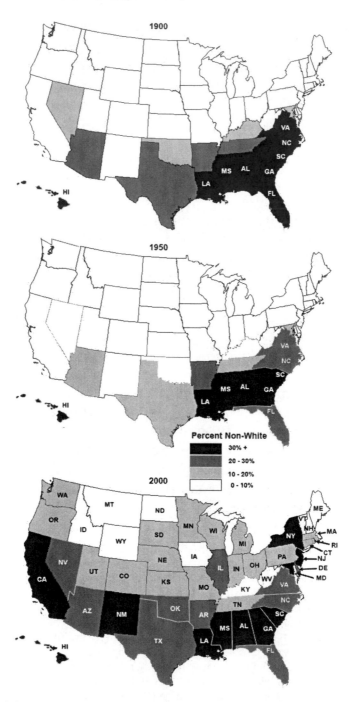

Exhibit 9.1.   Percent races other than White by state: 1900, 1950, 2000.

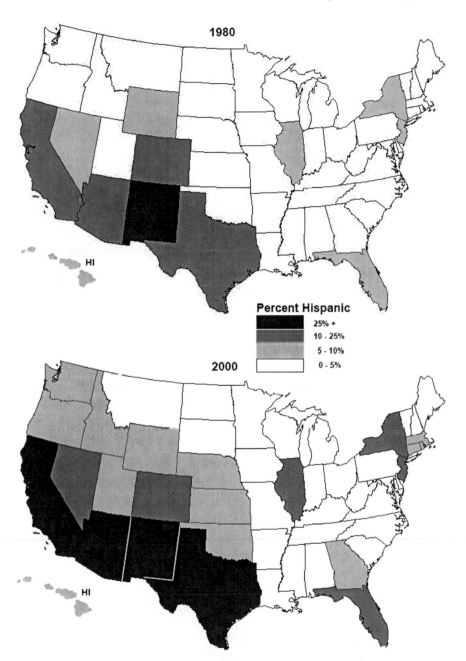

Exhibit 9.2.   Percent Hispanic by state: 1980, 2000. From U.S. Census. For more detailed information on the increase in percentage Hispanic population from the 1980 to the 2000 Census, see Appendix D.

last 25 years in the border states and the more heavily populated states in the Northeast. The nation of birth of these immigrants is generally different between the Southwest and the Northeast. The majority of Southwest Hispanics not born in the U.S. came from Mexico and Central America, whereas Hispanics of the Northeast derive primarily from Puerto Rico and the Caribbean.

The Accountability Hypothesis

I wish to advance the hypothesis that accountability pressures are adopted and applied selectively across the U.S. in response to the growth of racial and ethnic minorities in the populations of the individual states. The facts that such a hypothesis would explain if it were true is that the severity of education accountability measures varies in relation to the percentage Hispanic or Non-White population growth in the state. To support the plausibility of this hypothesis, Exhibit 9.3 is presented in which appear the U.S. states (absent Alaska) coded both by percent Hispanic population in the 2000 Census and by a specially derived measure of "accountability pressure."

The measure of "accountability pressure" displayed in Exhibit 9.3 was first reported in a work by my colleagues[4] and me in which we studied such pressure and student achievement in 25 states[5] with high-stakes testing programs. Our measurement approach to capturing this pressure was based on a more differentiated conceptualization of high-stakes

4.   Nichols, Sharon L.; Glass, Gene V.; & Berliner, David C. (2006). High-stakes testing and student achievement: Does accountability pressure increase student learning? *Education Policy Analysis Archives, 14*(1). Retrieved January 15, 2007, from http://epaa.asu.edu/epaa/v14n1/
5.   The choice of states in the Nichols-Glass-Berliner study was dictated in large part by the availability at several points in time of complete National Assessment of Educational Progress data. A few states, such as Florida, with highly visible and in some cases quite punitive high-stakes testing programs were excluded for this reason only.

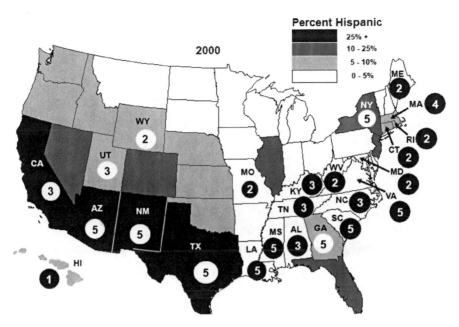

Exhibit 9.3.   High-stakes testing states coded for percentage Hispanic population and for Accountability Pressure Rating (*1 = least pressure, ... , 5 = most pressure*).

testing policy, practice, and implementation than had been previously carried out. Details of this procedure appear as Appendix C. Suffice it to say here that based on the judgments of approximately 250 graduate-level teachers and administrators and the validation of those judgments by two high-stakes testing policy researchers, each of the 25 states was assigned a rating of 1-5 based on detailed portfolios for each state which included reprints of enabling legislation, media accounts of the conduct of the high-stakes testing, and specially prepared summaries of rewards and sanctions as consequences of the testing. A rating of "1" represents essentially no threat or pressure exerted on teachers, administrators, students, and parents by the high-stakes testing program; "5" represents the highest level of accountability pressure. What is apparent in Exhibit 9.3 is that the severest accountability pressure is associated with the states with high percentages of Hispanic population. When accountability

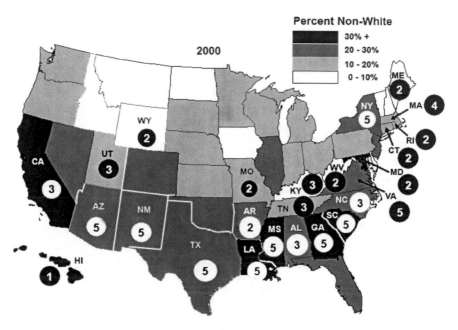

Exhibit 9.4.   High-stakes testing states coded by percentage of population non-White in 2000 and Accountability Pressure Rating (*1= Low, 5=High*). Adapted from Nichols, Glass, & Berliner (2006).

pressure is related to percentage of Non-White races by states, Exhibit 9.4 results.

In Exhibit 9.4, 25 states having implemented high-stakes testing programs by 2004 appear with codes representing two variables: the percentage of the population of the state that was reported to be "Non-White" in the 2000 Decennial Census, and the Nichols-Glass-Berliner Accountability Pressure Rating (APR), as a number between 1 and 5 in a circle. The coincidence of high pressure and above average ethnic and racial minority population across these 25 states is obvious without further analysis.

Focusing on those states with high-stakes testing programs that showed an increase in the percentage non-White population from below 20% in 1950 to above 20% in 2000, one sees the following distribution of accountability pressure ratings in 2004: CA = 3, AZ = 5, NM = 5, TX = 5, MD = 2, NY = 5.

These ratings average 4.2, considerably higher than the average rating assigned across all 25 states: 3.4. Taking a finer look at these data, the correlation between the APR and the gain in percent Hispanic from 1980 to 2000 by states is .2 when California is included in the calculation and .3 when it is not.[6] (Data and calculations appear in Appendix D.)

For the 25 states in Exhibit 9.4, most of the variation across states in the accountability pressure ratings is accounted for by recent rapid growth in the Hispanic population of the state and traditional levels of the Black (or African American) population. The multiple correlation of *APR in 2000* with *Gain in Percent Hispanic Population from 1980 to 2000* and *Percent Black (or African American) Population* for the 25 states in Exhibit 9.4 is .68 with California included, and .73 with California omitted.[7]

These data establish the suspicion that the hypothesis might be true: accountability pressures are adopted and applied selectively across the U.S. in response to the growth of racial and ethnic minorities in the populations of the individual states. Thorough qualitative work will be required to replace the suspicion with belief. A closer look at two representative states, one with a highly punitive accountability system and one with a nonpunitive system, will add some depth to the numbers and the correlations.

---

6.   While these correlations (.2, .3) may not seem large in some respects, they should be interpreted in light of the reminder that the 25 states on which they are based represent a "restricted sample" (see Glass, Gene V., & Hopkins, Kenneth D. (1996). *Statistical methods in education & psychology, Third edition.* Boston: Allyn & Bacon, pp. 121-123) in which correlations are typically attenuated. The 25 states missing from the calculation tend not to have had both high-stakes testing programs or large increases in Hispanic population during the period of time studied. If imputed values of 0 APR and 0% Hispanic population gain are substituted in the calculation of the correlation coefficient for the 25 missing states—a strategy that would likely place an upper bound on the relationship—a coefficient of nearly .6 is obtained.

7.   If the same strategy is followed of imputing 0s for the 25 missing states to obtain a sense of the effect of restriction of range on the multiple correlation, a value of .88 is obtained for the multiple *R*.

Accountability in Maine: A Low-Stakes State

Maine, a state with one Hispanic for every 200 persons in the 1980 Census and one in 140 persons in the 2000 Census, has implemented an accountability program with minimal threat to teachers, administrators, and students. The Maine Legislature established achievement standards for all public school students in 1996 in a program named Learning Results. Learning Results established curriculum based standards of test performance fro K-12 students. A new system of assessing performance against these standards was instituted at the same time. The Maine assessment system encompassed both a statewide criterion referenced exam—the Maine Educational Assessment (MEA)—and local district assessments.

MEA was first administered in 1984 at Grades 4, 8, and 11. It was redesigned periodically, particularly in 1990 and 1995, in light of shifting curricular emphases and changing standards. After the 1995 administration, there was wide spread criticism of the test as being inappropriately difficult. Objections were raised against changes in the MEA from being half multiple-choice and half open-ended questions to entirely open-ended. In 1996 when Learning Results was adopted by the legislature, the MEA became the tool for measuring progress relative to the state standards. The 1998-99 administration of the MEA was the first assessment coordinated to the Learning Results standards.

In 2004, "mini-assessments" in Grades 3, 5, 6, and 7 were added to meet the requirements of No Child Left Behind. All MEA tests can be taken in three different formats depending on such characteristics of the student as presence of handicaps, non-English background, and special education placement. The differing formats include the typical standard administration, administration with "accommodations," or an "alternative assessment." "Accommodations" in assessment are based on Individual Educational Plans (IEP) and include extended time limits, adult help in reading questions, and the like. States differ greatly in whether they will allow accommodations for special students in their assessment programs. Although nearly every state gives lip service to accommodations in assessment, some have failed to implement them and some have denied them altogether. Maine provided for such accommodations early on.

The Learning Result program originally reported test scores for individual students and aggregated to the level of individual schools in reading, writing, mathematics, science and technology, and social studies. In addition, school-level results, but not individual student scores, were reported in health and the visual and performing arts. In 2004, the MEA was redesigned to shorten the administration time; the sections of the test dealing with visual and performing arts, health, and social studies were dropped. Several other modifications were made to meet the mandates of the federal No Child Left Behind program. Throughout the history of Learning Results and its incorporation into the federal NCLB program, Maine has emphasized local assessments by school districts to honor differences among the districts in curriculum and type of students served.

Consequences of performance, that is, what is at stake, in the Learning Results program vary from school district to school district, and the stakes depend on a variety of factors, not just scores on the MEA. Among the most important consequence for an individual student in any accountability program is whether the child will be promoted to the next grade level at the end of the year. In Maine, this decision is based on policies set at the school district level and on local assessments rather than the MEA scores. The rate of retention in grade in the state of Maine is much lower than in other states with high levels of accountability pressure. The class of 2007 was the first class that was required to pass a local examination to receive a high school diploma. No significant difference in the rate of graduation from past rates was observed. Top performing students on the MEA are eligible to receive scholarships to in-state universities. Nor are teachers threatened with loss of job, reassignment, or public exposure for the performance of their students on the MEA. In a few districts, the local teachers union agreed to contracts in which teachers could be fired according to certain criteria that included poor student performance. No such firing has been recorded. Likewise, administrators are not significantly threatened with loss of job or reassignment in the Learning Results program. Schools that show marked improvement are publicly recognized; no monetary rewards are attached to school-level performance that exceeds expectations. Federal requirements under No Child Left Behind subject Title I schools in Maine to "reconstitution" (primarily, replacement of administrative personnel) if they fail to make "adequate yearly progress" for 2 years in a row. This has not happened in Maine. At worst, one or two schools experienced a year of "provisional status" while the state sought help in the form of consultants and administrative support.

Press coverage of Learning Results and its incorporation into NCLB was nearly uniformly supportive of the state's schools and educators. Arbitrary standards in need of re-examination were critiqued. Schools publicly cited for poor test performance were sympathetically portrayed as struggling with disadvantaged student populations. The *Bangor Daily News*, the states leading newspaper, credited the Maine Department of Education with dealing intelligently with the NCLB mandates:

> The state Department of Education decided this year that schools would be identified as low performing based only on the "doesn't meet" category on the MEAs. Last year, that category was combined with the "partially meets" category to determine low-performing schools.
>
> But using only the lowest performing scores "gives a more accurate accounting for the performance of students," Deputy Commissioner Judith Lucarelli said Tursday.[8]

---

8. *Bangor Daily News*, January 24, 2003. (p. A1)

Commissioner J. Duke Albanese was quoted in the same news article on the department's plans for helping low-performing schools:

> The department will work closely with the designated schools to improve scores, and will send three "knowledgeable educators" to review MEA data, instructional practices, curriculum design, assessment methods and local school policy, Albanese said. Assistance is available to the entire district.[9]

As NCLB began to impose requirements for more testing, Maine educators sought greater assurances of local control and ways of lessening the burden of too much testing:

> More Maine students likely will have to take annual standardized tests to comply with a new federal reform law, Commissioner Susan Gendron said....
>
> The new tests, shorter versions of the current MEAs, are the simplest way to meet the federal guidelines, Deputy Commissioner Patrick Phillips said.
>
> Separately, local school systems are being asked to develop another set of assessments by the end of the 2004 school year to measure achievement in meeting the state's new education standards, called Learning Results. The local assessments are expected to include student portfolios, projects and demonstrations.[10]

Reactions to public reporting at the school level of MEA scores were generally unfavorable. Educators in Maine saw little good coming from this form of accountability pressure. Persons outside Maine sought to convince the citizens and educators of Maine that this was the new "way we do business in education."

> Dawn Carrigan, principal of Portland's Longfellow School, should be celebrating. The state listed Longfellow—whose students live in a well-to-do neighborhood—as one of Maine's best schools.

---

9. *Bangor Daily News*, January 24, 2003. (p. A1)
10. *Bangor Daily News*, August 12, 2003. (p. A1)

But Carrigan instead is worried about teacher morale across town at Reiche, a school of mostly poor children. The state put Reiche on a list of schools failing to meet federal accountability standards. Carrigan believes there is no good reason to create public lists that compare schools, especially when students come from different backgrounds.

"It's harmful. It creates panic. It's discouraging," she said.

Maine educators like Carrigan have long fought the practice of grading schools based on student performance. When the Maine Educational Assessment—the state's standardized test—was established in the mid-1980s, state officials promised that the data would not be used "like a basketball score in the paper"....

Long before the federal No Child Left Behind Act arrived—and Maine was forced to create its own lists—many states were giving parents information on school performance. Some experts warn that unless Maine educators embrace public accountability, the state's schools are in danger of falling behind.

"It has become a way we do business in education in most places," said Kati Haycock of the Education Trust,[11] one of the groups that pushed for No Child Left Behind. "Maine is one of the last states to move in this direction."[12]

By and large, educators and politicians of the state of Maine have resisted pressures to centralize curriculum and assessment in the service of applying accountability pressure to teachers, administrators and students. In the Nichols, Glass, and Berliner study, raters gave Maine a score of 2 on the accountability pressure scale, one of only eights states rated at that level or lower on accountability pressure. Significantly, the combined Hispanic and African American population of Maine is less than 1.5% of the state's population. In 2005, the U.S. Census Bureau estimated the Maine population to be 98% White.

---

11.   The Education Trust, a Washington, DC based spin-off of the American Higher Education Association, is dedicated to improving the achievement of all students K-12 and closing the "achievement gap." "No federal education law has been more maligned or misunderstood than the No Child Left Behind Act. Yet, no federal education law has accomplished more," Haycock said. (http://www2.edtrust.org/EdTrust/Press+Room/NCLB+Recommendations.htm)
12.   *Portland Press Hearld*, November 2, 2003. (p. 1A)

Accountability in Texas: A High-Stakes State[13]

The state of Texas contrasts markedly with Maine, not incidentally in its demographic composition and in the way it treats public education. In essence, Texas was a hothouse in which the federal No Child Left Behind was nurtured before it was unleashed on the nation. George W. Bush was governor of Texas until he left office in 2000 to assume the Presidency of the U.S.; he was largely responsible for the shape of the Texas accountability program.

Texas, along with such border states as Arizona and California, could well be the bellwether leading the nation to its demographic future. Texas has an estimated population as of 2007 of approximately 24 million people. According to U.S. Census estimates, the population currently breaks down as follows by race: 84% White; 12% Black; 4% Asian; and 1% American Indian. Hispanics of any race constitute 35% of the total population. Many Hispanics are newly arrived from Mexico and Central America. Others, known as *Tejanos*, are descendants of families that have lived in the region since before Texas was admitted to the U.S. in 1845. Hispanics reside primarily in the southern, south-central, and western portions of the state. Northern portions of the state are primarily White Protestant descendants of English and Irish ancestors.

Historically, Texas politics were dominated by the Democratic party. Conservative Democrats held most elected offices in the state until the left leanings of the party drove many of them to the opposition in the late 20th century. The first Republican governor since immediately after the Civil War was elected in 1978. Currently, the governor, both U.S. Senators, and the majority of the Legislature are Republican. The last Democrat to be elected to a state office assumed

13.   This section draws heavily on the unpublished work of Sharon Nichols, University of Texas at San Antonio, and the published work of Walt Haney: Haney, Walt. (2000). The myth of the Texas miracle in education. *Education Policy Analysis Archives*, 8(41) Retrieved September 19, 2007 from http://epaa.asu.edu/epaa/v8n41/

duties in 1995. Texas politics swung right as its demographics turned Brown.

The public schools of Texas are organized into approximately 1,000 school districts administered by the Texas Education Agency. These school districts are largely separate from any municipal governments and cross county or city boundaries in many cases. There are numerous private and religious schools in the state over which the Texas Education Agency has no authority. Students in these schools are generally exempt from the TEA testing programs and no high school graduation test is required of students in them. Homeschooling is very popular in the state and no legislation places restrictions on such things as length of school day or minimum days per school year for home schools. Homeschooled students are not required to take graduating senior tests.

The history of educational accountability in Texas is replete with the creation and re-creation of high stakes achievement tests tied to severe sanctions of individual students, teachers, schools, and entire school districts. Beginning in 1980, state statute required the creation and administration of a basic skills test known as the Texas Assessment of Basic Skills (TABS). TABS measured minimal basic skills in math, reading, and language. TABS was rebuilt in 1985 and christened the Texas Educational Assessment of Minimum Skills (TEAMS), which was administered to students until 1989. The TEAMS test was adopted as a graduation requirement in 1985. As the standards movement swept the nation, TEAMS was remade into the Texas Assessment of Academic Skills (TAAS). The TAAS was mandated in 1990 as the primary measure of students and their schools. Students in Grades 3, 5, 7, 9, and 11 were first required to take the TAAS exam in the fall of both 1990 and 1991. These exams were designated "exit" exams for advancing from grade to grade or for graduating from high school. In 1994, the TAAS results were first used to assign accountability ratings to schools. In 1999, TAAS was thrown out and TAKS, the Texas Assessment of Knowledge and Skills, was instituted. TAKS is administered to students in the following subjects at the following grades: mathematics-Grades 3-10; reading-Grades 3-9; writing, spelling, and grammar-Grades 4 & 7; language arts-Grade 10; social studies-Grades 8 & 10; science-Grades 5 & 10. If the reader is confused by now, perhaps he or she can appreciate how confused the educators of Texas were too, since their reputations and public image depended on the results of these moving and shifting targets for more than 20 years.

The TAAS exam was very controversial among educators and parents. One complaint was that the "stakes" were low on the results of the test in the lower grades—students were said to be routinely passed from one grade to the next even when their performance was poor—but they were Draconian on the final high school graduation test. It was widely agreed that TAAS had little to do with the curriculum that was being taught in the grades at which it was administered. In an attempt to correct this shortcoming, the state education agency created several end of course exams more aligned with what was believed to be course content. Teachers in large numbers complained that TAAS narrowed the curriculum that could be taught and turned teaching into test preparation:

> We are so concerned about the TAAS & End of Course exam that we are teaching the test, but the kids are not learning the material. I can teach the test, and have a very high percentage pass, yet have kids that know no Algebra. Going to three years TAAS testing in the future will reduce education to completely teaching the test, and we will graduate an illiterate generation. (Case 130).[14]

TAKS was to correct many of the ills of the past. New teachers to the Texas system learn quickly that TAKS should be their main focus and *Sharpen Up*—a commercial test preparation program published by Buckle Down Publishing of Iowa City, Iowa[15]—is an important part of the curriculum.

---

14.   Haney, Walt. (2000). The myth of the Texas miracle in education. *Education Policy Analysis Archives, 8*(41). Retrieved September 19, 2007 from http://epaa.asu.edu/epaa/v8n41/

Texas has the most punitive sanctions of any state in the U.S. attached to performance on these tests. If results are not deemed acceptable by one or another arbitrary criterion, school districts may be placed on probation, have their state accreditation removed, have state monies withheld, have their superintendent replaced, or have the entire school district taken over by the State of Texas. Individual schools can suffer many of the same fates, including having the school "reconstituted" or closed by the state. Districts and individual schools strive to win the label of "Exemplary" or "Recognized" by the Texas Education Agency. The stakes for students are equally high, or even higher depending on one's perspective. Students can be held back in grade for poor TAKS scores (at Grade 3 in reading and Grades 5 and 8 in reading and mathematics). Students at Grade 11 can begin trying to pass the high school graduation test. The test is composed of 60 mathematics questions, 52 English questions including a written essay, 55 science questions, and 55 social studies questions. Students have. five tries to pass the test before graduation.

Failure rates on Texas high-stakes tests are as severe as those anywhere in the nation. Those who fail receive a "certificate of completion," which is not recognized as sufficient to gain admission to the university system. No alternate paths to the high school diploma are permitted. In the spring of 1999, 75% of high school sophomores passed the TAAS: the pass rates for the three major racial/ethnic groups were 60% of African Americans, 64% of Hispanics, and 86% of Whites (Anglos). Some felt that the TAAS was too easy. The TAKS was to prove more difficult. In 2003, the passing rates for the TAKS among 11th graders were 59% for "Anglos," 33% for African Americans, and 38% for Hispanics. Approximately 85% of the 11th grade students classified as Limited English Proficient (LEP) failed the TAKS that year. At the end of the

15.   Buckle Down Publishing bills itself as a "national leader in state-specific test preparation for Grades 2-12."

2006-2007 academic year, more than 40,000 high school seniors did not graduate because they failed to pass all four of the TAKS subtests. They constituted more than 15% of the senior class. (Florida denied diplomas to about 10% of its high school seniors in 2003 based on their having failed the state's exit exam.) Hispanic and African American students were disproportionately represented among those who failed to graduate. Testifying in a lawsuit brought by MALDEF, the Mexican American Legal Defense and Educational Fund, against the Texas Education Agency to stop the administration of TAAS, Walt Haney opined, "The adverse impact on Black and Hispanic students in Texas of the TAAS graduation test is extensive in time, pervasive in nature."

The impact of the TAKS was felt as early as the third grade. Students, primarily LEP or non-English speaking students, were being retained in grade (i.e., flunked) in large numbers. Politicians spoke of flunking children as if they were being handed a favor. To sustain such rhetoric, they had to ignore research that showed that flunking a grade confers no academic benefits to students, greatly increases their chances of eventually dropping out, and is experienced as extremely negative by most students, who feel a sense of shame and are teased by their peers.[16]

Monetary awards to schools are a part of the Texas accountability system, but they are seldom given and when they are, they amount to little more than a few hundred dollars. Most years, the legislature did not appropriate funds for this purpose. When a few individual Texas school districts in the 1980s instituted sizeable financial rewards for teachers and principals who raised students' test scores above predetermined levels, the program quickly erupted with cheating and scandal.[17] The power of the system is in withholding labels of

---

16.   Shepard, Lorrie A., & Smith, Mary Lee. (Eds.) (1989). *Flunking grades: Research and policies on retention.* London: Falmer Press. Holmes, Charles T. (1989). Grade level retention effects: A Meta-analysis of research studies. Pp. 16-33 in Lorrie A. Shepard & Mary Lee Smith (Eds.), *op. cit.* Grissom, James B., & Shepard, Lorrie A. (1989). Repeating and dropping out of school. Pp. 34-63 in *op. cit.*

approbation. The system punishes; it seldom rewards. As would be expected, punishment in the form of public shaming was liberally visited on poor schools enrolling predominantly Hispanic students.[18]

Many states have long and complicated lists of sanctions for less than acceptable performance on tests, but few apply them. Texas is an exception, as can be seen in the following excerpts from various newspapers that tracked the threat and anxiety aroused by Texas style accountability.

The damage done by punitive accountability measures was not limited to students being retained in grade (i.e., flunked) or high school students being denied diplomas. The curriculum taught was narrowed to basic skills subjects and intellectually challenging projects were replaced with drill and kill test preparation in all too many districts. Protagonists disagreed on the merits of having a high stakes test guide what is taught.

> "There are a lot of things we should be teaching kids in school that the TAAS doesn't measure," said Steve Antley, President of the Congress of Houston Teachers. "I think the real tragedy is that it has the whole effect of narrowing the curriculum."
>
> Jon Dansby, president of the Houston Education Association, has similar concerns that the TAAS is controlling what is being taught.
>
> Other subjects, including science and social studies, are being added to the testing program, but they are not yet part of the accountability system that determines whether a school is rated exemplary, recognized, acceptable or low-performing.
>
> While defenders of the accountability system acknowledge that the TAAS steers the curriculum, they don't consider that necessarily a

17.   Glass, Gene V. (1989). Using student test scores to evaluate teachers. In Jason Millman, & Linda Darling-Hammond (Eds.), *New handbook of teacher evaluation* (229-240). Beverly Hills, CA: SAGE.
18.   McNeil, Linda. (2005). Faking equity: High-stakes testing and the education of Latino youth. In A. Valenzuela (Ed.), *Leaving children behind: How "Texas-style" accountability fails Latino youth* (pp. 57-111). Albany: State University of New York Press. Padilla, Raymond. (2005). High-stakes testing and educational accountability as social constructions across cultures. In A. Valenzuela (Ed.), *op. cit.*, pp. 249-262.

bad thing. And although critics say that schools spend an inordinate amount of time preparing students to take the TAAS, defenders say it is relevant material—such as learning to add fractions—that is being taught, not test questions.

"I think it's completely natural that if you are going to be measured on something, you are going to put emphasis on it," said Houston Superintendent Rod Paige. "So the question is to me, is it what you are supposed to know and be able to do? What is the problem of teaching to that standard?"

Three years later, Rod Paige was to ask the same rhetorical questions defending No Child Left Behind as George W. Bush's Secretary of Education.[19]

The TAAS was not viewed so benignly by educators on the front lines. In Houston, resignations have been demanded and prosecutors are investigating whether criminal charges are warranted. In Austin, 17 indictments already have been issued and one person has entered a plea....

Their alleged crimes? Cheating on the very test state officials use to grade Texas's public schools and assess the academic performance of students.

The recent controversies with the Texas Assessment of Academic Skills, or TAAS, have prompted some to question whether the so-called cornerstone of the school accountability system is crumbling under the pressure to succeed.[20]

The Texas accountability system drew the attention of education policy researchers nationwide.

Two Harvard University studies ... criticized TAAS as a bad solution to serious public education problems involving poor and minority students.

"We're not disagreeing with the diagnosis," said Gary Orfield, director of the Civil Rights Project that released the studies. "We basically think of it as a very large civil rights issue.

19.   Markley, Melanie (1997, August 10). Texas system pushes better schools; Study pegs program as 'one of the better ones in the nation. *Houston Chronicle*, p. A37
20.   Arrillaga, Pauline (1999, April 13). Tampering allegations raise new questions about the role of TAAS. *Associated Press*.

Accountability is good. Smaller class size is good. But the TAAS test is a tremendously serious mistake," Orfield said.[21]

In spite of some of the highest failure rates for high stakes tests in the nation, the TAAS was seen as too easy by some. The TAKS would up the stakes.

The new, more difficult TAKS test and the practice of holding students back that don't pass the test in third grade next year is a daunting challenge. It may take some time and a few hard knocks," said Sheila Fields, a second-grade teacher and president of the Association of Texas Professional Educators.

This past school year [2001-2002], almost 14 percent, or 37,000 of the state's 267,000 third-grade pupils, did not pass the TAAS. That's down from 29 percent a year ago, but not good enough, especially considering next year's high stakes, [Texas Education Commissioner Felipe Alanis] said.

Alanis promised that the state would work with the educators to help the pupils, most of them non-English speakers, as early as possible.[22]

The hostility toward educators and even toward their students that characterized Texas education politics in the 1990s eventually found fertile ground in Washington, D.C.

In 1999, then-Gov. George W. Bush began speaking out against social promotion. State law already prohibited the practice of passing students along because of age rather than ability, but the governor thought the statute was weak.

Bush sought and won a measure that would tie advancement to student performance on a test, providing a uniform measure of whether pupils were ready to move ahead.

Starting with this year's [2002-2003] third-graders, children who cannot pass the exam will be held back until they master required skills. As they advance through school, they will have to pass state tests again in fifth and eighth grades to be promoted.

---

21.   Plaintiffs: Exit test unfair to minorities, contributes to dropouts. Associated Press. January 7, 2000.
22.   Mabin, Connie. Most schools get good grades; 162 rated low-performing. Associated Press. August 1, 2002.

"This is a bold step," said John Stevens, executive director of the Texas Business and Education Coalition. "There's no doubt about it. It looks harsh. But I can tell you, it's pretty damned hard to be a high school student who can't read."[23]

The TAKS instilled a new sense of fear and urgency in Texas educators.

Almost half of 10th-graders across the state flunked at least one segment of the new Texas Assessment of Knowledge and Skills. Many of those students are now juniors, and they must pass all four segments of the 11th-grade test to receive a diploma in 2005....

Some of the steps educators are taking are similar to what elementary schools did with third-graders last year as those pupils prepared for a test they had never seen....

Now, the pressure is on high school juniors, and the stakes are even higher.

"This is more serious than anything we've ever faced," said Kelly Crook, a director of instruction and accountability in the Del Valle district, where almost 70% of sophomores failed at least one segment of the TAKS. "There's no false sense of security about what we are up against."[24]

Race, Ethnicity, and Accountability

It is difficult to imagine the things that happen in Texas in the name of education accountability taking place in Maine and vice versa. There appears to be a link between accountability and ethnicity. Where highly punitive education accountability systems are installed, there one finds the politically weak and vulnerable members of society. The damage that is ignored in one state would never be tolerated in another, and who suffers the consequences may be of the greatest importance.

23.   Gutierrez, Bridget. (2003, March 2). Testing time for third-graders; Bar is raised on little kids; young pupils now must pass a state exam to advance. It might be a tough ride for some. *San Antonio Express-News*, p. A1.

24.   Blackwell, Kathy. (2003, November 20). Schools hustle to avert crisis. *Austin American-Statesman*, p. A1.

People are uncomfortable or worse in the presence of others who speak a different language. Those who look different are used as scapegoats when failure needs an excuse. These fears and antipathies are planted deep in the human psyche and facile suggestions for uprooting them are largely wasted breath. American society is thoroughly segregated along racial and ethnic lines, in part out of free choice and in part as a result of public housing policy. Location of domiciles has proven to be far more influential in determining the fate of public education over the last 60 years than has any instrument of education policy. Jean Anyon provided a vivid simile for those who would address education reform while ignoring the broader context in which schools operate: "attempting to fix inner city schools without fixing the city in which they are embedded is like trying to clean the air on one side of a screen door."[25]

George Lipsitz[26] has argued that "whiteness" has a cash value resulting from such factors as equity in houses acquired in discriminatory markets, unequal public schooling, privileged employments opportunities afforded by personal networks, and the transfer of wealth governed by inheritance laws and access to legal services, among others. It is this cash value that White Americans seek to maintain and expand through the instrument of public policy serving personal advantage. The result may be race-based hierarchies in American society even when the motives are not racist but are instead for material gain.

I close this chapter with a quotation from an article by Ernest House, an education policy researcher with extensive experience evaluating reform efforts in education. House does not need to be convinced of the existence of the motives and system of beliefs that could bring about the relationships shown here; he has observed them first-hand for 4 decades.

25.   Anyon, Jean. (1997). *Ghetto schooling: A political economy of urban educational reform*. New York: Teachers College Press. (p. 168)
26.   Lipsitz, George. (2006). *The possessive investment in whiteness: How white people profit from identity politics*. Philadelphia: Temple University Press.

For a long time, I have been puzzled by the connection between race and education policy.… I want to offer a tentative explanation of this connection. First, Americans hold deep-seated beliefs about democracy, equality, and fairness. These beliefs are sincere, I believe. Second, America is a deeply racist country in a particular way. Although many countries harbor racist beliefs, those in America are peculiar in some respects. Third, most "white" Americans don't fully comprehend that their country is racist, nor the extent of that racism, nor how that racism is embedded.

These beliefs result in seemingly contradictory policies. Given these beliefs, I would expect that policies with racial import will often be invisible or disguised as nonracial. That is, the intents and consequences of some policies will be taken to be something other than what they are, even to those who espouse them. This disguise enables the policies to seem fair and democratic, even when the policies have racial overtones. For example, the sociologist William Julius Wilson (1987) contends that Americans will not support policies that are believed to benefit minorities primarily.… I have a corollary to Wilson's thesis. Americans will support policies that are harmful to minorities that they would not tolerate if those same policies were applied to majority populations.[77]

---

27. House, Ernest R. (1999). Race and policy. *Education Policy Analysis Archives, 7*(16). Retrieved November 9, 2005, from http://epaa.asu.edu/epaa/v7n16.html

Part IV.
Looking
Forward

Chapter Ten

What is the Fate of Public Education in America

Fertilizers, pills, and magnetic strips have served as major forces shaping population, politics, and policy. How will population and politics shape public education in America for the next 2 or 3 decades? No one can claim to know the fate of public life much beyond that.

New technologies shape life in unpredictable ways.[1] Among the most significant inventions of the 20th century are fertilizers (agricultural technologies), pills (medical technologies), and magnetic strips (nonmoney based credit systems). These three areas of technological invention are responsible for a good deal of the character of American culture in the early 21st century. Public education is certain both to reflect and be shaped by that culture, far more than it itself is a shaper of culture.

American education policy at the beginning of the 21st century has grown out of powerful forces acting over decades. The rural to urban migration, the control of conception and the extension of life expectancy, and the spread of uncollateralized personal credit are among these powerful forces.

---

1. "We make our tools and then they shape us" (Kenneth Ewart Boulding).

Fertilizers, Pills, and Magnetic Strips: The Fate of Education in America
pp. 231–250
231

Undergirding these forces are fundamental human needs and desires: the pursuit of material self-interest, monetary advantage, comfort, and security. People's actions are scarcely comprehensible and predictions of their behavior are virtually impossible without thinking about what drives them and what personal interest is served by their acting in certain ways. How the American public will treat the education of young people in the future can not be anticipated in the absence of a description of how that public will be constituted (in terms of age, race, and culture) and what their needs are.

The rural-to-urban migration in industrialized societies was rooted in the increasing productivity of agriculture during the early 20th century. Increased productivity owed much to the invention of artificial fertilizers in 1910 and the rapid expansion of farm machinery around that time. The transition from a rural culture to an urban and suburban culture was accompanied by the choice to limit the number of children born to a family for economic reasons. The reduction of human fertility was made attainable by the invention of the birth control pill in 1953. Increased life expectancy began to be achieved by means of the extraordinary discoveries of medical science, including pharmaceuticals, inoculations, and improved surgical techniques. Baby booms at the end of WW II followed by baby busts in the 1960s and beyond have radically changed the nation's demographics.

Small uncollateralized loans by credit companies made possible by the development of the magnetic strip and cheap telecommunications have profoundly changed American's spending and saving habits. A hyperconsuming middle class quickly loses loyalty to expensive public institutions serving other people.

Robotics have had profound effects on the U.S. economy as well as the economies of all industrialized nations. While costs in the manufacturing sector decline in real dollars, the service sector of the economy, dependent as it is on human relationships, has shown no such increases in efficiency. Through their elected officials, voters apply increasing pressure on all public institutions for accountability. Education and other public institutions and services are being subjected to scrutiny and control of their finances and their effectiveness as never before.

In a democracy, demographics are destiny. The people's will is eventually expressed. At times this seems idealistic to the point of naiveté. But even presidential candidates change their positions in response to polling numbers to improve their chances; and they change to align with the majority, much to the chagrin of the very public whose interests are being served. It is as though the public would rather see a "foolish consistency" in their statesmen and divines than a leader who reflects their own interests. If demographics are destiny, then there are certain likely predictions that rest on the quite reasonable assumption that the majority will use government to promote material self-interest and secure safety and comfort.

It must be acknowledged that there are certain demographic imperatives. The retirees of mid-21st century America were born in the 1950s through the 1990s. The minority children born in the 21st century have entered elementary school, or soon will. They are alive today; that can not be changed. There is no turning back; the toothpaste is out of the tube; it can not be put back in.

American demographics have undergone a tectonic shift as a result of technological invention—a shift in ethnicity and a shift in age. Immigration and a differential birth rate account for the rise of Hispanics from a small minority class to a major social and political force. Nearly 70% of Hispanics identify themselves as Roman Catholics. Approximately 15% identify themselves as born-again or evangelical Protestants. Fewer than 1 in 10 do not identify with any religion. The connection between religion and fertility is too obvious to bear further mention. The authors of the Pew Hispanic Center study wrote,

> the prevalence of spirit-filled religious expressions and of ethnic-oriented worship ... combined with the rapid growth of the Hispanic population leave little doubt that a detailed understanding of religious faith among Latinos is essential to understanding the future of this population as well as the evolving nature of religion in the United States.[2]

And one might add, this same understanding of religious faith is essential to understanding the future of education in America.

The wealthier White majority—with fewer children and grandchildren than in the past, and with increasing debt and life expectancy—grows less willing to support financially the institutions that are stewards of poor minority children. Peter G. Peterson, who served as secretary of commerce under Richard Nixon and was once director of the Federal Reserve Bank of New York, proposed solutions to the inescapable fiscal crisis brought about by the aging of the American populace. Included in Peterson's proposals were increasing the eligibility age for receiving Social Security (FICA) benefits, raising taxes both on workers and on the percentage of Social Security benefits that can be taxed, reducing entitlements for the rich, and limiting costly care at the end of life.[3] Viewed in light of the voting power of the expected 75 million AARP members of mid-21st century America, these proposals, with the possible exception of raising current workers' contributions to FICA, appear quixotic.[4] Peterson has stirred imaginations in frightening ways as he has documented the

---

2.   Pew Hispanic Center and Pew Forum on Religion & Public Life. (2007). *Changing faiths: Latinos and the transformation of American religion.* Washington, DC: PEW Hispanic Center.
3.   Peterson, Peter G. (1996). *Will America grow up before it grows old: How the coming Social Security crisis threatens you, your family and your country.* New York: Random House.
4.   Morris, Charles R. (1996). *The AARP: America's most powerful lobby and the clash of generations.* New York: Times Books/Random House.

impending economic pressures on an aging populace, not just in America but throughout the world.

> I believe that global aging will become the transcendent political and economic issue of the twenty-first century. I will argue that—like it or not, and there's every reason to believe we won't like it— renegotiating the established social contract in response to global aging will soon dominate and daunt the public policy agendas of all the developed countries.[5]

The problem of an aging populace in America, far more so than in other developed nations, will be exacerbated by the existence of ethnophobia.

 Fate means destiny. Fate is the forces that predetermine an outcome. The word "fate" has a connotation of ruin or bad fortune—the three fates of mythology were Clotho, who spun the thread of life, Lachesis who measured it, and Atropos who cut it at its end. In this sense, fate is perhaps not inappropriately used in discussing the future of public education. It would be better to speak of possibilities or likely scenarios for public education rather than its fate in these pages were it not that the forces being discussed have a sense of inevitability about them. Thus we speak of demographic imperatives. In announcing the withdrawal of Israeli settlements from Gaza in 2005, Ariel Sharon spoke of the "demographic imperatives"—by which he meant the enormous growth in the Arab population in contrast to the virtual steady state of the Israeli population—that were shaping life in the Middle East. We live subject to the influence of certain demographic imperatives, and to ignore them is to forfeit understanding of one's own circumstances.

Assertions about the state of education in America are predictions or else they are historical facts of no significance whatsoever. No long-term predictions are being made here.

---

5.   Peterson, Peter G. (2000). *Gray dawn: How the coming age wave will transform Americaand the world.* New York: Three Rivers Press.

Several things could deflect or reverse these trends: changes in immigration policy; cultural shifts in the Hispanic population, particularly regarding religion and the choice between large families versus consumption of luxuries; international trade agreements; campaign financing; even such seemingly mundane things as the price of corn. A great deal of importance has been placed in this analysis on the burgeoning Hispanic population, their place on the economic ladder, and their relationship to public institutions. In the heat of the 2008 presidential campaign hardly any issues were more heatedly contested than health care and immigration. Whether the immigration debate was merely campaign rhetoric soon to be forgotten after the votes are counted is unclear. Suffice it to point out that the 25 million or so Hispanic citizens now residing in the U.S. are likely to maintain high fertility rates and their role in American politics and culture is likely to expand. This would be true even if all undocumented persons from Mexico and Central America were deported tomorrow, as some fanatics threaten. Currently, the Hispanic influence in politics is in its early stages. No Hispanic Supreme Court justice has ever been appointed. Hispanics serving in presidential cabinets have been far outnumbered by African Americans. The influence of Hispanics at the polls has yet to be felt. From 2000 to 2004, Hispanics accounted for 50% of U.S. population growth but only 10% of the increase in votes cast. Hispanic voting participation rates consistently trail voting rates for Whites or African Americans. Many Hispanics are either under the age of 18 or are ineligible to vote. Only one in five Hispanics voted in the 2004 presidential election, compared to 50% of Whites and 40% of African Americans. In 1984, 37% of Hispanic voters cast their ballot for Ronald Reagan. In 2000, a third voted for George W. Bush and in 2004, 40% voted for Bush. Party affiliation of Hispanic voters favors the Democratic party heavily: 50% Democratic, 25% Republican, 25% Independent.[6]

The aging White population and its economic circumstances will play an important role in the future of public life.

All of these things could change, or they might not. At most one might see with some acuity for a decade ahead; to claim to see further is false confidence. Where demographics are concerned, the view of the mid-range future is somewhat better. Nearly all Americans alive today at age 5 will be alive in 15 years at age 20. On such obvious assertions rests the ability to anticipate some of what the future has in store.

The Short-Range Future of American Public Education

Public education in America has always rested on a shared sense of common purpose, even when regrettably that sense was frequently shared only among a particular class or race. The sense of being one nation seems more threatened today than at any other time since the War Between the States. Political strategists are partly to blame for having intensified political differences in hopes of achieving power. It remains to be seen whether the "mosaic society" is truly the preferred alternative to the "melting pot." The demise of a sense of community about which Robert Putnam wrote so convincingly is likely to continue.[7] The powerful influence of television and other forms of entertainment will grow as the cost of display devices drops and the provision of materials (digitized movies and music) across the Internet spreads. With that demise comes the further erosion of a sense of common purpose and interconnectedness that for so long supported institutions like the public schools. Libraries, museums, parks and other traditional public venues are also likely to suffer diminished support. The further widening of the income distribution will continue to eat away at a sense of civic responsibility, already seriously weakened. The more people there are who live in gated communities, the fewer there are who care

6. Suro, Roberto; Fry, Richard; & Passel, Jeffrey. (2006). *Hispanics and the 2004 election: Population, electorate and voters.* Washington, DC: Pew Hispanic Center.
7. Putnam, Robert D. (2000). *Bowling alone: The collapse and revival of American community.* New York: Simon & Schuster.

about supporting a police force. The more families there are who drive two and three cars, the fewer families there are who care about public transportation. The more people there are who drink only Evian, the fewer people there are who care what comes out of other people's faucets. The more parents there are who send their children to private or quasi-private schools, the fewer persons there are who care what goes on in poor schools. The drive for lower taxes and for private privileges for one's children and grandchildren at public expense is likely to take several different forms in education. These forms have already emerged; in a real sense, they are now in their infancy.

Segregation will increase. Traditional public schools—neighborhood schools—will increasingly become the province of the poor and minorities, particularly in metropolitan areas. Two court cases challenging the use of race as a criterion in balancing the racial composition of K-12 public schools made their way to the U.S. Supreme Court in 2007.[8] One case was from Seattle, Washington, the other from Louisville, Kentucky. Each district had voluntarily chosen to desegregate their schools by using race as an assignment criterion. On June 28th, the Court issued a decision finding both school district's practices violated the equal protection clause of the 14th Amendment to the Constitution. The justices split sharply along ideological lines, with five finding the policies of the school districts unconstitutional. Dissenting justices branded the majority opinion a betrayal of the historic 1954 *Brown v Board of Education* decision. In an unusually scathing dissent, Justice Breyer wrote that the decision was one "the court and the nation will come to regret." It is safe to say that the national mood was aligned with the court's majority. The

---

8.   Linn, Robert L., & Welner, Kevin G. (Eds.). (2007). *Race-conscious policies for assigning students to schools: Social science research and the Supreme Court cases.* Washington, DC: National Academy of Education.

deep political divisions on the court affirmed once again the importance of elections.

It is now generally conceded by editorial writers, media pundits, and influential opinion makers that the attempt to desegregate public K-12 education has failed. Busing, magnet schools, and other instruments of desegregation dating back 50 years are alleged to have failed to improve the lot of minority students. In fact, where desegregation was accomplished on any significant scale for an extended period—namely, in the Southeastern U.S. —the best evidence[9] on the question of students' academic progress shows that young African American students benefited substantially. But this fact is buried under mounds of invective heaped on school desegregation. The national will to desegregate appears to be exhausted. More than 50 years after *Brown v Board of Education*, public education is becoming more segregated.[10] Voucher initiatives, largely rejected by voters in the past 30 years, will be looked on more favorably by an aging voting class. The push for vouchers may even be helped by the emerging Hispanic political faction; Hispanics expect a much greater role for religion in politics than do middle-class Whites.[11] Whether White majority scruples that have traditionally restrained the advance of the voucher movement will

---

9.   In summarizing their analyses of NAEP results tracked over a decade, Nancy Burton and Lyle V. Jones wrote, "The results summarized here show that during the 1970's the discrepancy in average achievement level between the nation's white and black youth has become smaller in five important learning areas at ages 9 and 13. Typically when achievement for white students has declined, that for black students has declined less; when whites have improved, blacks have improved more. The difference between the races has decreased at both ages in mathematics, science, reading, writing, and social studies." (p. 14) "Programs designed to foster equal educational opportunity may be among the factors that have contributed to the reduction in white black achievement differences" (p. 14). These trends were particularly pronounced in the Southeastern U.S. Burton, Nancy, & Jones, Lyle V. (1982). Recent trends in achievement levels of black and white youth. *Educational Researcher, 11* (4), 10-14.
10.   Boger, John Charles, & Orfield, Gary. (2005). *School resegregation: Must the South turn back?* Chapel Hill: University of North Carolina Press.

disappear under the strain of racial tensions and financial exigency is anyone's guess.

Homeschooling will probably continue to be the fastest growing trend on a percentage basis in education. Largely a White, middle-class movement, home chooling parents will seek and often succeed in gaining financial reimbursement from the state, either through organizing into ad hoc "schools" under the charter school movement or by securing education tax credits. The trend toward homeschooling will be augmented by virtual schools provided by private companies. Poorer families in which both parents must work or single-parent families will participate less in this trend, obviously.

Tax credits for tuition and other education expenses will spread from state to state as private providers of education services grow in popularity. A handful of states currently give tax credits for contributions to education agencies. In Florida, Pennsylvania, and Arizona these monies are distributed as vouchers largely redeemable at private or religious schools by middle and upper-income families. The laws have thus far withstood legal challenge, to the amazement of many scholars and observers. This avenue of funneling public monies to private and religious schools is likely to be traveled in several other states in the future. Wherever tried, tuition tax credits have favored the middle and upper economic classes, not the poor. Enclaves of older citizens—the Sun Cities and Boca Ratons of the sunbelt—will succeed increasingly in securing exemptions from property taxes that once supported public schools. Florida, Arizona, and 18 other states provide persons

11. "Two-thirds of Hispanics say that their religious beliefs are an important influence on their political thinking. More than half say churches and other houses of worship should address the social and political questions of the day." Pew Hispanic Center and Pew Forum on Religion & Public Life. (2007). *Changing faiths: Latinos and the transformation of American religion.* Washington, DC: PEW Hispanic Center.

over a certain age (e.g., 62) tax credits, deferrals, or "homestead exemptions" from property taxes, the major source of public school funding. These are likely to become popular in states other than those that currently have high concentrations of older citizens.

Virtual schooling (i.e., distance teaching and learning, schooling through the Internet), like corporate outsourcing, contract workers, and home offices, will grow as a means of reducing the costs of public schools. This mode of delivery can equal of exceed the effectiveness of face-to-face teaching in areas that are simply structured and tightly organized (e.g., mathematics, spelling, grammar, certain areas of the sciences, even reading of particular types); more "visceral" learning (e.g., literature, graphic arts, music, dance, ethics, philosophy) is likely to find a home in private or privatized venues (e.g., churches, clubs of various sorts, Boy Scouts and Girl Scouts, YMCA, YMHA, and the like).[12] Under the control of legislatures, which in turn are greatly influenced by corporate and commercial interests, virtual schooling is likely to be opened up to private, profit making companies. This can be no surprise to anyone who observes the growing encroachment of commercial interests into public institutions and public affairs.[13] The Public Broadcasting System runs more minutes of commercials each year. Public money builds arenas and stadiums that are branded with company logos as soon as they open. In Florida, a school district sold advertising space to McDonalds on children's report cards.[14]

---

12. Vrasidas, Charalambos, & Glass, Gene V. (2002). *Distance education and distributed learning*. Charlotte, NC: Information Age.

13. Molnar, Alex. (1996). *Giving kids the business: The commercialization of America's schools*. Boulder, CO: Westview/HarperCollins. Molnar, Alex. (2001). Calculating the benefits and costs of for-profit public education. *Education Policy Analysis Archives*, 9(15). Retrieved December 1, 2006 from http://epaa.asu.edu/epaa/v9n15.html. Molnar, Alex. (2005). *School commercialism: From democratic ideal to market economy*. New York: RoutledgeFalmer.

Philanthropy will rise to ever increasing prominence as a result of the "great divide"[15] between the rich and the poor. Because of the huge accumulation of wealth—due to tax policies—by the few in America in the last 25 years and the increasing percentage of the population living near poverty levels, philanthropy may be one of the last hopes for public institutions. But philanthropy is an uncertain patron. Donors have a way of shaping the institutions they support, as institutions willingly change their shape to attract donations. Philanthropy comes with strings attached. Who, then, will be the donors, and what is their conception of education?

Bill Gates, founder of Microsoft, is, of course, one of the richest persons in the world. Of late, he has taken an interest in K-12 education, through the Bill and Melinda Gates Foundation which has been enriched considerably by the beneficence of Warren Buffett, another of the richest persons in the world. One must commend Buffett's wisdom in turning over some $50 billion to the Gateses because he has neither the time nor the inclination to study how best to use his money for the good of society. Much depends on the wisdom of the latter couple.

To date, the Gates Foundation's conception of what makes for successful education has proved to be long on platitudes but short of innovative or fruitful ideas. In testimony before the U.S. Senate Health, Energy, Labor and Pensions Committee on March 7, 2007, Bill Gates stressed the importance of standards and high expectations, the contemporary clichés. In a newspaper supplement widely distributed with the Sunday news, he is quoted as saying, "Testing is the only objective measurement of our students. It's incredible that we

---

14.   Seminole County, Florida. Students receiving all As and Bs in academic subjects for Grades 2-5 could present their report card at a local McDonalds restaurant and receive a free Happy Meal (Cheeseburger or Chicken McNuggets); all this in a nation suffering rampant childhood obesity.
15.   Sperling, John; Helburn, Suzanne; George, Samuel; Morris, John; & Hunt, Carl. (2004). *The great divide: Retro vs. metro America*. Sausalito, CA: PoliPoint Press.

have no national standard." "When we gave up phonics, we destroyed the reading ability of kids."[16]

Gates called for high schools and universities to produce large numbers of math and science majors, without documenting that either the jobs would be available or that the jobs would require the skills of a math and science major.[17] When Dennis Redovich of the Center for the Study of Jobs & Education in Wisconsin and United States projected job growth in the U.S. to the year 2016, he arrived at the following conclusions:

> the majority of jobs in 2016 [will] require short term on the job training or experience or moderate length on the job training, experience or education. Technology makes jobs simpler not more difficult and makes workers more productive. The great majority of the jobs of the future are the same jobs of the 20th century with new technological tools making these jobs easier to do. A majority of jobs require only short or moderate length training or experience. The jobs of the future in the United States in 2016 are essentially the same jobs in existence in 2006. There is no crisis in math science education in the United States.... There is a surplus of highly educated workers for jobs that require higher levels of education and training.[18]

The Gates foundation joined with the Broad Foundation to invest $60 million in a venture named the Strong American Schools Partnership. Strong American Schools hopes "to inspire the American people to join an effort that demands more from our leaders and educators, while ensuring that all

---

16.   *Parade* magazine (2007, September 23).

17.   While Microsoft's need for a large pool of science and engineering majors to draw employees from may be clear, the nation's need for more science and engineering graduates is not. A National Science Foundation survey of science and engineering graduates in 1995 and 2001 revealed that among those who are employed and who earned better than a 3.75 GPA in college, only 64% were employed in a field related to science and engineering. National Science Foundation. (2004). *Science and Engineering Indicators 2004.* Washington, DC: National Science Foundation. (Appendix Table 2-9)

18.   Redovich, Dennis W. (2007). *Math & science employment and employment projections by required education and training levels in the United States 2006-2016.* Milwaukee, WI: Center for the Study of Jobs & Education in Wisconsin and United States.

of our children benefit from good teachers, high expectations and challenging coursework." Gates spoke most passionately about the need to reform immigration law so that companies like Microsoft can more easily import highly trained scientists and engineers from outside the U.S. Gates attributed the slow progress of education reform to a lack of political and public will.[19] If will power could reform education, its problem would have long ago been solved.[20]

Undeniably, philanthropy to education in the U.S. has a conservative bent. In a study of 1,200 foundations giving to education organizations, Rick Cohen determined that between 2002 and 2005, $380 million went to 104 organizations advocating school vouchers or K-12 tuition tax credits.[21] The Walton Family Foundation (Wal-Mart) gave $25 million to such organizations in 1 year, 2005. (See Exhibit 10.1 for a list of recipient organizations backing vouchers and other school choice movements.) Other ideologically conservative foundations funding school choice movement include the Lynde and Harry Bradley Foundation (motor parts), Sarah Scaife Foundation (banking, oil, and aluminum), and John Templeton Foundation (financial investments and spiritual endeavors, according to the foundation's Web site). It is understandable, perhaps, that those successful in the business world believe that their success is the result of hard work, competition, and freedom from regulations—rather than inheritance, litigiousness, and luck. Consequently, they see their own success as a model for all endeavors.

---

19.   Herszenhorn, David M. (2007, April 25). Billionaires start $60 million schools effort. *New York Times*.

20.   In this respect, Gates was echoing Herbert Walberg and other conservative voices. In chapter 2, Walberg was quoted as saying that the U.S. could equal the Japanese education system if only the U.S. had the will: "Gumption and will-power, that's the key."

21.   Cohen, Rick. (2007). *Strategic grantmaking: Foundations and the school privatization movement.* Washington, DC: National Committee for Responsive Philanthropy. Retrieved December 1, 2007 from http://www.ncrp.org/downloads/ NCRP2007-StrategicGrantmaking-FINAL-LowRes.pdf.

**Exhibit 10.1.   Major School Choice Advocates and
Foundation Support Received, 2002-2005**

Philanthropic Organization	Amount Contributed
Children's Scholarship Fund	$73,320,000
Heritage Foundation	34,250,000
Children First	31,540,000
American Enterprise Institute	28,060,000
Hoover Institution	16,860,000
Focus on the Family	16,520,000
Manhattan Institute	15,570,000
Cato Institute	12,710,000
Institute for Justice	10,990,000
National Center for Policy Analysis	8,060,000
Hudson Institute	7,450,000

Based on data in Cohen (2007, Table 2, p. 13).

In contrast to the type of philanthropy that captures media attention stands the small individual contributions to public schools that are collected into what are known as school or education foundations. Education foundations are nonprofit privately operated organizations assisting public schools that qualify as charitable organizations. The Internal Revenue Service considers them to be tax-exempt organizations under section 501(c)(3) of the Internal Revenue Code. School foundations began to appear in the 1980s in states like California and Massachusetts after these states adopted limits on property tax growth. In 2006, there were approximately 5,000 school foundations for the 90,000 public elementary and secondary schools in the U.S. Although the existence of these foundations is often justified as a response to declining tax support for schools, their expenditures appear to be made more for enriching an already adequately funded school than providing for necessities. A survey conducted by the New Jersey School Boards Association revealed that foundation monies tended to support the following types of activity:

teacher mini-grants, the arts, public relations, and technology enhancements.[22] School foundation contributions have shown a pattern of increasing funding inequities between rich and poor schools.[23]

Zimmer and colleagues studied school foundations in Los Angeles County and concluded as follows[24]:

> We observed some differences in the nature of private giving in schools and school districts depending on their socioeconomic status.... Schools located in the wealthiest communities (that is, those with the highest socioeconomic status) had very strong parental support in absolute terms, relative to other schools in the sample. While there was a greater level of parental support at schools in wealthier communities, some schools in the poorer communities were also successful in raising private support, although they needed to approach a relatively wide array of private donors.

Contributions in wealthier districts tend to be in the form of money while parents in poorer districts contribute *in kind*, that is, they volunteer their time.

Philanthropy that is conscious of the huge inequities in American education could mitigate, perhaps, the crushing effects of poverty. In an ironic twist, a credit card mogul recently gave back generously to the community on which he once enriched himself so abundantly. T. Denny Sanford, in his early 70s, is retired. The former CEO of First Premier Bank and Premier Bankcard is a part-time resident of Scottsdale, Arizona, Vail, Colorado, and Sioux Falls, South Dakota. In the early 1980s, he purchased United National Bank (now United National Corporation) and built it into a company with assets

22. New Jersey School Board Association. (1999). *Local education foundation survey results.* Trenton: New Jersey School Board Association.
23. Crampton, Faith E., & Bauman, Paul. (1998). *A new challenge to fiscal equity: Educational entrepreneurship and its implications for states, districts, and schools.* Paper presented at the Annual Meeting of the American Educational Research Association, San Diego, CA.
24. Zimmer, Ron; Krop, Cathy; Kaganoff, Tessa; Ross, Karen E.; & Brewer. Dominic. (2001). *Private giving to public schools and districts in Los Angeles County: A pilot study.* Santa Monica, CA: Rand. Retrieved October 25, 2007 from http://192.5.14.110/pubs/monograph_reports/MR1429/MR1429.sum.html

over $1 billion. Sanford's personal wealth—estimated at $2.5 billion—derives from the credit card side of the banking industry, wealth amassed in South Dakota's credit friendly environment. *Forbes* magazine listed Sanford as the 117th richest American in 2006. In 2007, Sanford donated $400 million to the Sioux Valley Hospitals and Health System of Sioux Falls in hopes of building a health complex to rival the Mayo Clinic and Johns Hopkins University's medical school. One can imagine that this benefaction could in theory be traced back to the interest payments of millions of persons carrying credit card debt over the past 30 years. Suppose a quarter million Premier card holds paid $1,600 a piece in interest charges over the years, and that money in 2007 ended up building a world-class medical clinic in Sioux Falls, South Dakota. Can one really say that the money would have brought about greater good to society in the pockets of middle class Americans, who likely would have spent it on cruises and trips to Atlantic City or Las Vegas? Or that government would have done better with the $400,000,000 collected in taxes from the same citizens? Will the philanthropy of the super-rich (Sanford is ranked 14th in the *Chronicle of Philanthropy*'s list of American donors) rescue public life in America?

I have been accused personally of being both a cynic and a pessimist, two not incompatible temperaments. I am often accused of cynicism by my educator friends, far less often by my economist or political scientist friends. Surely my temperament is irrelevant to the cause of public education. But I will plead guilty to the first accusation—cynicism—and innocent to the second—pessimism. Decades of talk about reforming the American K-12 education system have made me cynical about each new discovery that promises to close the achievement gap or make every kid a winner. I am convinced that the current rhetoric of education reform—whether it speaks of "systemic reform" or "effective education" or "standards-based education" or "inquiry based teaching"—and how it is imagined that reform will be delivered—through books, in workshops, by governmental directive—speaks only false promises and portends failure. There are in the nation's schools "points of light," hundreds if not thousands. But they will not be discovered by giving paper-and-pencil tests and analyzing statistics. They shine in the eyes of any impartial observer who takes the time to look for them.

Public education is an endeavor nearly unique in the nation's experience. Parents share the stewardship of their most precious possession with a few other adults. Those adults intend to influence these children in fundamentally important ways. This is not only a strange economic relationship, as Ken Boulding once pointed out, it is a complex human relationship fraught with possibilities for great success and great failure. Human relationships nearly as important as that between parents and their children take place between teachers and their students. In that relationship, nothing counts with such significance as the intelligence and character of those teachers. "Character" is not meant in the sense that a William Bennett might use it, where it is synonymous with moral rigidity and a smug confidence that the *Great Books of the Western World* are the guiding light for our times. But rather, character here refers to those attributes of personality that allow teachers to be authentic and nurturing in the relationships with their charges.

We celebrate "points of light" when we see them. A Deborah Meier in East Harlem or a Jaime Escalante at Garfield High School in East Los Angeles shine brightly in the media. Others then speak of "scaling up" their model, that is, finding the essential elements of their success, putting them into words, and sending out the message so that the entire world can do likewise. But they forget or never knew that these stars' successes come not so much from what they do as from what they are as persons. And it is not only about who they are as persons but also in part about who their students are at the times of their greatest successes. Their wonderfully successful schools can no more be "scaled up" than one can scale up great families, great marriages, or great love affairs. In this I am an optimist: that the only reform that stands any chance of making our public schools better is the investment in teachers—to aide them in their quest to understand, to learn, to become more compassionate, caring, and competent persons.

The Struggle Between Liberty and Justice

There are no answers here on how to repair the world of our public schools. If anything, the country has too many proposed solutions to education's supposed ills. I have tried to give explanations instead. I hope to have offered you, reader, a realistic view of how we have come to this state of affairs in education. If the effort changes our sense of the importance of various questions or brings us closer to a more rational assessment of the possibility of finding answers, then the effort has not been wasted. Will understanding—like that hopefully conveyed here—lead to some degree of introspection, some reflection by the very generations on whom the future of public education depends? If indeed the motives driving school reform are as selfish as is here claimed, can good consciences be awakened? There are no likely solutions to problems possible without knowledge of causes, even if it is only partial knowledge.

The strong currents sweeping U.S. public education toward its future arise in the headwaters of a free people's drive for comfort and a higher standard of living for themselves, that standard being measured primarily in material terms. Americans love freedom, and nothing rankles them as much as infringements of their liberties. We are limited in our ability to imagine ourselves in the place of other people or to care for their fate as much as our own; and yet justice demands it. When problems of fairness and equity arise, we are often at a loss for solutions. If liberty and justice are separated, neither is safe. If exercise of liberties denies liberty to others, it is unjust.[25]

---

25.   Nickel, James. (1997). The liberty dimension of historic and contemporary segregation. *Law and Philosophy, 16,* 259-277.

References and Web Sites

Ansary, Tamim. (2007, March). Education at risk. *Edutopia*, 49-53. Retrieved September 10, 2007, from http://www.edutopia.org/

Anderson, Gerard F. (2007). From "soak the rich" to "soak the poor": Recent trends in hospital pricing. *Health Affairs, 26*(3), 780-789.

Anyon, Jean. (1997). *Ghetto schooling: A political economy of urban educational reform.* New York: Teachers College Press.

Apple, Michael W. (1993). *Official knowledge: Democratic education in a conservative age.* New York: Routledge & Kegan Paul.

Apple, Michael W. (1996). *Education and cultural politics.* New York: Teachers College Press.

Apple, Michael W. (2001). *Educating the "right" way: Markets, standards, God, and inequality.* New York: Routledge/Falmer.

Arrillaga, Pauline. (1999, April 13). Tampering allegations raise new questions about the role of TAAS. *Associated Press.*

Astin, Alexander W. (1998). The changing American college student: Thirty year trends, 1966-1996. *The Review of Higher Education, 21*(2), 115-135.

Astin, Alexander W. (2000). The civic challenge of educating the underprepared. In Thomas Ehrlic (Ed.), *Civic responsibility and higher education* (pp. 124 -146).Westport, CT: Oryx Press.

Astin, Alexander W. (1991). The changing American college student: Implications for educational policy and practice. *Higher Education, 22*(2), 129-143.

Aud, S. (2007). *School choice by the numbers: The fiscal effect of school choice programs 1990-2006.* San Francisco: The Milton & Rose D. Friedman Foundation.

Averett, Nancy, & Wilkerson, James E. (2002, August 4). Tax law little aid to poor students. *The Morning Call*, p. A1.

Baker, Bruce. (2007). Review of *Education by the numbers: The fiscal effect of school choice programs, 1990-2006.* Retrieved August 25, 2007 from http://epsl.asu.edu/epru/ttreviews/EPSL-0705-235-EPRU.pdf.

Baum, Sandy, & Ma, Jennifer. (2007). *Trends in college pricing*. New York: College Board. Retrieved November 20, 2007 from http://www .collegeboard.com/prod_downloads/about/news_info/trends/ trends_pricing_07.pdf

Bauman, Kurt J. (2002). Home schooling in the United States: Trends and characteristics. *Education Policy Analysis Archives*, *10*(26). Retrieved November 23, 2005, from http://epaa.asu.edu/epaa/v10n26.html

Bauman, Kurt J. (2001). *Home schooling in the United States: Trends and characteristics* (Working Paper Series No. 53). Washington, DC: Population Division, U.S. Census Bureau.

Belfield, Clive R. (2006). *The evidence on education vouchers: An application to the Cleveland Scholarship and Tutoring Program*. New York: National Center for the Study of Privatization in Education, Teachers College, Columbia University.

Belfield, Clive R., & Levin, Henry M. (2005). *Privatizing educational choice: Consequences for parents, schools, and public policy*. Boulder, CO: Paradigm.

Bennett, William J. (1992). *The devaluing of America: Fight for our culture and our children*. New York: Simon & Schuster.

Berliner, David C. (1993). Educational reform in an era of disinformation. *Educational Policy Analysis Archives*, *1*(2). Retrieved November 8, 2005 from http://epaa.asu.edu/epaa/v1n2.html

Berliner, David C. (2006). Our impoverished view of educational reform. *Teachers College Record*, *108*(6), 949-995.

Berliner, David C., & Biddle, Bruce J. (1995). *The manufactured crisis: Myth, fraud and attack on America's public schools*. New York: Addison-Wesley.

Berliner, David C., & Biddle, Bruce J. (1996). Making molehills out of molehills: Reply to Lawrence Stedman's review of *The manufactured crisis*. *Educational Policy Analysis Archives*, *4*(3). Retrieved November 8, 2005, from http://epaa.asu.edu/epaa/v4n3.html

Bertola, Giuseppe; Disney, Richard; & Grant, Charles. (Eds.) (2006). *The economics of consumer credit*. Boston, MA: MIT Press.

Bestor, Arthur. (1985). *Educational wastelands: The retreat from learning in our public schools*. Urbana: University of Illinois Press. (Original work published 1953)

Bestor, Arthur. (1955). *The restoration of learning*. Urbana: University of Illinois Press.

Bivens, Josh. (2005, November 20). Trade deficits and manufacturing employment. *Economic Snapshot*. Retrieved June 20, 2006 http:// www.epi.org/content.cfm/webfeatures_snapshots_20051130.

Blackwell, Kathy. (2003, November 30). Schools hustle to avert crisis. *Austin American-Statesman* , p. A1.

Boe, Erling E., & Shin, Sujie. (2005). Is the United States really losing the international horse race in academic achievement? *Phi Delta Kappan, 86*(9), 688-695.

Boger, John Charles, & Orfield, Gary. (2005). *School resegregation: Must the South turn back?* Chapel Hill: University of North Carolina Press.

Boulding, Kenneth E. (1953). *The organization revolution: A study in the ethics of economic organization.* New York: Harper and Brothers.

Boulding, K. (1972). The schooling industry as a possible pathological section of the American economy. *Review of Educational Research, 42*(1), 129-143.

Bounds, Amy. (2007, November 13). Horizons Charter founder facing theft, embezzlement charges. *Boulder Daily Camera,* p. A1.

Bowles, Samuel, & Gintis, Herbert. (1976). *Schooling in capitalist america: educational reform and the contradictions of economic life.* New York: Basic Books.

Bracey, Gerald W. (1998). *TIMSS, rhymes with "dims," as in "witted," KAPPAN.* Retrieved November 8, 2005, from http://www.pdkintl.org/kappan/kbra9805.htm

Bracey, Gerald W. (2000). The TIMSS "final year" study and report: A critique. *Educational Researcher, 29*(4), 4-10.

Bracey, Gerald W. (2003). *On the death of childhood and the destruction of public schools: The folly of today's education policies and practices.* Portsmouth, NH: Heinemann.

Bracey, Gerald W. (2006, July/August). Believing the worst. *Stanford Magazine.* Retrieved February 23, 2007, from http://www.stanfordalumni.org/news/magazine/2006/julaug/features/nclb.html

Bracey, Gerald W. (2007). *Get rich: Be a school teacher.* Retrieved March 19, 2007, http://www.huffingtonpost.com/gerald-bracey/get-rich-be-a-school-tea_b_40506.html

Bracey, Gerald. (2007, December 3). Righting wrongs. *The Huffington Post.* Retrieved December 9, 2007 from http://www.huffingtonpost.com/gerald-bracey/righting-wrongs_b_75189.html

Bracey, Gerald W. (2007, December 5). Diane does Rush. *The Huffington Post.* Retrieved December 9, 2007 from http://www.huffingtonpost.com/gerald-bracey/diane-does-rush_b_75696.html

Bradley Center for Philanthropy and Civic Renewal. (2003). *Giving better, giving smarter: Six years later.* (Discussion transcript.) Washington, DC: Hudson Institute. Retrieved November 7, 2007, from http://www.hudson.org/files/pdf_upload/Transcript_2003_05_15.pdf

Brantlinger, Ellen. (2003). *Dividing classes: How the middle class negotiates and rationalizes school advantage.* New York: RoutledgeFalmer.

Bronner, Ethan. (1998, February 25). U.S. twelfth-graders rank poorly in math and science study. *New York Times,* p. A-1.

Burton, Nancy, & Jones, Lyle V. (1982). Recent trends in achievement levels of Black and White youth. *Educational Researcher, 11*(4), 10-14.

Callahan, Raymond E. (1962). *Education and the cult of efficiency.* Chicago: University of Chicago Press.

Camarota, Steven A. (2005a). *Birth rates among immigrants in America comparing fertility in the U.S. and home countries.* Washington, DC: Center for Immigration Studies. Retrieved November 28, 2005, from http://www.cis.org/articles/2005/back1105.html

Camarota, Steven A. (2005b). *Immigrants at mid-decade: A snapshot of America's foreign-born population in 2005.* Washington, DC: Center for Immigration Studies. Retrieved December 13, 2005, from http://www.cis.org/articles/2005/back1405.html

Camilli, Gregory. (2006). Review of Kosar, Kevin R. *Failing grades: The federal politics of education standards. Education Review, .* Retrieved May 1, 2007, from http://edrev.asu.edu/reviews/rev469.htm

Carasso, Adam; Steuerle, C. Eugene; & Reynolds, Gillian. (2007). *Kids' share 2007: How children fare in the federal budget.* Washington, DC: Urban Institute. Retrieved March 19, 2007, from http://www.urban.org/UploadedPDF/411432_Kids_Share_2007.pdf

Carnoy, Martin; Jacobsen, R.; Mishel, L.; & Rothstein, Richard. (2005). *The charter school dust-up: Examining the evidence on enrollment and achievement.* Washington, DC: Economic Policy Institute and Teachers College Press.

Carnoy, Martin, & Loeb, Susanna. (2002). Does external accountability affect student outcomes? A cross-state analysis. *Educational Evaluation and Policy Analysis, 24*(4), 305–331.

Chubb, John E., & Hanushek, Eric A. (1990). Reforming Educational Reform. In Henry J. Aaron (Ed.), *Setting national priorities: Policy for the nineties* (pp. 213-247). Washington, DC: Brookings Institution.

Clark, T. (2001). *Virtual schools: A study of virtual schools in the United States.* Retrieved November 15, 2005, from http://www.wested.org/online_pubs/virtualschools.pdf

Cobb, Casey D., & Glass, Gene V. (1999). Ethnic segregation in Arizona charter schools. *Education Policy Analysis Archives, 7*(1). Retrieved November 15, 2005, from http://epaa.asu.edu/epaa/v7n1/

Cohen, Rick. (2007). *Strategic grantmaking: Foundations and the school privatization movement.* Washington, DC: National Committee for Responsive Philanthropy. Retrieved December 1, 2007 from http://www.ncrp.org/downloads/NCRP2007-StrategicGrantmaking-FINAL-LowRes.pdf

Compact edition of the Oxford English Dictionary. (1971). Oxford, United Kingdom: Oxford University Press.

Conant, James Bryant. (1970). *My several lives* New York: Harper & Row.

Crampton, Faith E., & Bauman, Paul. (1998, April). *A new challenge to fiscal equity: Educational entrepreneurship and its implications for states, districts, and schools.* Paper presented at the annual meeting of the American Educational Research Association, San Diego, CA.

Crawford, James. (2002). *Census 2000: A guide for the perplexed.* Retrieved November 16, 2007, from http://ourworld.compuserve.com/homepages/jWCRAWFORD/census02.htm

Cremin, Lawrence A. (1990). *Popular education and its discontents.* New York: HarperCollins.

Cronbach, Lee J., & Associates. (1980). *Toward reform of program evaluation.* San Francisco: Jossey-Bass.

Cummins, Jim. (1999). *Language, power and pedagogy.* Retrieved April 25, 2007, from http://www.iteachilearn.com/cummins/lpp.html

Darling-Hammond, Linda. (2000). Teacher quality and student achievement: A review of state policy evidence. *Education Policy Analysis Archives, 8*(1). Retrieved April 24, 2007, from http://epaa.asu.edu/epaa/v8n1/.

Darling-Hammond, Linda; Holtzman, Deborah J.; Gatlin, Su Jin; & Heilig, Julian V. (2005). Does teacher preparation matter? Evidence about teacher certification, Teach for America, and teacher effectiveness. *Education Policy Analysis Archives, 13*(42). Retrieved April 26, 2007, from http://epaa.asu.edu/epaa/v13n42/

de Graaf, John; Waan, David; & Naylor, Thomas H. (2001). *Affluenza: The all-consuming epidemic.* San Francisco: Barrett-Koehler.

Delpit, Lisa D. (1988). The silenced dialogue: Power and pedagogy in educating other people's children. *Harvard Educational Review, 58*(3), 280–298.

Delpit, Lisa D. (1996). *Other people's children: Cultural conflict in the classroom.* New York: The New Press.

Dew-Becker, Ian, & Gordon, Robert J. (2005). *Where did the productivity growth go? Inflation dynamics and the distribution of income* (Working Paper No. 11842). New York: National Bureau of Economic Research.

Diamond, Jared. (1997). *Guns, germs, and steel: The fates of human socities.* New York: W. W. Norton.

Dorn, Sherman. (2007). *Accountability Frankenstein: Understanding and taming the monster.* Charlotte, NC: Information Age.

Draut, Tamara. (2007). *Borrowing to stay healthy.* New York: Demos Retrieved March 6, 2007, from http://demos.org/page495.cfm

Draut, Tamara. (2005). *The plastic safety net: The reality behind debt in America.* New York: Demos: A Network for Ideas & Action.

Easterlin, Richard A. (2004). *The reluctant economist: Perspectives on economics, economic history, and demography.* Cambridge, United Kingdom: Cambridge University Press.

Egan, Timothy. (2006). *The worst hard time: The untold story of those who survived the Great American Dust Bowl.* Boston: Houghton Mifflin.

Ehrenreich, Barbara (1989). *Fear of falling: The inner life of the middle class.* New York: Harper Collins.

Ellwein, Mary Catherine, & Glass, Gene V. (1989). Ending social promotion in Waterford: Appearances and reality. In Lorrie A. Shepard & Mary Lee Smith (Eds.), *Flunking grades: Research and policies on retention* (pp. 151-173). London: Falmer Press.

El Nassar, Haya. (2006, March 2). Report: Hispanics lagging in education. *USA Today*, p. 3A.

Epsey, David K. (2007). *Annual report to the nation on the status of cancer, 1975-2004, featuring cancer in American Indians and Alaska Natives.* Retrieved October 15, 2007, from http://www.cancer.org/docroot/NWS/content/NWS_1_1x_Decline_in_Cancer_Deaths_Doubles.asp

Escamilla, Kathy; Shannon, Sheila; Carlos, Silvana; & Garcia, Jorge. (2003). Breaking the code: Colorado's defeat of the anti-bilingual education initiative (Amendment 31). *Bilingual Research Journal, 27*(3), 357-382.

Espenshade, Thomas J. (1984). *Investment in children.* Washington, DC: Urban Institute Press.

Farhi, Paul. (2007, January 21). Five myths about U.S. kids outclassed by the rest of the world. *Washington Post*, p. B2.

Federal Reserve. (2006). *Flow of funds accounts, balance sheet tables: Total household liabilities.* Retrieved December 3, 2007 from http://www.federalreserve.gov/releases/z1/

Fetler, Mark. (1997a). Where have all the teachers gone? *Education Policy Analysis Archives, 5*(2). Retrieved April 24, 2007, from http://epaa.asu.edu/epaa/v5n2.html

Fetler, Mark. (1997b). Staffing up and dropping out: Unintended consequences of high demand for teachers. *Education Policy Analysis Archives, 5*(16). Retrieved April 24, 2007, from http://epaa.asu.edu/epaa/v5n16.html

Finer, Lawrence B.; Frohwirth, L. F.; Dauphinee, L. A.; Singh, S., & Moore, A. M. (2005). Reasons U.S. women have abortions: Quantitative and qualitative perspectives. *Perspectives on Sexual and Reproductive Health, 37*(3), 110-118.

Flesch, Rudolph. (1955). *Why Johnny can't read.* New York: Harper & Row.

Flesch, Rudolph. (1956). *Teaching Johnny to read.* New York: Grosset and Dunlap.

Flesch, Rudolph. (1981). *Why Johnny still can't read: A new look at the scandal of our schools.* New York: Harper & Row.

Ford, Larry R. (1986). Multiunit housing in the American city. *Geographical Review, 76*(4), 390-407.

Frankenberg, Erica, & Lee, Chungmei. (2003). Charter schools and race: A lost opportunity for integrated education. *Education Policy Analysis Archives, 11*(32). Retrieved November 15, 2005, from http:// epaa.asu.edu/epaa/v11n32/

Frey, William H. (2007). *Mapping the growth of older America: Seniors and boomers in the early 21st century.* Washington, DC: Brookings Institution.

Friedman, Milton. (1955). The role of government in education. In R. A. Solo (Ed.), *Economics and the public interest* (pp. 123-144). New Brunswick, NJ: Rutgers University Press.

Friedman, Thomas L. (2005). *The world is flat: A brief history of the twenty-first century.* New York: Farrar, Straus & Giroux.

Fry, R. (2005). *The high schools Hispanics attend: Size and other key characteristics.* Washington, DC: Pew Hispanic Center. Retrieved November 8, 2005, from http://pewhispanic.org/reports/report.php?ReportID=54

Fuller, Bruce. (Ed.) *Inside charter schools: The paradox of radical decentralization.* Cambridge, MA: Harvard University Press.

Gándara, Patricia. (1994). Choosing higher education: Educationally ambitious Chicanos and the path to social mobility. *Education Policy Analysis Archives, 2*(8). Retrieved June 19, 2005 from http:// epaa.asu.edu/epaa/v2n8.html

Gándara, Patricia. (1995). *Over the ivy walls: The educational mobility of low-income Chicanos.* Albany: State University of New York Press.

General Accounting Office. (1993). *Educational achievement standards: NAGB's approach yields misleading interpretations.* Washington, DC: Author.

Gibson, Campbell, & Jung, Kay. (2002). *Historical census statistics on population totals by race, 1790 to 1990, and by Hispanic origin, 1970 to 1990, for the United States, regions, divisions, and states* (Working Paper Series No. 56). Washington, DC: Population Division, U. S. Census Bureau.

Gilbert, Dennis. (1997). *American class structure in an age of growing inequality* (5th ed.). Belmont, CA: Wadsworth.

Glass, Gene V. (1970). *Proceedings of the 1970 International Conference on Testing Problems.* Princeton, NJ: Educational Testing Service.

Glass, Gene V. (1978). Standards and criteria. *Journal of Educational Measurement, 15*(4), 237-261. A revised version retrieved March 5, 2007, from http://glass.ed.asu.edu/gene/papers/standards/

Glass, Gene V. (1987). What works: Politics and research. *Educational Researcher, 16,* 5-10.

Glass, Gene V. (1989). Using student test scores to evaluate teachers. In Jason Millman & Linda Darling-Hammond (Eds.), *New handbook of teacher evaluation.* Beverly Hills, CA: Sage.

Glass, Gene V. (1994). School choice: A discussion with Herbert Gintis. *Education Policy Analysis Archives*, 2(6). Retrieved April 10, 2007, from http://epaa.asu.edu/epaa/v2n6.html

Glass, Gene V., & Edholm, Cheryl A. (2002). *The AIMS test and the mathematics actually used by Arizona employees* (Document #EPSL-0210-122-EPRU). Tempe: Education Policy Studies Laboratory, Arizona State University.

Glass, Gene V., & Hopkins, Kenneth D. (1996). *Statistical methods in education & psychology* (3rd ed.). Boston: Allyn & Bacon.

Glass, GeneV.; McGaw, Barry; & Smith, Mary Lee. (1981). *Meta-analysis in social research*. Beverly Hills, CA: SAGE.

Glass, G. V.; Cahen, Leonard S.; Smith, Mary Lee; & Filby, Nikola N. (1982). *School class size: Research and policy*. Beverly Hills, CA: Sage.

Goe, Laura. (2002). Legislating equity: The distribution of emergency permit teachers in California. *Education Policy Analysis Archives*, 10(42). Retrieved April 23, 2007, from http://epaa.asu.edu/epaa/v10n42/

Green, Thomas F., with Ericson, David P., & Seidman, Robert H. (1980). *Predicting the behavior of the educational system*. Syracuse, NY: Syracuse University Press.

Greene, Jay P., & Winters, Marcus A. (2007). *How much are public school teachers paid? Civic Report No. 50*. New York: Manhattan Institute for Policy Research. Retrieved April 1, 2007, from http://www.manhattan-institute.org/html/cr_50.htm

Grissom, James B., & Shepard, Lorrie A. (1989). Repeating and dropping out of school. In Lorrie A. Shepard & Mary Lee Smith (Eds.), *Flunking grades: Research and policies on retention* (pp. 34-63). London: Falmer Press.

Gutierrez, Bridget. (2003, March 2). Testing time for third-graders; Bar is raised on little kids; young pupils now must pass a state exam to advance. It might be a tough ride for some. *San Antonio Express-News*, p. A1.

Hagewen, Kellie J., & Morgan, S. Philip. (2005). Intended and ideal family size in the United States, 1970-2002. *Population and Development Review*, 31(3), 507-527.

Hakuta, Kenji; Butler, Yuko Goto; & Witt, Daria. (2000). *How long does it take English learners to attain proficiency?* Retrieved April 22, 2007, from http://www.stanford.edu/~hakuta/Docs/HowLong.pdf

Haney, Walt. (2000). The myth of the Texas miracle in education. *Education Policy Analysis Archives*, 8(41) Retrieved September 19, 2007 from http://epaa.asu.edu/epaa/v8n41/

Hanushek, Eric A. (2002, Fall). The seeds of growth. *Education Next*, 10-17.

Happy talk on school reform. (2005, October 25). *New York Times.* Retrieved June 12, 2006 from http://www.nytimes.com/2005/10/22/opinion/22sat3.html?_r=1&oref=slogin.

Hargraves, J. Lee. (2004). *Trends in health insurance coverage and access among Black, Latino and White Americans, 2001-2003* (Tracking Report No. 11). Washington, DC: Center for Studying Health System Change.

Harris, Marvin. (1979). *Cultural materialism: The struggle for a science of culture.* New York: Random House.

Harris, Marvin. (1987). *Why nothing works: The anthropology of daily life* (Original title *America now: The anthropology of a changing culture*). New York: Touchstone Books.

Henry, Tamara. (1998, February 25). Poor academic showing hurts U.S. high schoolers. *USA Today,* p. 1-A.

Herszenhorn, David M. (2007, April 25). Billionaires start $60 million schools effort. *New York Times.*

Higham, John. (1955). *Strangers in the land: Patterns of American nativism, 1860-1925.* New Brunswick, NJ: Rutgers University Press.

Hinchey, Patricia H., & Cadiero-Kaplan, K. (2005). The future of teacher education and teaching: Another piece of the privatization puzzle. *Journal for Critical Education Policy Studies,* 3(2). Retrieved December 20, 2005, from http://www.jceps.com/index.php?pageID=article&articleID=48

Hobbs, F., & Stoops, N. (2002). *Demographic trends in the 20th century.* Washington, DC: U.S. Census Bureau, Census 2000 Special Reports, Series CENSR-4, U.S. Government Printing Office.

Holmes, Charles T. (1989). Grade level retention effects: A meta-analysis of research studies. In Lorrie A. Shepard & Mary Lee Smith (Eds.), *Flunking grades: Research and policies on retention* (pp. 16-33). London: Falmer Press.

House, Ernest R. (1999). Race and policy. *Education Policy Analysis Archives,* 7(16). Retrieved November 9, 2005, from http://epaa.asu.edu/epaa/v7n16.html

Howe, Kenneth, & Eisenhart, Margaret. (2000). *A study of Boulder Valley School District's open enrollment system.* Boulder, CO: Boulder Valley School District. Retrieved November 27, 2005, from http://www.bvsd.k12.co.us/downPdf/openenroll_report.pdf

Howe, Kenneth; Eisenhart, Margaret; & Betebenner, Damian. (2001). School choice crucible: A case study of Boulder Valley. *Phi Delta Kappan,* 83(2), 137-146. (Condensed and reprinted, 2002, under the title Research scotches school choice. *Education Digest,* 67(5), 10-17.) Retrieved November 27, 2005, from http://www.pdkintl.org/kappan/k0110how.htm

Hudson Institute's Bradley Center for Philanthropy and Civic Renewal, "Giving Better, Giving Smarter: Six Years Later" (edited transcript of a breakfast discussion, May 15, 2003, Washington, DC), http://www.hudson.org/files/pdf_upload/Transcript_2003_05_15.pdf

Huerta, Luis A. (2000). Losing public accountability: A home schooling charter. In Bruce Fuller (Ed.), *Inside charter schools: The paradox of radical decentralization* (pp. 177-202). Cambridge, MA: Harvard University Press.

Huerta, Luis A.; Gonzalez, Maria-Fernanda; & d'Entremont, Chad (2006). Cyber and home school charter schools: Adopting policy to new forms of public schooling. *Peabody Journal of Education, 81*(1), 103-139.

Hutchins, Robert Maynard. (1972). The great anti-school campaign. *The great ideas today.* Chicago: Encyclopedia Britannica.

Ingersoll, Richard. (2001). Teacher turnover and teacher shortages: An organizational analysis. *American Educational Research Journal, 38*(3), 499-534.

Joint Center for Housing Studies of Harvard University. (2006). *The state of the nation's housing 2006.* Cambridge, MA: Harvard University.

Jones, Lyle V., & Olkin, Ingram. (Eds.). (2004). *The nation's report card: Evolution and perspectives.* Bloomington, IN: Phi Delta Kappa Educational Foundation.

Kirp, David L. (2005). This little student went to market. In R. H. Hersh & J. Merrow (Eds.), *Declining by degrees: Higher education at risk* (pp. 116-124). New York: Palgrave Macmillan.

Klesmer, H. (1994). Assessment and teacher perceptions of ESL student achievement. *English Quarterly, 26*(3), 5-7.

Klopfenstein, Kristin. (2004a). The advanced placement expansion of the 1990s: How did traditionally underserved students fare? *Education Policy Analysis Archives, 12*(68). Retrieved December 2, 2005, from http://epaa.asu.edu/epaa/v12n68/

Klopfenstein, Kristin. (2004b). Advanced Placement: Do minorities have equal opportunity? *Economics of Education Review, 23*(2), 115-131.

Kosar, Kevin. R. (2005). *Failing grades: The federal politics of education standards.* Boulder, CO: Lynne Rienner.

Kossan, Pat. (2002, March 23). School tax credits fail poor. *Arizona Republic,* p. A1.

Kossan, Pat. (2007, March 24). Charter scores slide despite NFL funding. *Arizona Republic,* pp. A1, A19.

Kossan, Pat. (2007, May 3). 'Traditional' schools making a comeback. *Arizona Republic,* p. B1.

Kossan, Pat. (2007, September 4). Arizona's charters overstate their enrollments, audits show. *Arizona Republic,* p. A1.

Kossan, Pat. (2007, September 12). Principal keeps job after failing to report molest. *Arizona Republic*, p. A1.

Kossan, Pat. (2007, December 21). Schools misused funding, state says. *Arizona Republic*, p. A1.

Kozol, Jonathan. (1991). *Savage inequalities: Children in America's schools.* New York: HarperCollins.

Krugman, Paul. (2006, February 27). Graduates versus oligarchs. *New York Times*, p. A20.

Kuhn, Thomas S. (1962). *The structure of scientific revolutions.* Chicago: University of Chicago Press.

Laczko-Kerr, Ildi, & Berliner, David C. (2002). The effectiveness of "Teach for America" and other under-certified teachers on student academic achievement: A case of harmful public policy. *Education Policy Analysis Archives, 10*(37). Retrieved April 26, 2007, from http://epaa.asu.edu/epaa/v10n37/

Leo, John. (1998, March 9). Hey! We're No. 19! *U.S. News & World Report*, p. 14.

Levin, Henry M. (1990). The theory of choice applied to education. In W. H. Clune & John F. Witte (Eds.), *Choice and control in American education, Vol. I. The theory of choice and control in education* (pp. 247-284). New York: Falmer Press.

Levin, Henry M. (2002) A comprehensive framework for evaluating education vouchers. *Educational Evaluation and Policy Analysis, 24*(3), 159-174.

Lichten, William. (2000). Whither advanced placement? *Education Policy Analysis Archives, 8*(29). Retrieved December 2, 2005, from http://epaa.asu.edu/epaa/v8n29.html.

Lilly, Scott. (2007). *Beyond justice: Bush administration's Labor Department abuses labor union regulatory authorities.* Washington, DC: Center for American Progress.

Lines, P. (1998). *Homeschoolers: Estimating numbers and growth.* National Institute on Student Achievement, Curriculum, and Assessment, Office of Education Research and Improvement: U.S. Department of Education.

Linn, Robert L., & Welner, Kevin G. (Eds.). (2007). *Race-conscious policies for assigning students to schools: Social science research and the Supreme Court cases.* Washington, DC: National Academy of Education.

Lippmann, Walter. (1982). Conversation with Eric Sevareid, February 22, 1965. Quoted in *Bartlett's familiar quotations*, p. 1013.

Lipsitz, George. (2006). *The possessive investment in whiteness: How white people profit from identity politics.* Philadelphia: Temple University Press.

Lowell, B. Lindsay, & Salzman, Hal. (2007). *Into the eye of the storm: Assessing the evidence on science and engineering education, quality, and workforce demand*. Washington, DC: The Urban Institute.

Lubienski, Christopher, & Gulosino, Charisse. (2007). *Choice, competition, and organizational orientation: A geo-spatial analysis of charter schools and the distribution of educational opportunities*. New York: National Center for the Study of Privatization in Education, Columbia University.

Mabin, Connie. (2002, August 1). Most schools get good grades; 162 rated low-performing. *Associated Press*.

Madaus, George, & Clarke, Marguerite. (2001). The adverse impact of high-stakes testing on minority students: Evidence from one hundred years of test data. In Gary Orfield & Mindy L. Kornhaber (Eds.), *Raising standards or raising barriers? Inequality and high-stakes testing in public education* (pp. 85-106). New York: Century Foundation.

Markley, Melanie. (1997, August 10). Texas system pushes better schools; Study pegs program as "one of the better ones in the nation." *Houston Chronicle*, p. A37

McDevitt, T. M. (1999). *World population profile: 1998*. Washington, DC: U.S. Government Printing Office.

McNeil, Linda. (2005). Faking equity: High-stakes testing and the education of Latino youth. In Angela Valenzuela (Ed.), *Leaving children behind: How "Texas-style" accountability fails Latino youth* (pp. 57-111). Albany: State University of New York Press.

Meehl, Paul E. (1967). Theory-testing in psychology and physics: A methodological paradox. *Philosophy of Science, 34*, 103-15.

Meehl. Paul E. (1978). Theoretical risks and tabular asterisks: Sir Karl, Sir Ronald, and the slow progress of soft psychology. *Journal of Consulting and Clinical Psychology, 46*, 806-834.

Milanowski, Anthony. (2003). An exploration of the pay levels needed to attract students with mathematics, science and technology skills to a career in K-12 teaching. *Education Policy Analysis Archives, 11*(50). Retrieved April 25, 2007, from http://epaa.asu.edu/epaa/v11n50/

Millman, Jason, & Darling-Hammond, Linda. (Eds.) *New handbook of teacher evaluation*. Beverly Hills, CA: Sage.

Miron, Gary; Cullen, Anne; Applegate, E. Brooks; & Farrell, Patricia. (2007). *Evaluation of the Delaware charter school reform: Final report*. Kalamazoo, MI: The Evaluation Center, Western Michigan University.

Mishel, Lawrence. (2007). *Jay Greene's persistent misuse of data for teacher pay comparisons*. Washington, DC: Economic Policy Institute. Retrieved April 5, 2007, from http://www.epi.org/content.cfm/webfeatures_viewpoints_teacher_pay_comparions

Mishel, Lawrence, & Eisenbrey, Ross. (2006). *What's wrong with the economy*. Washington, DC: Economic Policy Institute. Retrieved March 7, 2007, from http://www.epi.org/content.cfm/pm110

Mishel, Lawrence; Ettlinger, Michael; & Gould, Elise. (2004). *Less cash in their pockets: Trends in incomes, wages, taxes, and health spending of middle-income families*. Washington, DC: Economic Policy Institute. Retrieved February 13, 2006 from http://www.epi.org/content.cfm/bp154

Molnar, Alex. (1996). *Giving kids the business: The commercialization of America's schools*. Boulder, CO: Westview/HarperCollins.

Molnar, Alex. (2000). *Vouchers, class size reduction, and student achievement: Considering the evidence*. Bloomington, IN: Phi Delta Kappa.

Molnar, Alex. (2001). Calculating the benefits and costs of for-profit public education. *Education Policy Analysis Archives, 9*(15). Retrieved December 1, 2006 from http://epaa.asu.edu/epaa/v9n15.html

Molnar, Alex. (2005). *School commercialism: From democratic ideal to market economy*. New York: RoutledgeFalmer.

Mora, Jorge, & Taylor, J. Edward. (2006). Determinants of migration, destination, and sector choice: Disentangling individual, household, and community effects. In Maurice Schiff & Çaglar Özden (Eds.), *International migration, remittances and the brain drain* (pp. 21-51). Washington, DC: World Bank and Palgrave Macmillan.

Morris, Charles R. (1996). *The AARP: America's most powerful lobby and the clash of generations*. New York: Times Books/Random House.

Murnane, Richard. (1986). Comparisons of private and public schools: The critical role of regulations. In D. Levy (Ed.), *Private education studies in choice and public policy*. New York: Oxford University Press.

Nambury, S. R.; Pellegrino, James W.; Bertenthal, Meryl W.; Mitchell, Karen J.; & Jones, Lee R. (Eds.). (2000). *Grading the nation's report card: Research from the evaluation of NAEP*. Washington, DC: National Academies Press.

National Center for Education Statistics. (1995b). *America's teachers ten years after "A nation at risk."* Washington, DC: U. S. Department of Education Office of Educational Research and Improvement, NCES 95-766.

National Center for Education Statistics. (2006). *Digest of Education Statistics 2006*. Washington, DC: U.S. Department of Education. Retrieved September 19, 2007, from http://nces.ed.gov/programs/digest/

National Center for Education Statistics. (2007). *Mapping 2005 state proficiency standards onto the NAEP scales* (NCES 2007–482). Washington, DC: U.S. Government Printing Office.

National Commission on Excellence in Education. (1983). *A nation at risk: The imperative for educational reform*. Washington, DC: U.S. Department

of Education. Retrieved June 19, 2007 from http://www.ed.gov/pubs/
NatAtRisk/index.html

National Commission on Mathematics and Science Teaching for the 21st
Century. (2000). *Before it's too late: A report to the nation from the National
Commission on Mathematics and Science Teaching for the 21st Century.*
Washington, DC: U.S. Department of Education.

National Science Foundation. (2004). *Science and engineering indicators 2004.*
Washington, DC: National Science Foundation.

New Jersey School Board Association. (1999). *Local education foundation survey results.* Trenton: New Jersey School Board Association.

Nichols, Sharon L., & Berliner, David C. (2007). *Collateral damage: How high-
stakes testing corrupts America's schools.* Cambridge, MA: Harvard Education Press.

Nichols, Sharon L.; Glass, Gene V.; & Berliner, David C. (2006). High-
stakes testing and student achievement: Does accountability pressure
increase student learning? *Education Policy Analysis Archives, 14*(1).
Retrieved January 15, 2007, from http://epaa.asu.edu/epaa/v14n1/

Nichols, Sharon L., & Good, Thomas. (2004). *America's teenagersmyths and
realities: Media images, schooling, and the social costs of indifference.* Mahwah, NJ: Erlbaum.

Nickel, James. (1997). The liberty dimension of historic and contemporary
segregation. *Law and Philosophy, 16,* 259-277.

O'Connor, James. (1987). *The meaning of crisis: A theoretical introduction.*
New York: Basil Blackwell.

Odden, Allan R. (Ed.) (1992). *Rethinking school finance: An agenda for the
1990s.* San Francisco, CA: Jossey-Bass.

Orfield, Gary, & Kornhaber, Mindy L. (Eds.). (2001). *Raising standards or
raising barriers? Inequality and high-stakes testing in public education.* New
York: Century Foundation.

Orfield, Gary. (2003). Foreword to Frankenberg, Erica & Lee, Chungmei.
(2003). Charter schools and race: A lost opportunity for integrated
education. *Education Policy Analysis Archives, 11*(32). Retrieved
November 15, 2005, from http://epaa.asu.edu/epaa/v11n32/

Packard, Vance. (1957). *The hidden persuaders.* New York: David McKay.

Padilla, Raymond. (2005). High-stakes testing and educational accountability as social constructions across cultures. In Angela Valenzuela
(Ed.), *Leaving children behind: How "Texas-style" accountability fails Latino
youth.* (pp. 249-262). Albany: State University of New York Press.

Paulson, A. (2004). Virtual schools: Real concerns. *Christian Science Monitor.*
May 4, 2004. Retrieved November 15, 2005, from http://www
.csmonitor.com/2004/0504/p11s02-legn.html.

People for the American Way. (2003). *Who gets the credit? Who pays the consequences? the Illinois tuition tax credit.* Washington, DC: People for the American Way.

Peterson, Peter G. (1996). *Will America grow up before it grows old: How the coming Social Security crisis threatens you, your family and your country.* New York: Random House.

Peterson, Peter G. (2000).*Gray dawn: How the coming age wave will transform Americaand the world.* New York: Three Rivers Press.

Pew Hispanic Center. (2006). *Modes of entry for the unauthorized migrant population.* Retrieved February 26, 2007, from http://pewhispanic.org/files/factsheets/19.pdf

Pew Hispanic Center and Pew Forum on Religion & Public Life. (2007). *Changing faiths: Latinos and the transformation of American religion.* Washington, DC: PEW Hispanic Center.

Putnam, Robert D. (2000). *Bowling alone: The collapse and revival of American community.* New York: Simon & Schuster.

RAND. (2005). *Future health and medical care spending of the elderly.* Washington, DC: RAND Corporation. Retrieved October 5, 2005, from http://www.rand.org/publications/RB/RB9146/

Raspberry, William. (1998, March 12). American 12th-graders scored at the very bottom of the rankings. *Washington Post*, p. A-15.

Ravitch, Diane. (2007, December 5). Is U.S. education better than ever? *The Huffington Post.* Retrieved December 9, 2007 from http://www.huffingtonpost.com/diane-ravitch/is-us-education-better-_b_75441.html

Reimers, David M. (1985). *Still the golden door: The Third World comes to America.* New York: Columbia University Press.

Renzulli, L., & Evans, L. (2005). School choice, charter schools, and white flight. *Social Problems, 52*(3), 398-418.

Richburg, Keith B. (1985, October 19). Japanese education: Admired but not easily imported. *Washington Post*, pp. A1, A4.

Rickover, Hyman. (1959). *Education and freedom.* New York: E. P. Dutton.

Rickover, Hyman. (1962). *Swiss schools and ours: Why theirs are better.* Boston, MA: Little Brown & Co.

Rickover, Hyman. (1963). *American education, a national failure: The problem of our schools and what we can learn from England.* New York: E. P. Dutton.

Rolstad, Kellie; Mahoney, Kate; & Glass, Gene V. (2005). The big picture: A meta-analysis of program effectiveness research on English Language Learners. *Educational Policy, 19*(4), 1-23.

Rothstein, Richard. (1998). *The way we were? the myths and realities of America's student achievement.* Washington, DC: The Century Foundation.

Rothstein, Richard; Jacobsen, Rebecca; & Widler, Tamara. (2006, November). *"Proficiency for all": An oxymoron.* Paper prepared for the symposium, Examining America's Commitment to Closing Achievement Gaps: NCLB and Its Alternatives, sponsored by the Campaign for Educational Equity, Teachers College, Columbia University.

Rudner, Lawrence M. (1999). Scholastic achievement and demographic characteristics of home school students in 1998. *Education Policy Analysis Archives, 7*(8). Retrieved November 23, 2005, from http://epaa.asu .edu/epaa/v7n8/

Sandia National Laboratories. (1993). Perspectives on education in America: An annotated briefing. *Journal of Educational Research, 86*(5), 259-310.

Sax, L. J.; Astin, A. W.; Korn, W. S.; & Mahoney, K. M. (2000). *The American freshman: National norms for fall 2000.* Los Angeles: Higher Education Research Institute, UCLA.

Schor, Juliet B. (1998). *The overspent American: Upscaling, downshifting, and the new consumer.* New York: Basic Books.

Shepard, Lorrie A., & Smith, Mary Lee. (Eds.). *Flunking grades: Research and policies on retention.* London: Falmer Press.

Silberman, Charles E. (1970). *Crisis in the classroom.* New York: Random House.

Smith, Adam. (2000). *The theory of moral sentiments.* Amherst, NY: Prometheus Books.

Smith, Mary Lee, with Miller-Kahn, Linda; Heinecke, Walt; Jarvis, Patricia F.; & Noble, Audrey. (2003). *Political spectacle and the fate of American schools.* New York: Routledge/Falmer.

Snyder, Thomas D. (1993). *120 years of American education: A statistical portrait.* Washington, DC: US Department of Education, National Center for Education Statistics.

Sperling, John; Helburn, Suzanne; George, Samuel; Morris, John; & Hunt, Carl. (2004). *The great divide: Retro vs. metro America.* Sausalito, CA: PoliPoint Press.

Spencer, Jason. (2006, January 1). Schools accused of cheating: Three low-income Acres Homes elementaries had big TAKS gains. *Houston Chronicle,* p. 1.

Stake, Robert E. (1970). National Assessment. In Gene V. Glass (Ed.), *Proceedings of the 1970 International Conference on Testing Problems* (pp. 53-66). Princeton, NJ: Educational Testing Service.

Stake, Robert E. (2007, February 4). NAEP, report cards and education: A review essay. *Education Review, 10*(1). Retrieved February 17, 2007, from http://edrev.asu.edu/essays/v10n1index.html

Statistical Abstract of the United States: 2004-2005. Washington, DC: Government Printing Office. Retrieved November 15, 2005, from http://www.census.gov/prod/www/statistical-abstract-04.html

Stedman, Lawrence C. (1996). Respecting the evidence: The achievement crisis remains real. *Education Policy Analysis Archives, 4*(7). Retrieved November 8, 2005 from http://epaa.asu.edu/epaa/v4n7.html

Steinhauer, Jennifer. (2007, February 16). A school district with low taxes and no schools. *New York Times.* Retrieved February 20, 2007, from http://www.nytimes.com/2007/02/16/us/16scottsdale.html

Stevens, D. (2005, August 12). On every box of cake mix, evidence of Freud's theories. *New York Times.* Retrieved November 24, 2005 from http://movies2.nytimes.com/2005/08/12/movies/12self.html?ex=1132894800&en=50eefa3934e4d1da&ei=5070

Streater, J. (2005, June 2). Stratification is inevitable result. *Boulder Daily Camera,* p. 33.

Stufflebeam, Daniel L.; Jaeger, Richard M.; & Scriven, Michael. (1991). *Summative evaluation of the National Assessment Governing Board's inaugural effort to set achievement levels on the National Assessment of Educational Progress.* Washington, DC: National Assessment Governing Board.

Sullivan, Teresa A.; Warren, Elizabeth; & Westbrook, Jay Lawrence. (2000). *The fragile middle class: Americans in debt.* New Haven, CT: Yale University Press.

Suro, Robert; Fry, Richard; & Passel, Jeffrey. (2006). *Hispanics and the 2004 election: Population, electorate and voters.* Washington, DC: Pew Hispanic Center.

Thomas, W. P., & Collier, V. P. (2002). *A national study of school effectiveness for language minority students' long-term academic achievement.* Retrieved April 22, 2007 from http://www.crede.org/research/llaa/1.1es.html

Thompson, Holland. (1921). *The age of invention: A chronicle of mechanical conquest. Chronicles of America, Volume 37.* Retrieved February 13, 2006, from the Gutenberg Project: http://www.gutenberg.org

Thompson, William, & Hickey, Joseph. (2005). *Society in focus.* Boston: Pearson.

Tienda, Marta, & Mitchell, Faith. (Eds.). (2006). *Hispanics and the future of America.* Washington, DC: National Academies Press.

Torgerson, Warren S. (1958). *Theory and methods of scaling.* New York: John Wiley.

Torney-Purta, J.; Lehmann, R.; Oswald, H.; & Schulz, W. (2001). *Demokratie und Bildung in 28 Ländern: Politisches Verstehen und Engagement bei Vierzehnjährigen* [Democracy and education in 28 nations: Political understanding and engagement among 14-year-olds]. Amsterdam:

International Association for the Evaluation of Educational Achievement.

U.S. Department of Education. (2000). *Trends in educational equity of girls and women.* Washington, DC: Office of Educational Research and Improvement. National Center for Education Statistics, 2000-030.

U.S. Department of Labor. (2006). *100 Years of U.S. consumer spending: Data for the nation, New York City, and Boston* (Report 991). Washington, DC: Author.

Valenzuela, Angela. (Ed.). (2005). *Leaving children behind: How "Texas-style" accountability fails Latino youth.* Albany: State University of New York Press.

Vandevoort, Leslie G.; Amrein-Beardsley, Audrey; & Berliner, David C. (2004). National board certified teachers and their students' achievement. *Education Policy Analysis Archives, 12*(46). Retrieved February 15, 2007, from http://epaa.asu.edu/epaa/v12n46/

Vinovskis, Maris A. (1998). Overseeing the Nation's REPORT CARD: The creation and evolution of the National Assessment Governing Board (NAGB). Retrieved February 17, 2007, from http://www.nagb.org/pubs/95222.pdf

Vrasidas, Charalambos, & Glass, Gene V. (2002). *Distance education and distributed learning.* Charlotte, NC: Information Age.

Warren, Elizabeth; Sullivan, Teresa A.; & Jacoby, Melissa B. (2000). Medical problems and bankruptcy filings. Retrieved March 5, 2007, from the Social Science Research Network: http://papers.ssrn.com/sol3/papers.cfm?abstract_id=224581

Warren, Elizabeth, & Tyagi, Amelia Warren. (2003). *The two-income trap: Why middle-class mothers and fathers are going broke.* New York: Basic Books.

Wells, Amy S.; Holme, J. J.; Lopez, A., & Cooper, C. W. (2000). Charter schools and racial and social class segregation: Yet another sorting machine? In R. Kahlenberg (Ed.), *A notion at risk: Preserving education as an engine for social mobility* (pp. 169-222). New York: Century Foundation Press.

Welner, Kevin G. (2000). Taxing the establishment clause: The revolutionary decision of the Arizona Supreme Court in *Kotterman v. Killian. Education Policy Analysis Archives, 8*(36). Retrieved November 27, 2005, from http://epaa.asu.edu/epaa/v8n36.html

Welner, Sylvia, & Welner, Kevin G. (2005). Small doses of arsenic: A Bohemian woman's story of survival. Lanham, MD: Hamilton Books.

Wirt, John; Choy, Susan; Gerald, Debra; Provasnik, Stephen; Rooney, Patrick; Watanabe, Satoshi; et al. (2002). *The condition of education, 2002.* Washington, DC: U.S. Department of Education.

Will, George. (2007, May 31). The case for conservatism. *Washington Post*, p. B7.

Willinsky, John. (2000). *If only we knew: Increasing the public value of social science research*. New York: Routledge.

Wilson, Glen Y. (2000). Effects on funding equity of the Arizona Tax Credit Law. *Education Policy Analysis Archives, 8*(38). Retrieved November 27, 2005, from http://epaa.asu.edu/epaa/v8n38.html

Wilson, William Julius. (1987). *The truly disadvantaged*. Chicago: University of Chicago Press.

Witte, John. (1997). *Achievement effects of the Milwaukee Voucher Program*. Paper presented at the American Economics Association Annual Meeting, New Orleans, LA. Retrieved April 20, 2007, from http://www.disc.wisc.edu/choice/aea97.html.

Wraga, William G. (2000). *The comprehensive high school in the United States: A historical perspective*. Paper presented at the meeting of the John Dewey Society, New Orleans, Louisiana. (ERIC Document # ED443170)

Yankelovich, Daniel. (2005, November 25). Ferment and change: Higher education in 2015. *The Chronicle of Higher Education*. Retrieved December 7, 2005, from http://chronicle.com/weekly/v52/i14/14b00601.htm

Zakaria, Fareed. (2006, January 9). We all have a lot to learn. *Newsweek International Edition*. Retrieved February 17, 2007, from http://www.msnbc.msn.com/id/10663340/site/newsweek/

Zimmer, Ron; Krop, Cathy; Kaganoff, Tessa;Ross, Karen E.; & Brewer, Dominic. (2001). *Private giving to public schools and districts in Los Angeles County: A pilot study*. Santa Monica, CA: RAND. Retrieved October 25, 2007 from http://192.5.14.110/pubs/monograph_reports/MR1429/MR1429.sum.html

The following Web sites were frequently accessed for information or data:

http://www.cancer.org
    American Cancer Society

http://www.epi.org
    Economic Policy Institute

http://www.america-tomorrow.com/bracey/EDDRA/
    The Education Disinformation and Detection Reporting Agency

http://epaa.asu.edu/epaa/
Education Policy Analysis Archives, an open access, peer-reviewed journal for education policy analysis

http://edrev.asu.edu/
Education Review, an open access journal of scholarly reviews of books in education

http://www.huffingtonpost.com/gerald-bracey/
Gerald Bracey's blog at the Huffington Post

http://www.nass.usda.gov
National Agricultural Statistics Service of the United States Department of Agriculture

http://nces.ed.gov/
The National Center for Education Statistics of the United States Department of Education

http://www.cdc.gov/nchs/
National Center for Health Statistics

http://www.ncrp.org/
National Committee for Responsive Philanthropy

http://www.pbs.org/
Public Broadcasting System

http://pewhispanic.org
Pew Hispanic Center

http://www.prb.org
Population Reference Bureau

http://www.rand.org/
RAND Organization

http://www.bea.gov
United States Bureau of Economic Analysis

http://www.census.gov
United States Census Bureau

http://www.federalreserve.gov
United States Federal Reserve

http://www.urban.org
The Urban Institute

Listing of Exhibits

Acknowledgments

 The work reported here started in what is increasingly an unusual way. In February 2005, a friend asked if I would make a presentation about education to her current affairs group. This group had convened each month since the mid-1930s in the homes of the various participants in Boulder, Colorado, to listen to talks by experts and thus keep current with what is going on in the world. Such gatherings for educational purposes were common in the 1920s and into the 1930s, often put together by labor unions. Academics often took seriously their responsibility to teach a broader audience than just their tuition paying students. Intellectual life was not confined to the universities, and labor unions convened meetings to learn from speakers who took seriously their responsibility to educate a public that was broader than the matriculated members of public universities. The phenomenon is nearly extinct today. Fortunately, my friend's group was keeping the tradition alive. I gathered that they had recently had a couple of bad experiences, one with a volcanologist and another with an economist, and perhaps they would give an educationist a try with hopes of finding a more engaging message. The experience of attempting to represent one's work to those who are not specialists and, who therefore, have every right to be both skeptical of its unfounded claims and impatient with its jargon and technical dissembling is one that I heartily recommend to all scholars. I worked diligently on the talk which lasted a little over an hour. I strove for explanations that were more fundamental than I had ever reached for before. Such an audience had every right not to be impressed with the technical minutia that make up a good bit of how we scholars communicate with each other. The result was beneficial for me; I can only hope that the current affairs group derived some value from it. The outline of that talk became the outline for this book.

The second incarnation of the talk was at the annual meeting of the American Educational Research Association in San Francisco on April 8, 2006. I had been fortunate enough to have been awarded the Distinguished Contributions to Educational Research Award of that organization in 2005, and the award recipient is obliged to give an hour-long speech the following year. I suspect that most past recipients would agree that this is a daunting prospect that haunts them for 12 months. So it was with me. Such a great award demands nothing less than a great speech. This is the sort of pressure that regularly drives academics to fits of grandiosity, a tendency from which I suffer even under less exalted circumstances. The speech I gave on that day was titled "Fertilizer, Pills, & Robots." The "robots" stood for the amazing technological changes in industrial production that have transformed the American economy from a manufacturing economy to a service economy, with consequent pressures to hold down the rising proportion of the GDP devoted to services (among which education is one of the more expensive). Robots have survived and appear in chapter 7 of the present book, although they disappeared from the title.

My children and grandchildren were present at this address. We transported the entire family not already living in San Francisco to the event. It was to be, and has been so far, my last big speech to an audience of considerable size. I spoke about fertilizers, pills, robots, and American education. The speech went well, I think, though I am too much a skeptical empiricist to take completely on faith the limited eye contact, facial expressions, and handshakes that often accompany talks to large audiences. I can, however, attest to one extraordinary experience on that occasion that gave me some hope that these ideas are on the right track. Each of my adult children and stepchildren and their spouses engaged me in a discussion of the speech afterwards, an experience at once both threatening and deeply reassuring. I owe a particular debt to my stepson Kyle, age 30 at the time, a Silicon Valley inhabitant, who listened politely to the speech and then was quiet for a few days, apparently mulling over what he had heard. Then from the back seat of the rental car while wending our way through San Francisco streets with their promiscuous assortment of the homeless and the opulently housed in a seemingly endless search for a parking place, he said, "You know, it might be about robots, but it's also about magnetic strips." It took a young person, attuned to the financial habits of a culture several generations away from the rural to urban migrants or even the women of his grandmother's generation newly liberated from the uncertainties of conception to see that his generation was being shaped by the magnetic strip, that invisible line of information on the back of the plastic credit card. The more I thought about it, the more it became clear that magnetic strips, making possible the invention of the plastic credit card, thus making possible the extension of small amounts of personal credit to individuals, have greatly altered spending habits, and of course saving habits. These ubiquitous occupants of wallets and purses have brought about a culture of consumption that is profoundly influencing public institutions in America. These mundane inventions—fertilizers, pills, robots, magnetic strips—began to fit together. They came for me to represent the technological advances in production and consumption that have so profoundly shaped life in industrialized society in ways that threaten the common good.

My son-in-law Piet's addiction to the *New York Times* has been a boon to the research that went into this volume. My sister-in-law, Janice Friedman, interrupted her studies for her doctor of pharmacy degree to answer my naïve questions on several occasions. The historian Stephen Ambrose was once accused of using his children as research assistants; claims were even made that perhaps some of what he wrote might even have been the ideas of his children. I say, "good on him" and his family.

In the spring of 2007, I conducted a seminar for advanced PhD students in the education policy program at Arizona State University, my home institution. The students and I discussed drafts of chapters and I benefited greatly from their written comments. They deserve my gratitude and more credit than students typically receive: Joseph Axel, Jeff Bale, Gerald Blankson, James Hazard Hall III, Rucheeta Kulkarni, Gina Pazzaglia, Barbel Singer-Bon, and Yun Teng.

One's colleagues contribute in ways largely unknown. Among my many colleagues, Gustavo Fischman, Sherman Dorn, Terrence Wiley, the late Thomas F. Green, and Gerald Bracey deserve special recognition, the latter two for their writings, utterly different in tone and style, undeniably important in their own way. My colleague at Arizona State University, Alex Molnar, has helped me in many ways to see what lies at the bottom of so many education policy proposals; his worldliness, born of his tough upbringing in Chicago, prepared him for his role as one of the foremost education critics of the decade. The less obvious ways colleagues contribute to each other's work is by withholding criticism that when delivered early would staunch the flow of ideas. Ursula Casanova kindly encouraged my pursuit of the topics in this book at a time when encouragement was needed. A more obvious contribution is made when colleagues pour on criticism when ideas need to be cut down to size. My long-time friend Ernest R. House and I have talked about the ideas that led to this book on many occasions. I took some satisfaction from the fact that he did not disagree with me completely after scanning an early précis. Ernie always has a way of evaluating my attempts at a comprehensive account of education policy with the statement, "Well, that's part of it." I hope that this time I've got a bit more of it. Robert E. Stake and Michael Scriven have been especially influential in my life as a researcher, the former for more than 45 years, the latter for more than 42. Their extraordinary contributions to scholarship in education have constantly reminded me that unless intelligence is joined with creativity nothing but conventional thinking and pedantry can result. Casey Cobb kindly read a draft and made helpful suggestions. Sharon Nichols dug up raw materials from an earlier research project on which she and I and David Berliner collaborated. I have learned much from each of them, but especially from the last mentioned. David Berliner and I have been colleagues and friends for more than 20 years now. Our careers have many things in common. We were a part, indeed active participants, in the heady days of the 1960s and 1970s when solutions to the world's problems seemed near at hand; just a few well-done experiments brought off with all the right methods and new knowledge would unlock doors to immense possibilities. I think it is safe to say that we both have been disabused of these fantasies for some time now. Where we once thought that science would lead education, we now understand that politics is in the driver's seat. And in place of the discovery of great truths that will revolutionize society, perhaps I speak for him too when I say that we will settle for simple justice.

I have had the good fortune during my 45 years in the academic world to have served about equal time in two institutions: first at the University of Colorado at Boulder, and since 1986 at Arizona State University in Tempe. Both universities pride themselves on freedom of inquiry. Kenneth Boulding[1]

1. Kenneth Ewart Boulding (1910-1993); economist, educator, peace activist, poet, and interdisciplinary scholar. "Somewhere … between the specific that has no meaning and the general that has no content there must be, for each purpose and at each level of abstraction, an optimum degree of generality." Boulding, Kenneth. (1956). General systems theory: The skeleton of science. *Management Science, 2*(3), 197-208.

had much to do with setting the intellectual tone of the campus when I taught at Colorado. Boulding had come to Colorado from the University of Michigan in 1967; his impact on the intellectual life of the campus was immediate. Established, very successful universities are sometimes spoiled by their success; they repeat superstitiously the thinking that brought them their laurels in the past. Creative thinking suffers. Boulding surely was never stifled at Ann Arbor, but his arrival in Boulder brought fresh air to an institution in the process of finding its own identity. Both at CU and ASU, wanderings outside one's "field" in search of more general explanations were never punished, as they would have been and frequently are in more rigid universities. I owe them much.

One can find many reasons not to write a book. I have thought up several; my critics will, no doubt, think of others. This book would not have been written were it not for my wife, Sandra Rubin Glass, politely asking and not expecting "No" for an answer to the often posed question, "Are you going to finish that book?"

Appendixes

Appendix A: Notes on Theory, Research, and Policy

Readers steeped in the scholarship of education or those who know my personal contributions in the area may well wonder why there is so little reference to research in the analysis that I have presented and even less reference to theory. And because in the minds of many, policy is closely linked with theory and research, they might wonder how a discussion of education policy can be sustained for so many pages without dealing with the relationship among all three.

The word "theory" has many meanings. A dictionary will list several. Paul Meehl at the time of his death was working on a paper in which he was examining 16 different uses of the term "theory" in the social and behavioral sciences. In the simple and well-developed sciences, a theory must be capable of generating testable ideas and, according to the generally accepted arguments of the philosopher Karl Popper, capable of being empirically disproven. Stephen Hawking described this idea of theory quite succinctly:

> A theory is a good theory if it satisfies two requirements: It must accurately describe a large class of observations on the basis of a model which contains only a few arbitrary elements, and it must make definite predictions about the results of future observations ...

Fertilizers, Pills, and Magnetic Strips: The Fate of Education in America
pp. 281–298
Copyright © 2008 by Information Age Publishing

281

any physical theory is always provisional, in the sense that it is only a hypothesis; you can never prove it. No matter how many times the results of experiments agree with some theory, you can never be sure that the next time the result will not contradict the theory. On the other hand, you can disprove a theory by finding even a single observation which disagrees with the predictions of the theory.[1]

Nothing in the realm of education, or even in a much more limited domain like the learning of meaningful text, can satisfy this definition of theory. Meehl has made this point quite clear in his critique of the use of the notion of theory in the "soft sciences."[2]

In the soft sciences, theory often means little more than a collection of a few names for vaguely delineated concepts, linked, perhaps, by arrows indicated ambiguous flows of influence. Self-concept leads to, causes, influences, or modifies academic achievement in some way or other, and maybe achievement affects self-concept too. Little is accomplished by these lines of argument. The intellectual fashion in scholarship today is to contextualize everything; everything is embedded in something else and the opportunities for saying anything of even marginal relevance are endless. But some contexts are important and others are not. The inability to distinguish important from trivial contexts is a symptom of an absence of any overarching theory of society and education. There is no grand theory of education in its social circumstances that is even worth talking about[3]; and consequently, any one can say almost anything they want about both. Lacking a theory, one must pick a context based on common sense, or an ordinary sense of what is important and what isn't.

---

1.   Hawking, Stephen. (1988). *A brief history of time*. London: Bantam Books. Pp. 10-11.
2.   Meehl, P. E. (1967). Theory-testing in psychology and physics: A methodological paradox. *Philosophy of Science, 34*, 103-15. Meehl. P. E. (1978). Theoretical risks and tabular asterisks: Sir Karl, Sir Ronald, and the slow progress of soft psychology. *Journal of Consulting and Clinical Psychology, 46*, 806-34.
3.   Dershimer, Richard. (circa 1970). Personal communication of Thomas Kuhn's opinion expressed in an interview with Dershimer.

Another use of the word theory denotes what some call a "conceptual framework." Such theories resemble theories in the soft sciences but without the pretensions of measurements and supposed empirical tests. The "conceptual" suggests that indeed such things involve concepts, but the "framework" is only something these concepts are loosely tied to. These conceptual frameworks generally have no dynamic character; they are incapable of generating "definite predictions"—in Hawking's phraseology—but rather at most they might assert that two things are correlated or related, and since almost everything is related to something else, they can not be disproven and consequently have no value as scientific theory. Academic research on education is replete with these conceptual frameworks that move in and out of favor with dizzying rapidity. Theories of organizational change, theories of leadership, theories of teaching; they are seldom little more than neologisms bundled together in loose confederations.

Nonetheless, it is at the level of a conceptual framework that I have chosen to work here. To pretend to anything more precise, or to act as though any theory explains the extraordinarily complex evolution of modern life in the past century is a supererogation of which I wish not to be guilty. My conceptual framework comprises a small number of concepts grounded in ordinary language without exotic meanings. Thomas Green used to refer to philosophy as the analysis of the ordinary. There is much in that approach that appeals to me. I have relied primarily on everyday concepts of economics and politics. However, I am not referring to such things as school finance policies—in fact, these are among the least interesting things to say about education—or the politics of who gets elected to the local school board, or even who gets elected to the White House. Rather, I have looked at American society more generally as it has been shaped by basic economic considerations of production and consumption and how the public's will has been expressed through the political process.

Much has been made in the analysis presented here of *demography*, the description of the population of people; but demography is not a theory, rather it is a set of methods that describe collections of people. There are economic concepts in the analysis, but only of the simplest sort, namely, that people are motivated by *material self-interest*. The notion of material self-interest is quite distinct from the Adam Smith notion of self-interest, which involves the interests of society as a whole.[4] Material self-interest in my conceptual framework is akin to Adam Smith's notion of selfishness, and appears to be a much more potent force in modern societies that depend so greatly on economic growth and consumption of material goods. At the root of those forces shaping contemporary culture in America is technological invention and change. Much about how people live their lives today can be traced to the influence of such fundamental circumstances as food production, human fertility, the advent of the concept of organization,[5] the creation of bureaucracies and oligopolies.[6] Here I wish to single out just one aspect of contemporary life and connect it to these fundamental forces. As for political concepts, nothing more complicated than America's ambivalent courtship with both *oligopoly* and *democracy* has been invoked to account for the influence of the *demos* on education policy. No matter how powerful is the influence of huge corporations on the political process in the United States, at a point the sheer weight of opinion of the voting class will exert itself and prevail. Whether the issue is the war in Viet Nam, the war in Iraq, or Social Security, numbers matter. Finally, my personal preference for psychoanalysis to explain many of the most important aspects of human behavior has not played much of a role in this attempt

4.   Smith, Adam. (2000). *The theory of moral sentiments*. Amherst, NY: Prometheus Books.

5.   Boulding, Kenneth E. (1953). *The organization revolution: A study in the ethics of economic organization*. New York: Harper and Brothers.

6.   Harris, Marvin. (1987). *Why nothing works: The anthropology of daily life* (Original title *America now: The anthropology of a changing culture*). New York: Touchstone Books.

to account for current education policy or extrapolate public education today into the future. However, I do see something akin to the *defense mechanisms* at work in the intellectualizing of motives of both experts and ordinary people around questions of racial and ethnic segregation in public education. No one likes to be accused of being prejudiced, but most of us are. Too often, a policy that segregates *my* children from the children of those *other* people will be rationalized in terms of the superior academic performance of students in "schools of choice" or the need to receive the very best preparation for college so that America can remain internationally competitive.

Those who know of my life-long involvement with empirical research[7] may wonder at its relative absence in these pages. Nothing has been made of a study that claims charter schools outperform traditional public schools or a different study that alleges to show that homeschooled students do better in college than their counterparts in public schools. In the first place, I do not believe that these studies, mired as they are in debates between research methods experts, have any determinative value in shaping the current nature of public education or its future. No proponent of school vouchers ever changed positions based on a study that showed nonvoucher students 2 months ahead in mathematics. When extremely well-controlled experiments show that differences in outcomes exist between competing policies, they are without exception small. Decades of research on class size show tiny benefits can be expected from economically feasible size reductions, but the debate over class size goes on.[8] When poorly controlled comparisons are presented in support of one policy or another, they are discounted by the opposition, as they should be.

7. Glass, Gene V.; McGaw, Barry; & Smith, Mary Lee. (1981). *Meta-analysis in social research*. Beverly Hills, CA: Sage.
8. Glass, Gene V.; Cahen, Leonard S.; Smith, Mary Lee; & Filby, Nikola N. (1982). *School class size: Research and policy*. Beverly Hills, CA: Sage.

Research is used rhetorically in policy debates. Not to advance research in support of one's position is often tantamount to conceding the debate—as if the prosecution put its expert on the stand and the defense called no expert. In rare instances so recondite and far from the public's ability to understand and in instances where a small group of individuals exercises strict control ("contexts of command" as Cronbach[9] and his associates spoke of them) or in places where the stakes are so low that almost no one cares about them, research may actually determine policy. But even these contexts are surprisingly and increasingly rare. Research evidence is marshaled *against* such seemingly "scientific" practices as vaccinating against flu viruses, preventing forest fires, the use of antibiotics, tonsillectomies, global warming, and cutting fat out of your diet. For the most part, research in education functions in a "context of accommodation" where interests are in conflict and the stakes are relatively high. There, research virtually never determines policy. Instead, it is used in the adversarial political process to advance one's cause. Ultimately, the policy will be determined through democratic procedures (direct or representative) because no other way of resolving the policy conflicts works as well. Votes are taken as a way of forcing action and tying off inquiry, which never ends. (As an observer once remarked concerning trials, they end because people get tired of talking; if they were all conducted in writing—as research is— they would never end.)

Research does not determine policy in the areas in which we are interested—human services—in large part because such research has no boundaries, that is, its concerns are virtually unlimited. Such research lacks a "paradigm" in the strict Kuhnian sense: not in the sense in which the word has come to mean virtually everything and nothing in popular pseudointellectual speech, but "paradigm" in the sense that

---

9.   Cronbach, Lee J., & Associates. (1980). *Toward reform of program evaluation*. San Francisco: Jossey-Bass.

Kuhn used it, meaning having an agreed upon set of concepts, problems, measures and methods. On one of the rare occasions when Kuhn was asked whether educational research had a paradigm, or had experienced any recent "paradigm shifts," he seemed barely to understand the question. In *Structure of Scientific Revolutions*, he opined that even psychology was in a "pre-paradigm" state.[10] Without boundaries, a body of research supporting policy A can always be said to be missing elements X, Y and Z, that just happen at the moment to be of critical importance to those who dislike the implications of whatever research has been advanced in support of policy A.

This lack of a paradigm for social scientific and educational research not only makes them suffer from an inability to limit the number of considerations that can be claimed to bear on any one problem, it also means that there are no guidelines on what problems the research will address. The questions that empirical research addresses do not come from (are not suggested by) theories or conceptual frameworks themselves, but rather reflect the interests of the persons who choose them. For example, administrators in one school district choose to study "the culture of absenteeism" among teachers, in so doing they ignore the possibility that sabbaticals for teachers might be a worthy and productive topic for research. The politics of this situation are almost too obvious to mention.

If anything, scholars such as myself tend to study the broad sweep of education in piecemeal fashion, with the result that we delude ourselves through suboptimization—elegant answers to the wrong or unimportant questions—into thinking that we are solving important problems. It has always been my inclination and often my failing to seek broader answers, aggregations, views of whole landscapes. Producing a coherent view of a larger scene always seemed more useful than a high resolution snapshot.

---

10. Kuhn, Thomas S. (1962). *The structure of scientific revolutions*. Chicago: University of Chicago Press.

Appendix B: Programme for International Student Assessment (PISA)

This appendix supplements Chapter Two's section titled "International Assessments 'Prove' There Is an Education Crisis in the U.S."

Exhibit B-1.   PISA 2003 & 2006 Average Scores in Science for 15 Year-Olds

Nation	Science 2003	Science 2006	Gain or Loss
Finland	548	563	15
Hong Kong-China	539	542	3
Canada	519	534	15
Japan	548	531	−17
New Zealand	521	530	9
Australia	525	527	2
Netherlands	524	525	1
Liechtenstein	525	522	−3
Korea	538	522	−16
Germany	502	516	14
Czech Republic	523	513	−10
Switzerland	513	512	−1
Macao-China	525	511	−14
Austria	491	511	20
Belgium	509	510	1
Ireland	505	508	3
Hungary	503	504	1
Sweden	506	503	−3
Poland	498	498	0
Denmark	475	496	21
France	511	495	−16
Iceland	495	491	-4
Latvia	489	490	1
United States	491	489	−2
Slovak Republic	495	488	−7
Spain	487	488	1
Norway	484	487	3
Luxembourg	483	486	3
Russian Federation	489	479	−10

(exhibit continues on next page)

Exhibit B-1. (continued)

Nation	Science 2003	Science 2006	Gain or Loss
Italy	486	475	−11
Portugal	468	474	6
Greece	481	473	−8
Serbia	436	436	0
Uruguay	438	428	−10
Turkey	434	424	−10
Thailand	429	421	-8
Mexico	405	410	5
Indonesia	395	393	−2
Brazil	390	390	0
Tunisia	385	386	1

Exhibit B-2.   PISA 2003 & 2006 Average Scores in Mathematics for 15-Year-Olds

Nation	Math 2003	Math 2006	Gain or Loss
Finland	544	548	4
Hong Kong-China	550	547	−3
Korea	542	547	5
Netherlands	538	531	−7
Switzerland	527	530	3
Canada	532	527	−5
Macao-China	527	525	−2
Liechtenstein	536	525	−11
Japan	534	523	−11
New Zealand	523	522	−1
Belgium	529	520	−9
Australia	524	520	−4
Denmark	514	513	−1
Czech Republic	516	510	−6
Iceland	515	506	−9
Austria	506	505	−1
Germany	503	504	1
Sweden	509	502	−7
Ireland	503	501	−2
France	511	496	−15

(exhibit continues on next page)

Exhibit B-2. (continued)

Nation	Math 2003	Math 2006	Gain or Loss
Poland	490	495	5
Slovak Republic	496	492	−4
Hungary	490	491	1
Luxembourg	493	490	−3
Norway	495	490	−5
Latvia	483	486	3
Spain	485	480	−5
Russian Federation	468	476	8
United States	483	474	−9
Portugal	466	466	0
Italy	466	462	−4
Greece	445	459	14
Serbia	437	435	−2
Uruguay	422	427	5
Turkey	423	424	1
Thailand	417	417	0
Mexico	385	406	21
Indonesia	360	391	31
Tunisia	359	365	6

Exhibit B-3.
PISA 2003 Average Scores in
Reading for 15-Year-Olds

Nation	Average
Finland	543
Korea	534
Canada	528
Australia	525
Liechtenstein	525
New Zealand	522
Ireland	515
Sweden	514
Netherlands	513
Hong Kong-China	510
Belgium	507

(exhibit continues on next page)

Exhibit B-3. (continued)

Nation	Average
Norway	500
Switzerland	499
Japan	498
Macao-China	498
Poland	497
France	496
United States	495
Denmark	492
Iceland	492
Germany	491
Austria	491
Latvia	491
Czech Republic	489
Hungary	482
Spain	481
Luxembourg	479
Portugal	478
Italy	476
Greece	472
Slovak Republic	469
Russian Federation	442
Turkey	441
Uruguay	434
Thailand	420
Serbia	412
Brazil	403
Mexico	400
Indonesia	382
Tunisia	375

Errors in the printed directions on the
Reading test for U.S. students rendered
their data unusable.

Appendix C: The Accountability Pressure Rating[11]

This appendix supplements Chapter Nine.

The determination of our APR relied on a set of portfolios constructed to describe in as much detail as possible the past and current assessment and accountability practices of each state. These portfolios were crafted to tell the "story" of accountability; and therefore, they include a wide range of documentation describing the politics, legislative activity, and impact of a state's high-stakes testing program. The purpose of creating the portfolios was to describe the varied nature, impact, and role of high-stakes testing in each of the 25 study states. Although a concrete description of the laws in each state would provide a summary of accountability activities at the legislative level, they fail to more fully describe the impact of these laws. Therefore the portfolios also included newspaper articles that served as a proxy for legislative implementation and impact. What follows is a more detailed description and rationale of the portfolio contents which included three main sections: (a) an introduction essay, (b) a rewards/sanction sheet, (c) and newspaper stories. These are described in more detail next.

Context for assessing state-level stakes.   The first document in each portfolio was a summary essay of the state's past and current assessment and accountability plan. These essays included some background information (e.g., name of past and current assessment system, implementation strategies), (b) a description of the most current assessment system, and (c) a summary of the rewards and sanctions (e.g., the current and past laws). The goal of this initial portfolio document was to contextualize that state's accountability plan.

---

11.   Based on Nichols, Sharon L.; Glass, Gene V.; & Berliner, David C. (2006). High-stakes testing and student achievement: Does accountability pressure increase student learning? *Education Policy Analysis Archives, 14*(1). Retrieved January 15, 2007, from http://epaa.asu.edu/epaa/v14n1/

Rewards/sanction worksheet. Each portfolio also contained a table that presented a range of questions and answers about what the state can do legally by way of consequences to districts, schools, and students. The structure and content of this table drew heavily on data compiled by the Education Commission of States as of 2002 that described many of the accountability laws on state books as of 2001.[12] In addition to laws, the rewards/sanctions worksheet also provided more detailed information about the law's impact. For example, it might be the case that a teacher can be fired legally, but in reality a state may never have done this. This contrasts with another state where firing a teacher might not only be legal, but the state has already enacted the law and fired some teachers

Media. Newspaper articles were included because they provide a description of local cultural norms. Its value has been noted by others. "Documents are studied to understand culture—or the process and the array of objects, symbols, and meanings that make up social reality shared by members of a society" (Altheide, 1996, p. 2). In addition to their evidentiary role, newspapers reflect societal beliefs, reactions, values, and perspectives of current and historical events and thereby contribute substantially to our shared cultural knowledge of local, national, and international events. Their inclusion represents a unique strategy for measuring the impact of high-stakes testing pressure.

David Altheide's (1996) Ethnographic Content Analysis (ECA) strategy guided the newspaper article selection process. Given the scope and range of newspaper reporting, ECA provided a strategic framework from which a logical and representative selection process emerged. Newspaper selection

---

12. Nichols inquired about how Education Commision of States obtained the information provided in their table. Personal correspondence revealed that the lead researcher in charge of maintaining this database on state-level accountability laws consulted a variety of sources including legal briefs, laws, discussions with state department of education representatives and state department of education Web sites.

strategies based in ECA maximize the probability that all themes represented throughout newspaper documentation are included because the universe of possible newspaper stories are reviewed and re-reviewed with an eye toward themes, content, and emphasis.

> ECA follows a recursive and reflexive movement between concept development-sampling-data, collection-data, coding-data, and analysis-interpretation. The aim is to be systematic and analytic but not rigid. Categories and variables initially guide the study, but others are allowed and expected to emerge throughout the study, including an orientation toward *constant discovery* and *constant comparison* of relevant situations, settings, styles, images, meanings, and nuances (Altheide, 1996, p. 16).

ECA was ideal for this purpose because it allowed the reader to make coding and selection decisions based on her interaction with the documents. This is critical because the range of issues/concerns facing individual states varied widely, and therefore the selection system had to be flexible enough to capture the ongoing changes in reporting styles and content over time and from state to state.

In general, the process of selecting newspaper stories for inclusion in state portfolios involved two major steps. The first step was a two-part pilot process (a) to identify the "searchable" universe of media coverage and relevant themes and content of that coverage and (b) to determine the feasibility of our measurement strategy across five of our study states. The second step grew out of the first and was the systematic application of a news media selection strategy for the remaining 20 study states. The end result was a cross section of thematically representative newspaper articles selected for inclusion in each of the 25 study states' portfolios.

Scaling. The method of "comparative judgments" was adopted for scaling the 25 study states along a hypothetical continuum of accountability pressure (Torgerson, 1958). This scaling method was appropriate for assigning relational values among stimuli with complex, abstract psychological properties. The value of this approach is that judges do not have to assign an *absolute* rating to each stimulus. Rather, it is only necessary that judges make a judgment about which of only two stimuli exhibits *more* of the construct of interest. The "stimulus" in this study is the construct of "pressure" as reflected in the portfolio documentation.

Judges' Ratings

Independent judgments of the pressure associated with each of the 300 possible state pairings were collected. To the judges' data (averaging entries where there were more than one entry per cell), the least-squares solution for unidimensional scale values due to Mosteller[13] was used to calculate rating scores (referred to as the Accountability Pressure Rating, or APR). The judges' estimates of the directed distance between any two states on a hypothetical scale of "high-stakes pressure" were taken as the raw distance data and formed a skew symmetric matrix of order 25 with entries on the interval −4 to +4.

Validity Analysis

As a check on the validity of the rating scale, two expert educators (blind to the APR results) also reviewed all 25 portfolios and independently rated them on a scale of "pressure" from 1-5.

Results of a correlation analysis are presented in Exhibits B-1 and B-2. Our APR was positively correlated (above .60) with both experts' judgments. Interestingly, correlations were much lower among experts' rating judgments and Carnoy

13.   Torgerson, Warren S. (1958). *Theory and methods of scaling.* NY, NY: John Wiley. Pp. 170-173.

and Loeb's[14] index (e.g., at one extreme, Expert 2 and Carnoy and Loeb 2 correlated only .29).

In Exhibit B-2, among the correlations bearing on the validity of the APR is the correlation between the newly derived APR rating and the average of the ratings given by Expert 1 and Carnoy and Loeb 1 (.72), and the correlation of the APR with the average of Expert 1 and Carnoy and Loeb 2 (.70). In this system, there is significant overlap in judgment on the level of pressure associated with high-stakes testing as measured by our APR and the pooled judgments of our expert 1 and Carnoy and Loeb's systems. The high correlations between some of the other measures (e.g., Amrein & Berliner with either expert averaged with Carnoy & Loeb ratings) most likely resulted from the fact that both Amrein and Berliner and Carnoy and Loeb were essentially counting provisions in the same set of laws.

Exhibit C-1. Correlations of APR, Experts', and Carnoy and Loeb's Rating Systems

	APR	*Expert 1*	*Expert 2*	*Carnoy & Loeb 1*	*Carnoy & Loeb 2*	*Average Expert 1 & 2*
APR	1.00					
Expert 1	0.68	1.00				
Expert 2	0.63	0.57	1.00			
Carnoy 1	0.53	0.44	0.51	1.00		
Carnoy 2	0.45	0.34	0.29	0.85	1.00	
Average Expert 1 & 2	0.77	0.89	0.87	0.52	0.34	1.00

---

14.   Carnoy, M., & Loeb, S. (2002, Winter). Does external accountability affect student outcomes? A cross-state analysis. *Educational Evaluation and Policy Analysis, 24*(4), 305-331.

Exhibit C-2. Correlations of APR, Averaged Ratings, Boston, ECS, and Amrein and Berliner

	A	B	C	D	E	F	G	H	I
A: APR	1.00								
B: Average Expert 1 & Carnoy & Loeb 1	0.72	1.00							
C: Average Expert 1 & Carnoy & Loeb 2	0.70	0.95	1.00						
D: Average Expert 2 & Carnoy & Loeb 1	0.66	0.85	0.75	1.00					
E: Average Expert 2 & Carnoy & Loeb 2	0.67	0.83	0.83	0.95	1.00				
F: Amrein & Berliner	0.54	0.75	0.74	0.82	0.85	1.00			
G: Policy Activism	−.18	−.01	0.09	0.00	0.10	0.22	1.00		
H: Boston Rating 1	0.51	0.71	0.66	0.77	0.75	0.79	0.14	1.00	
I: Boston Rating 2	0.59	0.63	0.62	0.67	0.68	0.64	0.18	0.61	1.00
J: ECS	0.49	0.67	0.77	0.67	0.80	0.82	0.38	0.76	0.53

Appendix D: Race and Ethnicity Data With Accountability Pressure Ratings

This appendix supplements chapter 9.

Exhibit D-1. Gain in Percent Hispanic 1980-2000, Percent Black 2000, and Accountability Pressure Rating 2000 and 2004 for the 25 States of the Nichols, Glass, and Berliner Study

State	% H-80	% H-00	Gain H %	% Black	APR ('00)	APR ('04)
Alabama	0.9	1.7	0.8	26	3	3
Arizona	16.2	25.3	9.1	3.1	4	5
Arkansas	0.8	3.3	2.5	15.7	2	2
California	19.2	32.4	13.2	6.7	2	3
Connecticut	4	9.4	5.4	9.1	1	2
Georgia	1.1	5.3	4.2	28.7	5	5
Hawaii	7.4	7.2	−0.2	1.8	0	1
Kentucky	0.8	1.5	0.7	7.3	3	3
Louisiana	2.4	2.4	0	32.5	5	5
Maine	0.5	0.7	0.2	0.5	2	2
Maryland	1.5	4.3	2.8	27.9	2	2
Massachusetts	2.5	6.8	4.3	5.4	2	4
Mississippi	1	1.4	0.4	36.3	4	5
Missouri	1.1	2.1	1	11.2	1	2
New Mexico	36.6	42.1	5.5	1.9	4	5
New York	9.5	15.1	5.6	15.9	4	5
North Carolina	1	4.7	3.7	21.6	3	3
Rhode Island	2.1	8.7	6.6	4.5	1	2
South Carolina	1.1	2.4	1.3	29.5	4	5
Tennessee	0.7	2.2	1.5	16.4	3	3
Texas	21	32	11	11.5	5	5
Utah	4.1	9	4.9	0.8	1	3
Virginia	1.5	4.7	3.2	19.6	3	5
West Virginia	0.7	0.7	0	3.2	1	2
Wyoming	5.2	6.4	1.2	0.8	1	2

Derived from http://www.censusscope.org/us/map_hispanicpop.html

Author Index

Subject Index